SOLDIERS, STATECRAFT, AND HISTORY

SOLDIERS, STATECRAFT, AND HISTORY

Coercive Diplomacy and International Order

JAMES A. NATHAN

 PRAEGER

Westport, Connecticut
London

Library of Congress Cataloging-in-Publication Data

Nathan, James A.
    Soldiers, statecraft, and history : coercive diplomacy and international order /
James A. Nathan.
        p. cm.
    Includes bibliographical references and index.
    ISBN 0–275–97635–1 (alk. paper)—ISBN 0–275–97641–6 (pbk. : alk. paper)
    1. Intervention (International law)—Political aspects. I. Title.
JZ6360.N38   2002
327.1'17—dc21   2001058942

British Library Cataloguing in Publication Data is available.

Library of Congress Catalog Card Number: 2001058942
ISBN: 0–275–97635–1
        0–275–97641–6 (pbk.)

First published in 2002

Praeger Publishers, 88 Post Road West, Westport, CT 06881
An imprint of Greenwood Publishing Group, Inc.
www.praeger.com

Printed in the United States of America

∞™

The paper used in this book complies with the
Permanent Paper Standard issued by the National
Information Standards Organization (Z39.48–1984).

10 9 8 7 6 5 4 3 2 1

Copyright Acknowledgments

The author and publisher are grateful for permission to reproduce material from the following:

Carl von Clausewitz, *On War* (Michael Howard and Peter Paret, eds. and trans.), with introductory essays by Peter Paret, Michael Howard, and Bernard Brodie, and a commentary by
Bernard Brodie (Princeton, N.J.: Princeton University Press, 1984). Reprinted with permission.

Every reasonable effort has been made to trace the owners of copyright materials in this book,
but in some instances this has proven impossible. The author and publisher will be glad to
receive information leading to more complete acknowledgments in subsequent printings of
the book, and in the meantime extend their apologies for any omissions.

Contents

Introduction

Professional students of military power often learn the great theorists of war and diplomacy only epigrammatically, without much context.[1] Most military studies concentrate on specific tactics, battles, and battlefield technologies. Similarly, diplomacy, if it is taught at all in universities, is rarely broached as the historical essence of statecraft. Rather, diplomacy has been identified either as a rather baroque, atavistic methodology—the stuff of calling cards, top hats, and morning coats—or, as a synonym for the intricacies of various alliances and configurations of power; or, in some cases, as the study of an American problem in administrative and bureaucratic theory.

This book is devoted to what I consider the essence of diplomacy and statecraft. It is informed by two propositions: first, that limited force has enduring utility; and second, that force, to be judged successful, needs to be informed by more than a narrow definition of the national purpose. The historical definition of the national purposes that follow are designed to illustrate how power can be used, mitigated, and tamed. The book is also meant as something of an admonition regarding the consequences of power-seeking that is unmindful of the benefits of international order. As some of the narratives in this book illustrate, power used for the purpose of burnishing national ego is filled with the potential for disaster.

This book is little concerned, directly, with abstract "schools" of thought, though it might be comfortably shelved with other works by "neorealist" authors. I should note, however, that this work is somewhat more concerned with "grand strategy" and domestic politics than is usual in the contemporary study of international relations.

The argument I advance would seem commonsensical: The successful management of foreign policy requires the conscious integration of force and diplomacy. Alas, it is less an ordinary academic observation than one would suppose; for some decades past the initial scholarly excavations on the structure of international relations, most students come away with a sense that the study of international relations is closer to geometry and calculus than the real stuff of conflict or the nature of epoch-changing ideas.[2]

WAR, ORDER, AND DIPLOMACY: THEME ENOUGH?

Periods of international order have two distinguishing characteristics. First, they have usually arisen as a kind of collective revulsion to cataclysmic violence, such as was the case in the Thirty Years War (Chapter 1). Order has also emerged as a result of powerful states achieving some kind of consensus regarding the limits of ambition and conduct. The periods of stability that have followed Europe's episode of extreme violence, if not ideal, have at least been more acceptable than the apparent alternatives (Chapters 3 and 4). Yet, it is an ironic truth that at those moments when there is some cohesion and stability to international society—such as just prior to the rise of Frederick the Great (Chapter 3) and the half-century or so after the Napoleonic Wars (Chapter 4)—states have been the most vulnerable to "spoilers" and "rogues."

Force has always presented a challenge to international order. But it is only an apparent contradiction that force is also the precondition of order. Force is an ambiguous, yet essential instrument. The abilities of states to control benefits and injuries—material, financial, and political—all count. Trade and economic wealth share a place with force in underpinning statecraft. For economic power, like military power, can be an agent of injury or an instrument of international cohesion.

Indeed, some have hoped and continue to hope that force can be replaced by economics. As David Star Jordan, president of Stanford University, declared in 1913: "[T]he great war of Europe, ever threatening, . . . will never come. . . . the bankers will not find the money for such a fight, the industries will not maintain it, the statesmen can not . . . there will be no general war."[3] Dr. Jordan's poignant optimism reflected a real consensus among the member states of international society that was soon to be betrayed by Europe's startling self-immolation.

Carl von Clausewitz, the authority so frequently referenced in this book, was especially afraid that the force, once unleashed, would eclipse the purposes of those who called it forth in the first place. Both the Napoleonic Wars and the "Great War," as Europeans still call it, were the very antitheses of a rational, limited undertaking. Instead—in Clausewitz's terms—the conflagrations initiated by Revolutionary France and World War I were times of "elemental fury," fueled by masses and machines that had somehow escaped "from . . . ancient diplomatic and economic bonds." As a result, "sensible policy [was] eclipsed by violence"[4] (Chapter 4).

World War I and its aftershocks blew apart the great balance of power that emerged after the Napoleonic Wars. But even in Europe's years of relative repose, bloodshed and war were hardly banished. The only experience modern states have of a long-lasting peace among the dominant powers is the Cold War. Despite an intense nuclear fear at the apogee of the Cold War, overall deaths from conflict among states were fewer in the Cold War than at any other time since the conclusion of Europe's Thirty Years War in the middle of the seventeenth century.[5]

The Cold War and its inflexible nuclear peace are past, and its remarkable interstate stability is unlikely to return. Many observers, including myself, view the world that is emerging as historically familiar in the sense that there will be a continuing call on coercive instruments.

The examples in this book are meant to serve as a warning. There is real peril in letting force separate itself from rational ends (and, hence, international order itself). For when war has become a matter of ego, as we shall see was the case in the time of Louis XIV (Chapter 2), Frederick the Great (Chapter 3), Napoleon (Chapter 4), and Kaiser Wilhelm (Chapter 5), or when force turns into a kind of violence which ceases to know any limits (as was the case in the searing Thirty Years War), the use of force then becomes, as Clausewitz put it, "absurd."[6] This was Clausewitz's enduring specter—conflict expanding to the point of mindless mayhem, and thence "devoid of sense . . . a thing unto itself."[7]

STATE INTERESTS, LIMITED WAR, AND INTERNATIONAL ORDER

International politics was not always guided by "state interests." After 1648, and the Treaty of Westphalia that marks its conclusion (Chapter 1), dynastic war and religious confessional violence continued as both "ornamental" and substantive features of international relations.[8] But the notion that states were something apart from the personalities of the kings and emperors themselves became more common. New conceptions of objective and lasting state interests arose. If the idea of state interests did not displace the demands of ruling families and their religion, then, by and large, it was true that the logic of "reason of state" edged out the continuing temptations of personal aggrandizement and regal patrimony. A statecraft predicated on interests necessarily places a premium on longer term and more tangible results rather than personal or family considerations.

The passionate and absolute truths of religious orthodoxy were at odds with compromise. It was hard to meet "evil" and heresy on middle ground. But the emergence of the national "interests" allowed more flexibility. Interests are susceptible to negotiation. Matters of honor and faith are harder to compromise. Interests are contingent, and function to great degree on circumstances. And interests are usually limited, and hence defensible by limited force.

After the Thirty Years War, a secular profession of diplomats emerged. Before, the usual practice was to send prelates, messengers, or even singing heralds as envoys overseas. But as Cardinal Richelieu's confidant, Rohan, wrote, this new class of diplomats, informed by "interests guided by reason alone," seemed capable of restraining the "disorderly appetites" of princes and potentates.[9] The process of bending power to the ends of secular politics, abetted by a new class of professional negotiators, held out real promise: Even in "systems" of states that recognized no superior or common power, some kind of meaningful international order seemed possible.

DIPLOMATS, SOLDIERS, AND STATECRAFT

From the age of 12, Carl von Clausewitz spent his life in the profession of arms. As a witness to the roiling waves of the French Revolution, nationalism, and the epoch-destroying tides that washed over Europe, Clausewitz was well positioned to develop a set of original insights regarding the necessity of a synergy between warriors and diplomats. For Clausewitz, just as a professionalization of arms could mitigate wanton behavior and unbridled destruction, so too do might competent professional diplomats palliate interstate rivalry through studied, stylized discourse.

Like warriors, diplomats are ultimately responsible to civil authority. Diplomats, in turn, both interpret and sustain international rules. Hence, just as magistrates and police help define and sustain procedures that give domestic society a modicum of cohesion, so do diplomats and the modern profession of arms contribute to sustaining international "order"[10] (Chapter 1).

Order has a similar meaning to both domestic society and international society. For the opposite of order is anarchy, the banishment of rules; anarchy, as the philosopher Thomas Hobbes put it, holds the frightening potential for a war of all against all. The fusion of force and diplomacy is the essence of statecraft. War, to Clausewitz, was but a "stronger form of diplomacy."[11] Just as the object of war is, as Clausewitz knew, to obtain a better peace, it is critical to conduct peacetime diplomacy with an eye to the possibility of ensuing conflict.[12]

Clausewitz was appalled that France's revolutionary wars had compelled such intense animosities and carnage, and he yearned to return warfare to a limited sphere.[13] The times Clausewitz wished to recreate were when "[w]ar . . . [was] solely the concern of the government."[14] For Clausewitz, the democratization and "massification" of war were a prescription for mayhem. War, Clausewitz felt, was only "rational" when it was controlled, finite in its means, methods, and ends. The regulation of war seemed possible after the defeat of Napoleon with the development in Europe of the

"Concert System," which included an explosion of new diplomatic and legal designs geared to moderate international relations[15] (Chapter 5). But by the end of the nineteenth century it was clear—or at least it should have been clear, if for no other reason than the example of the American Civil War—that mass participation in government and war were not about to go away. The potential of violence to escape the bounds of policy and reason and become a "thing unto itself"—a permanent feature of international relations.

A NEW KIND OF INTERNATIONAL RELATIONS?

Even at the apogee of the Cold War, academic observers were starting to notice that the legal, moral, and even the factual bases of sovereignty were subject to new challenges. Something of a "transitional movement" away from the Westphalian system of relationships was under way.[16] Today we have termed this "globalization"—a trend identified in the 1970s by university observers of international relations who argued that economic integration and digital communication constitute a powerful "web of constraints on the foreign policy behavior."[17]

Those who accentuated the novelty of the new international environment have pointed to three features of contemporary international society:

1. *A significant transcendence of geography.* The United States, once hard to reach except by oceangoing ships, is now host to over 51 million visitors a year, and some 25 million Americans travel overseas every year.[18] The erosion of geographic verities has been made plain by the advent of rockets and assorted means and mechanisms of mass havoc.[19]

2. *The consequence of global trade and communications.* Trade has been displacing security worldwide as a means of determining priorities and interests since the end of the Cold War. Once, for instance, New Zealand saw itself bound in an intimate relationship to U.S. security. This relationship was New Zealand's foreign policy obsession from the first part of World War II until well into the 1970s. In the past quarter-century or so, however, New Zealand has developed a bipartisan consensus that no matter how valued the relationship with the United States, security in the antipodes must be dictated by the necessities of economics and not by the connection with Washington.

The ascendance of trade in world politics is apparent from the numbers. World exports in 1998 were 18 times those in 1950, while world gross domestic product (GDP) in 1998 was six times that of world GDP in 1950.[20] One estimate suggests that even a rather small (10 percent) rise in the ratio of trade to GDP between any given group of nations over the last 20 years accounts for as much as a 3.3 percent rise in per capita incomes.[21] In sum, trade has become an integral part of the developed world economy and is increasingly at the forefront of American foreign policy.

It is not surprising, therefore, that for the first time since the administration of William Howard Taft, commercial policy and exports, more than
any other consideration, shaped American foreign policy in the Clinton
years. Both of President Clinton's secretaries of state, Warren Christopher
and Madeleine Albright, underscored their belief that foreign policy obli-
gations had become substantially different than they were in the heyday of
the Cold War.

"First," Madeleine Albright told a Rice University audience in 1997,

foreign policy creates jobs: The Clinton Administration has negotiated more than
200 trade agreements since 1993. Those agreements have helped exports to soar
and boosted employment by more than 1.6 million. . . . And we have opened the
doors of embassies around the world to U.S. entrepreneurs. . . . Have no doubt,
these efforts will continue. For as long as I am Secretary of State, America's diplomatic influence will be harnessed to the task of helping America's economy to
grow.[22]

International trade reshaped "high politics" in the 1990s, and the bureaucratic franchise in American foreign policy widened to include the
Commerce Department, the Treasury Department, and representatives of
business, labor, science, and technology.[23]

   3. *International politics have become susceptible to what historically had
been considered private interests.* Walter Wriston, the former head of Ci-
ticorp, said not long ago:

Money goes where it's wanted, and only stays where it's well treated, and once
you tie the world together with telecommunications and information, the ballgame
is over. It's a new world, and the fact is, the information standard is more draconian
than the gold standard. . . . It's beyond the political control of the world, and that's
good news.[24]

Private groups and individual interests have made for a different kind of
international relations. Once, only states were a proper "subject" of international law. But in recent times, individuals have become the subject and
object of law. For instance, George Soros, an American billionaire, has
spent 123 million U.S. dollars—five times more than the U.S. government—
in order to support democracy in central Europe, and he has outspent the
United States in several countries in Central America as well.[25] And another
individual, Osama bin Laden, a stateless terrorist, has become a unique
object of international law, and the focus of vast coalitional war in the
latter part of 2001.

The stark example of the rising importance of nongovernmental groups
was vivified by the outrage perpetrated on the United States on the morning
of September 11, 2001. The minions of terror declared war. The murder
of more than 3,000 Americans by the capture of four large aircraft which

were turned into huge bombs is said to be the opening salvo of new kind of enemy at the dawn of a new politics. Or is it?

WHAT'S NEW, REALLY?

A New International Economy?

To the economists, there are two essential features of global interdependence. The first is the flow of goods and services, and the second is the flow of capital. Although a number of current observers have tended to describe trends in economics as unique, a second look suggests that today's global integration has only just returned to levels attained at the eve of World War I. Paul Krugman, for instance, reports that between 1850 and 1913, world merchandise exports rose from around 5 percent to about 12 percent of world domestic product. At the start of 1950, world merchandise trade stood at about 7 percent of world domestic product, recovered to pre–World War I levels of 12 percent only in the early 1970s, and reached about 17 percent in the early 1990s.[26] In the case of the United States, exports and imports as a percentage of American gross national product exceeded 20 percent just after World War I; it then fell to about 8 percent during the depression years of the 1930s. Trade returned to and exceeded its original high point in the mid-1990s and now stands, by some estimates, at over 30 percent of GDP at the start of the third millennium.[27]

Prosperity

Common for the last few decades, and reinforced by the dismissal of the Soviet threat, is the view that conflict between developed states diminishes with prosperity. Simply put, prosperous states have more to lose; hence, simple cost-benefit analysis yields the calculation that war is less desirable, hence "sub-rational," "unthinkable," and "obsolete" among developed states.[28] But this, in fact, is a view that characterizes American diplomacy from the onset. Most of the American Founders felt that "civilization . . . encompassed the whole world."[29]

To be sure, the diffusion of prosperity and American market values to a growing middle class—in countries once desperately poor and ruled wholly from above—is important; the 1990s strain of celebration was reflective, in part, of a sustained period of growth for large sections of the world.[30] But fast growth in countries like Germany in the past century (Chapter 5) and China (growing its GDP at an astonishing 8–12 percent per year for most of the 1990s) is no necessary bar to political expansion and military conflict. The perpetual conflicts in Asia—over territory, political influence, and military and economic advantage—are evidence.

Modernization, moreover, has been uneven, and much of the Islamic world has benefited little from globalization. The average annual income in the Arab world is less than half the world average. The record of modernization, with the exception of Turkey in the Moslem world, Bermand Lewis despaired in late 2001, is one of "almost unrelieved failure."[31]

The depredations of Osama bin Laden were not wholly unanticipated. Raymond Aron, one of the great French intellectuals of the twentieth century, noted some years ago that this "illusion, . . . that [there is] a single rationality to all peoples and to those who govern them . . . would like to leave behind history with a capital H, which writes its letters in blood."[32]

A response to an unconventional attack will almost certainly have, at its core, a "conventional" response. U.S. President George W. Bush said the Tuesday, September 11, 2001 attacks on the World Trade Center and the Pentagon were "an act of war"* and immediately set about rallying the world to defeat those who had carried out and abetted the attacks. NATO ambassadors invoked the Article V mutual defense clause in the organization for the first time in its 52-year history.[33]

In a sense, the struggle against terrorism may be novel in its scope; but terror's remedy will involve the mobilization of instruments familiar in the Cold War—the orchestration of alliances, the direction of limited force, and the management of intelligence and the "dark arts" of espionage, as well as the use of economic sanctions, propaganda, and development assistance.

Geography

Factors like geography, frequently said to be "obliterated" by missiles and communication, remain significant, even defining.[34] How else can you explain the upsurge of American interest in the plight of Haiti in the mid-1990s while sustaining a studied indifference to far greater displacement and suffering in Central Africa? Even in the age just passed, frozen by a nuclear standoff, one might speculate that shooting could well have broken out had not so much space separated the two Cold War antagonists.

Some point to Robert McNamara's epiphany at the time of the Cuban Missile Crisis—when the American Secretary of Defense averred to his colleagues that "a missile is a missile"—as evidence that geography had been transcended by missile technology. It was true that in McNamara's view nuclear weapons mattered only in terms of who commands them (and, of course, where they land). Far less significant is the precise geography from which they were launched (Chapters 5 and 6). But it was also true that McNamara did not gainsay the political and psychological significance of Soviet weapons so close to the United States in a hemisphere the United States had always considered an American preserve.[35]

Geography counts. The fact is that the United States took Cuban-based missiles far more seriously than the Russian nascent capacity to launch a

---

*These words were penned in mid-October 2001, just prior to U.S. and allied assaults on Afghan terrorist bases.

missile from ships on the high seas or from distant fields in Europe and Asia. Similarly, the Russian apprehension of a threat from American missiles in Turkey was also a significant ingredient of the crisis, and relevant to the justification Nikita Khrushchev presented for the Soviet nuclear deployment to the Caribbean.[36]

History and Culture

In recent years, some Americans have suggested we are at an end of the meaningful, "exciting" history of great national and cultural differences.[37] But ties of history do forge politically meaningful bonds.[38] When the great scourge who masterminded the September 11, 2001 attack on America spoke of his reasons, he referred to the need to avenge true faith against "crusader states." Osama bin Laden's reasoning was extreme, but hardly emerged like the surprising appearance of fully grown and armored Athena from the head of Zeus after Hephaistos struck him in the skull with an axe. After all, the usually unarticulated reasoning behind Europe's long rebuff of Turkey's long-standing petition for "full" membership in the European Community was nearly Jungian. One German diplomat said privately, "[The recent war in] Yugoslavia was a lesson for us. Europe can best stay together if it remains white and Christian." "Let us be honest about it," said Hans van Mierlo, the Dutch Foreign Minister, at a European meeting in February 1997, "there is a problem of a large Moslem state. Do we want that in Europe?"[39]

Sovereignty?

In fact, classic repertoires are reemerging after the long sleep of the Cold War. Even alliance aggregation—Britain's great talent for several hundred years and the unrequited goal of Germany in the late nineteenth century (Chapter 5)—is coming to resemble its classic form; for instance, President Clinton's priority in the "enlargement" of NATO. Yet, though alliances may be expanded, their substance seems more contingent, ad hoc, and problematic (as was the case in the 1991 Gulf War and the Kosovo campaign) than at any time since the end of World War I.

A fashionable depreciation of the classic basis of international relations (i.e., a "system" of "sovereign" states) stems from the observation that states have been fatally sabotaged by the "facts" of globalization and interdependence. But in many ways, states defend themselves more effectively than ever before. In some ways, developed states have never seemed more "sovereign." In the United States and the developed world, the same technology that allows states to receive goods, services, and ideas from abroad also makes possible, at least in theory, the security of frontiers.[40] As Robert Keohane, a leading explicator of global interdependence, once explained in this regard, "sovereignty of states, or even their autonomy" is not threatened by interdependence. In fact, if anything, globalization probably accentuates differences among states when measured in terms of effectiveness.[41]

It is an empirical truth: Sovereignty is rarely challenged. Even during the Cold War, no American official ever denied that adversary states have a right to exist. If in the recent conflicts of the 1990s (Haiti, Somalia in 1992–1993, and Iraq and the former Yugoslavia) some aspects of formal sovereignty seem to have been compromised, the process is hardly different from the constant adjustments of peoples and territory that were the hallmark of conference chambers from the Treaty of Westphalia to Yalta in February 1945—or, for that matter, the rearrangement of the former Soviet bloc in Communism's last hours.

Force

We no longer say, as Baron Von Humbolt declared, that "diplomacy is potential war."[42] But force remains. In fact, force was never far from the period through which we have just passed, the Cold War. In Yale historian John Lewis Gaddis' words, "the long peace of the Cold War is far and away one of the most stable kinds of peace ever to emerge between well-armed hostile states engaged in what many feared would be a cataclysmic arms race."[43]

The essence of the peace of the last half of the twentieth century was American "hegemony" combined with the nuclear threat. The current Western allergy to arms has seemed a function of participatory democracy, low birthrates, and, in the American case, an excessive sensitivity to the humiliation at arms in Vietnam. But the need for purposive force in international relations remains. In the former Yugoslavia, it was only collective force, willfully, albeit reluctantly, led by the Clinton administration, that put an end to the worst transnational violence in Europe since World War II (Chapter 6). It was only collective force that pushed Saddam Hussein away from a position of cruel extortion in the Persian Gulf (Chapter 6). And it will be primarily instruments of force that will address the terrorist outrage of September 11, 2001.

Strategy

A. J. Beceivich notes that the purposes "upon which soldiers embark bear small resemblance to . . . the lofty one of saving the world . . . the best one can hope for is a modicum of stability."[44] Beceivich's forecast is a rare academic echo of Clausewitz's injunctions regarding the inextricable union of force and policy.

The study of Clausewitz, the author who is referenced so extensively herein, enjoyed something of a renaissance in the wake of Vietnam. But in recent years, the case for banishing the Clausewitzian approach appeared in the heady glow of the 1991 Gulf War.[45] For example, Admiral William Owens, a recent vice chairman of the U.S. Joint Chiefs, explained that the U.S. technological edge erases Clausewitz's principle of "friction" in war. Now, said Owens, commanders stand confident of their ability "to see and understand everything on the battlefield . . . and to 'dissipate the fog' of war."[46]

Nowhere has Clausewitz's reputation been more thoroughly repudiated than in the U.S Air Force. Colonel John A. Warden III, the man who designed the air campaign in the Persian Gulf, took Clausewitz head on.[47] To Warden (Chapter 6), Clausewitz was "right, but only at . . . a time when communications were almost nonexistent, weapons had little range or accuracy . . . , most movement was at a walking pace." To Warden, the psychological side of war—a factor that Clausewitz held would count more than two times the physical side—has been banished.[48] To Warden, the ability to target economic and political structures has simply overwhelmed everything else.[49]

The confidence in the utility of technology and an unwillingness to devote resources to the "unpredictable" human side of politics are now reflected in American military doctrine.[50] The breach between force and policy is accentuated by a growing autonomy of the American profession at arms from the rest of society, on the one hand, and on the other a disturbing tendency of civilian elites to acquiesce in allowing the military to define its own agenda and, as one military academy commandant lyricized, its own "counterculture" (Chapter 6).[51]

To be sure, some elements of power and force are different today. No state today could place some 80 percent of revenues in the military, as Frederick the Great did (Chapter 3).[52] State motives today are rarely characterized by the simple opportunism that drove Louis XIV's ceaseless search for "gloire," and that which stimulated Frederick to bedevil Europe, offering as an excuse only, "[I] was young, had plenty of money, a big army, and wanted to see my name in the newspapers."[53] But there is little evidence—from the behavior of the members of European Union, Japan in its recent defense plans, or in the plans and arms aquisition of China, Russia, or the United States, to say nothing of the developing world—that force has been vanquished or that its integration into policy is no longer a critical issue of statecraft.

The "Democratic Peace"

The celebratory mood of the 1990s arose, in fact, from the pronounced success of the American economy. Although it ended in 2001, the United States had achieved a period of growth that, starting in 1991,[54] was the longest expansion since World War II.[55] The widespread optimism of the

U.S. policy community also finds a unique validation in having seen the loser of one of the greatest struggles of history simply defect to "our side." Of significance was the banner in one of the last May Day parades of the old Soviet Union: "Workers of the World," it said, "We Are Sorry!"

As important is the recent profusion of democracies in Asia, Latin America, and Eastern Europe. Like Woodrow Wilson, who held that "[d]emocracy is the best preventative of such jealousies and suspicions and secret intrigues that produce wars among nations,"[56] President Clinton argued for eight years that to a free people comes the boon of peace—and nearly all other virtues:

[W]hen people live free and they're at peace, they're much less likely to make war or abuse the rights of their own citizens, much more likely to be good trading partners and partners in the struggle against terrorism, international crime, and drug trafficking, working with us to prevent global environmental decay.[57]

The proponents of a "democratic peace" hold that democracy and well-being mitigate war.[58] The problem with the asssertion of the democratic peace as fact is that the number of democracies that fit the proponents' definitions over time had never been that large before the mid-twentieth century. From what evidence we do have, like the man who fell out of the window and was asked how he was doing, we might be able to reply, "so far so good." Nonetheless, close calls such as those between the United States and Great Britain in 1895 (Chapter 5) and Britain and France in 1898 on the upper Nile are usually explained away by advocates of the new era of "democratic peace" with the observation that, in the end, conflict did not occur; or, as in the case of the 1970s "cod war" disputes in the North Sea between Britain and Iceland, casualties were few.[59]

One wonders if the vision of a "democratic peace" can be sustained, even if democratic states do well and continue to expand in numbers. After all, American policy advisors and officials have occasionally contemplated and even counseled preventive wars. In the nineteenth century, in order to avoid war, Secretary of State William Seward counseled President Abraham Lincoln to make war anywhere he could to save the United States from civil war:

I would demand explanations from Spain and France at once over Spain having re-acquired Santo Domingo. I would seek explanations from Great Britain and Russia and send agents into Canada, Mexico, and Central America, to rouse a vigorous continental spirit of Independence on this continent against European intervention. And, if satisfactory explanations are not offered from Spain and France, I would convene Congress and declare war against them.[60]

In the twentieth century, the United States seriously contemplated "preventive war" against nondemocratic regimes such as Soviet Russia, Maoist

China, occasional Gulf potentates, Communist Cuba, and various nuisances in Latin America as well. As President Dwight Eisenhower mused to Secretary of State John Foster Dulles in early 1953, one day in the not-too-distant future the United States might "be forced to consider whether or not our duty to future generations did not require us to initiate war at the most propitious moment we could designate," rather than bankrupt the United States in a ruinous arms race.[61]

Sometimes there are wars between arguably democratic countries, such as the war between the United States and Spain in 1898, and sometimes there are less clear-cut examples, such as the U.S. covert intervention against the democratically elected governments of Guatemala in 1954 and Chile in 1973; and sometimes it is a matter of real debate whether a society is or is not "really" democratic. After all, Woodrow Wilson, until the coming of World War I, was on record as stating that Germany was an estimable democracy.[62]

The current flood of democracies may well have crested in the early 1990s, with an understandable reaction to the failure of collectivist ideals to deliver. One awaits in anticipation the transformation of the polities of Africa, the Arab world, and Asia. Even Western democracy may not always endure its present shape. One U.S. expert, Ethan B. Kapstein, writing as Director of Studies of the Council on Foreign Relations, went so far as to liken Europe's current stability to that in Germany during the Weimar years preceding the appointment of Hitler as chancellor.[63]

If there is a severe and widespread economic downturn, outbursts of distemper—like those that characterized the European politics of the 1920s—are conceivable. And it is possible to conjecture that "real" democratic governments would then be more prone to seek the traditional diversions of foreign policy "emergencies" in order to distract from insurmountable domestic woes.

Even if a diffusion of democracy and prosperity deepens and spreads, and even if the future is increasingly defined by technocrats and ballots rather than, in the famous words of Bismarck, "blood and iron," no sensible policy maker would either abandon the templates of international sovereignty or deny the requirement of security.[64]

For however hopeful policy makers and academics become about the prospects for and linkage between democracy and peace,[65] few would argue the proposition that there is an immutable law that a preponderance of democratic states will beget international order. Hence, even if modern democratic states do suffer great inhibitions in resorting to armed force (at least among themselves)—and if they do in fact, now more than ever, lack a stomach for war (Chapter 6)—a substantial requirement for constabulary, deterrent, punitive, and expeditionary forces will not soon simply evanesce.[66] Nor is it likely that issues of ideology and international order will simply slink into the shadows.[67]

ACKNOWLEDGMENTS

This book was started over 20 years ago when Jim King, one of the seminal intellects of the Cold War, asked me to work at the Naval War College's Center for Advanced Research. The work continued with grants from the Army War College, NATO, the University of Delaware, and, most recently, by the generous help of Auburn University at Montgomery and the rather splendid resources that have attended the Khaled bin Sultan Chair of international policy, which resides in AUM's political science department.

None of these organizations, of course, bear the least responsibility for the ideas expressed herein. To even a casual reader, it will be apparent that my intellectual debts are legion. The framework developed herein is not a little derivative of the extensive counsel, friendship, and written work of Robert E. Osgood and Robert W. Tucker. Others who helped substantially include Barton Bernstein, Philip Brenner, Will Curtis, Richard Ned Lebow, Edward L. Morse, Richard Remy, Geoff Stern, Elaine Thompson, and Charles Tien. Not to be neglected, of course, is the debt I owe James K. Oliver for two decades of close collaboration. The insight and enthusiasm of my editor, Dr. Heather Staines, was uniquely helpful. A common thank-you to all cited herein and many more unmentioned is inadequate. And I am more than a little embarrassed and profoundly grateful in having so much help from so many over so many years.

In any work of this breadth there will be errors. I have tried to cull as many as possible from the successive drafts. But in the end, of course, those lapses and mistakes that remain are my responsibility alone.

The book is dedicated to my wife, Lisa, and my sons, Alex and Michael, and to my father—not an educated man, but gentle, generous, and learned in ways that are still a beacon to all who knew him.

NOTES

1. An obvious exception is the first part of Henry Kissinger's engaging and magisterial *Diplomacy*, up until his exculpatory passages on Vietnam and the Nixon era (about half the book) and the classic essays by Herbert Butterfield and Martin Wright. See Henry Kissinger, *Diplomacy* (New York: Simon & Schuster, 1994). See Herbert Butterfield and Martin Wright (eds.), *Diplomatic Investigations: Essays in the Theory of International Politics* (Cambridge, Mass.: Harvard University Press, 1968). These latter essays reflect the "English school," which did much to define international relations as a separate field of study. To the earliest students of international relations, the field of international relations was a meld of rigorous, classic, cross-disciplinary studies infused particularly by philosophy, history, and the realities of the Cold War.

2. See Judith Goldstein and Robert O. Keohane, *Ideas and Foreign Policy: Beliefs, Institutions, and Political Change* (Ithaca, N.Y.: Cornell University Press,

1993), p. 4. The best current book on the place of ideas in the Cold War is John Lewis Gaddis, *Now We Know: Rethinking Cold War History* (New York: Oxford University Press, 1997).

3. Cited by John Mueller, *Retreat from Doomsday: The Obsolescence of Major War* (New York: Basic Books, 1989), p. 50.

4. Carl von Clausewitz, cited by Peter Paret and Daniel Morgan, *Carl von Clausewitz: Historical and Political Writings* (Princeton, N.J.: Princeton University Press, 1992), p. 356ff; and Carl von Clausewitz, *On War* (Michael Howard and Peter Paret, eds. and trans.), with introductory essays by Peter Paret, Michael Howard, and Bernard Brodie, and a commentary by Bernard Brodie (Princeton, N.J.: Princeton University Press, 1984), Book One, chapter 1, section 26, p. 88ff.

5. See Alex Roland, "Keep the Bomb," *Technology Review* (August/September 1995): 67–69, for the observation that deaths in war are declining. The percentage of deaths due to conflict was 1.5 percent of the population for the years from 1490 to 1900, and that percentage grew to 2.5 percent during World War II. However, in the years after World War II the percentage dropped to less than one-half of one percent of the population. These numbers do not dismiss the real carnage in Korea and Vietnam, which were, it is now more plain than before, surrogate contests between East and West. For something of a caveat on Korea, see Bruce Cummings, *The Origins of the Korean War* (Princeton, N.J.: Princeton University Press, ca. 1981–1990), Vol. 1, "Liberation and the Emergence of Separate Regimes, 1945–1947," and Vol. 2, "The Roaring of the Cataract." See also Cummings, "Revising Postrevisionism, or, the Poverty of Theory," *Diplomatic History* 17(4) (Fall 1993): 539–569.

6. Clausewitz, *On War*, Book Six, chapter 8, p. 607.

7. Ibid., Book One, chapter 1, p. 88; Book Eight, chapter 6B, p. 605.

8. Paul Schroeder, *The Transformation of European Politics* (Oxford: Clarendon Press, 1994), p. 579.

9. "On the Interests of Princes and States of Christendom," cited by Albert I. Hirschman, *The Passions and the Interests: Political Arguments for Capitalism before Its Triumph* (Princeton, N.J.: Princeton University Press, 1977), p. 34.

10. B. H. Liddell Hart, *Strategy*, 2nd rev. ed. (New York: Praeger, 1972). To Liddell Hart, a renowned English military commentator, this was the essential understanding necessary for any "grand strategy," that is, "to conduct war with constant regard to the peace you desire. The truth underlying Clausewitz's definition of war as a 'continuation of policy by other means' is that the prolongation of that policy through the war and into the subsequent peace must be borne in mind" (p. 366).

11. Clausewitz, *On War*, Book One, chapter 2, pp. 90–91 and Book Two, chapter 2, p. 143.

12. Raymond Aron, *Clausewitz, Philosopher of War* (Englewood Cliffs, N.J.: Prentice Hall, 1985), p. 62; Paul Kennedy, "The United States and Grand Strategy," in Paul Kennedy (ed.), *Grand Strategies in War and Peace* (New Haven, Conn.: Yale University Press, 1991), pp. 168–169; Clausewitz, *On War*, Book 8, chapter 6B, pp. 602–610, 706: "we also want to make it clear that war in itself does not suspend poltical intercourse or change it into something different."

13. Clausewitz, *On War*, Book One, chapter 2, p. 647.

14. Ibid., Book Eight, chapter 8, pp. 583, 589–591.

15. After the Cold War, the United States flirted for a decade or so with resur-

recting a large sort of "concert system" (much like that led by Britain in the mid-nineteenth century). The "new international order" propounded by President George H. W. Bush and elaborated by President Clinton was predicated on American leadership in the context of multilateral institutions. But as the third millennium unfolded, the old unilateral instincts and routines emerged.

16. Edward L. Morse, *Modernization and the Transformation of International Relations* (New York: Free Press, 1976), pp. 192–193.

17. Thomas L. Friedman, *The Lexus and the Olive Tree* (New York: Farrar, Straus & Giroux, 1999), p. 197; see also pp. 195–196 and 248. For Friedman's defense, see his "DOS CAPITAL 2.0," *Foreign Policy* (Fall 1999): 110–127. One of Friedman's more startling observations from these new forces is that war for those "plugged into the international system" is practically impossible. "[N]o two countries that both had McDonald's had fought a war against each other since each got its McDonald's," observes Friedman to illustrate this point. Of course Friedman's observation may now require a caveat in the case of the 1999 NATO campaign against Belgrade. See Katrina Kratovich, "Even McDonald's Can Survive Belgrade War," *Houston Chronicle*, October 1, 1999, http://www.chron.com/cs/CDA/story.hts/world/kosovo/351843.

18. U.S. Department of Commerce, ITA, "Tourism Industries: Statistics Canada; & Secretaria de Turismo (Mexico)," April 2001, http://tinet.ita.doc.gov/view/f-2000-203-001/index.html?ti_cart_cookie=20010906.120637.13355.

19. See Report of the Institute of Medicine, U.S. National Academy of Sciences, in the *Washington Post*, June 22, 1997, p. 14. The classic statement of this position is John Herz, "The Rise and Demise of the Territorial State," *World Politics* 9 (1957): 473–493, and his "The Territorial State Revisited," *Polity* 1 (1968): 12–34.

20. Martin Wolf, "World Economy: Trade Expansion Remains the Engine of Growth," *Financial Times* (London) World Trade Survey, November 29, 1999, http://specials.ft.com/ln/specials/sp3c52.htm.

21. Jeffrey A. Frankel and Andrew K. Rose, "Estimating the Effect of Currency Unions on Trade and Output," *NBER Working Paper 7857*, August 2000, http://papers.nber.org/papers/W7857.

22. Madeleine K. Albright, "Building a Bipartisan Foreign Policy," Address by Secretary of State, Rice Memorial Center, Rice University, February 7, 1997, http://www.rice.edu/projects/reno/speeches/19970207_Albright_Baker.htm.

23. For the distinction between high policy and low policy see Morse, *The Modernization and the Transformation of International Society*, pp. 85–100, passim. President Clinton campaigned on linking economics to policy at the presidential level by means of a coordinating body "similar the National Security Council." See *Washington Post*, August 14, 1992, p. 1, cited in I. M. Destler, *The National Economic Council: A Work in Progress* (Washington, D.C.: Institute for International Economics, 1997), p. 1.

24. See Stephen D. Krasner, "Economic Interdependence and Statehood," in Robert H. Jackson and Alan James (eds.), *States in a Changing World* (Oxford: Clarendon Press, 1993), p. 311.

25. Judith Miller, "A Promoter of Democracy Angers Authoritarians," *New York Times*, July 12, 1997, p. A4. By the same token, there is the current and disturbing trend of policy makers to bid out foreign policy to private contractors, ostensibly on grounds of efficiency, but with considerable costs if measured in terms

of accountability. See the investigative piece by Ken Silverstein, "Privatizing War: How Affairs of State Are Outsourced to Corporations Beyond Public Control," *The Nation*, July 28/August 4, 1997, pp. 11–17. See also James A. Nathan, "The New Feudalism," *Foreign Policy* 41 (Spring 1981).

26. Paul Krugman, "Growing World Trade: Causes and Consequences," *Brookings Papers on Economic Activity*, Issue 1 (1995), p. 3; see also Richard E. Baldwin and Philippe Martin, "Two Waves of Globalization: Superficial Similarities, Fundamental Differences," *NBER Working Papers Series*, Paper 6904, January 1999; and Michael D. Bordo, Barry Eichengreen, and Douglas A. Irwin, "Is Globalization Today Really Different than Globalization a Hundred Years Ago?" *NBER Working Papers Series*, Paper 7195, June 1999.

27. U.S. Council on Economic Advisers, *Economic Report of the President* (Washington, D.C.: GPO, February 2000), p. 203. Capital flows, in part because of the sheer size of today's movements, are harder to estimate. Some economists, however, suggest that national "current account" balances offer some insight into the overall movement of capital compared to other economic activity. Hence, one economist, Maurice Obstfeld, reports that out of 12 leading nations, the value of their respective current accounts stood at 3.3 percent of GDP prior to World War I; it then fell to 1.2 percent during the 1932–1939 years of the Great Depression. Between 1990 and 1996, capital accounts stood at some 2.3 percent of GDP. If Obstfeld is correct, international capital flows have yet to achieve the weight they had prior to World War I. However, by using an alternative measure the U.S. Council of Economic Advisers reports that cross-border capital inflows and outflows (both portfolio and foreign direct investment) grew from about 2 percent of U.S. gross national product during the 1960s to about 14 percent of U.S. GNP during the mid- to late 1990s, a figure that is probably higher than it stood at the end of the nineteenth century. Maurice Obstfeld, "The Global Capital Market: Benefactor or Menace?" *Journal of Economic Perspectives* 4(12) (Fall 1998), pp. 11–12; U.S. Council on Economic Advisers, *Economic Report of the President* (Washington, D.C.: GPO, February 2000), p. 206. See also John O'Neal and Bruce Russett, "Assessing the Liberal Peace with Alternative Specifications: Trade Still Reduces Conflict," *Journal of Peace Research* 41(2): 267–294.

28. John Mueller, *Retreat from Doomsday: The Obsolescence of Major War* (New York: Basic Books, 1989).

29. Felix Gilbert, *To the Farewell Address* (Princeton, N.J.: Princeton University Press, 1961), p. 57

30. Zbigniew Brzezinski, *The Grand Chessboard: American Primacy and Its Geostrategic Imperatives* (New York: Basic Books, 1997).

31. Barnard Lewis, "The Revolt of Islam," *The New Yorker*, November 19, 2001, p. 58.

32. Raymond Aron, *Clausewitz: Philosopher of War* (Englewood Cliffs, N.J.: Prentice Hall, 1985), p. 410; John A. Vasquez, *The War Puzzle* (Cambridge: Cambridge University Press, 1993); and Jack S. Levy, "The Causes of War: A Review of Theories and Evidence," in Philip Tetlock, Roy Radner, and Robert Axelrod (eds.), *Behavior, Society, and Nuclear War*, Vol. 1 (New York: Oxford University Press, 1991), pp. 209–333; Henry Farber and Joanne Gowa, "Polities and Peace," *International Security* 20(2) (Fall 1995): 123–146; David E. Spiro, "The Insignificance of the Liberal Peace," *International Security* 19(2) (Fall 1994): 50–86.

33. http://news.bbc.co.uk/hi/english/world/americas/newsid_1537000/1537534. stm, September 13, 2001; Rowan Scarborough, "Officials Talk of Military Response," *Washington Times*, September 13, 2001, http://www.washtimes.com/national/20010913-4292639.htm.

34. For a careful consideration of geography and nuclear weapons, see John H. Herz, *The Nation-State and the Crisis of World Politics: Essays on International Politics in the Twentieth Century* (New York: David McKay, 1976).

35. See James A. Nathan, "The Heyday of the New Strategy," *Diplomacy and Statecraft* 3(2) (July 1992): 303–342; and James A. Nathan, *Anatomy of the Cuban Missile Crisis* (Westport, Conn.: Greenwood Press, 2000).

36. See the essays in James A. Nathan (ed.), *The Cuban Missiles Revisited* (New York: St. Martin's Press, 1992). See also Aleksandr Fursenko and Timothy Naftali, *One Hell of a Gamble: Khrushchev, Castro, and Kennedy, 1958–1964* (New York: W. W. Norton, 1997).

37. Francis Fukuyama, "The End of History?" *The National Interest* (Summer 1989), reprinted in Fareed Zakaria, *The New Shape of World Politics* (New York: Council on Foreign Relations and W. W. Norton, 1997), pp. 1–26.

38. Samuel P. Huntington, *The Clash of Civilization and the Remaking of World Order* (New York: Simon and Schuster, 1996).

39. Stephen Kinzer, "Turkey Finds European Door Slow to Open," *New York Times*, February 23, 1997, p. A3; Stephen Kinzer, "Brussels Meeting Dims Turk's Hopes," *New York Times*, March 11, 1997, cited in James A. Nathan, "Turkey on the Edge," *International Relations* (the David Davies Memorial Institute of International Studies, London) 14(3) (August 1997).

40. See Barbara W. Tuchman, *The Proud Tower* (New York: Bantam Books, 1979), pp. 171–173, for a good review, and James A. Nathan, "Terrorism and International Morality," in Robert Rapport and Yonah Alexander (eds.), *The Rationalization of Terrorism* (Washington, D.C.: University Publications of America, 1982).

41. Robert Keohane, "International Institutions," in Linda B. Miller and Michael Joseph Smith (eds.), *Ideas and Ideals: Essays in Honor of Stanley Hoffman* (Boulder, Colo.: Westview Press, 1993), pp. 92–93.

42. Quoted by Edward L. Woodward, *War and Peace in Europe, 1815–1870* (London: Constable & Co, 1931), p. 12.

43. John Gaddis, "The Long Peace," *International Security* 10 (1986): 99–142; and John Lewis Gaddis, *The United States and the End of the Cold War: Implications, Reconsiderations, Provocations* (Oxford: Oxford University Press, 1992), p. 168ff.

44. A. J. Baceivich, "Tradition Abandoned: America's Military in a New Era," *The National Interest* 48 (Summer 1997): 20; James A. Nathan, "The Rise and Decline of Coercive Statecraft," *Proceedings of the United States Naval Institute*, October 1995, pp. 59–66; and James A. Nathan, "Force, Statecraft, and American Foreign Policy," *Polity* 28(2) (Winter 1995–1996): 237–259.

45. The evidence now suggests that Saddam's goal was the retention of power, while his method was sheer piracy: the looting of Kuwait. While that effort to hold and or dismantle Kuwait proved unsuccessful, eleven years on, the undertaking seems, from Saddam's point of view, not so bad. His hold on power was vindicated, and if anything strengthened, although the living standards of Iraqis, once at the

high end of the Arab world, have been reduced (according to UN workers) to the level of Uganda. Meanwhile, Saddam and his closest associates, through currency manipulation and the selling of contraband, have become, if anything, only richer. See Efraim Karsh, "Rethinking the 1990–91 Gulf Conflict," *Diplomacy & Statecraft* 7(3) (November 1996): 729–769; and the report of Eric Weiner, *National Public Radio*, "All Things Considered," July 17, 1997.

46. William Owens, quoted in Thomas Duffy, "Breakthrough Could Give Forces Total Command of Future Battlefield," *Inside the Navy*, January 23 1995; cited by Williamson Murray, "Clausewitz out, Computer in: Military Culture and Technological Hubris," *The National Interest* 48 (Summer 1997): 62, 64, passim.

47. See, for instance, the remarkable narrative in Lt. Col. Richard Reynolds, USAF, *Heart of the Storm: The Genesis of the Air Campaign against Iraq* (Montgomery, Ala.: Air University Press, January 1995).

48. See Col. John Warden III, "The Enemy as a System," *Airpower Journal* (Spring 1995): 40–55. For an attempt to contort Clausewitz to the new doctrines of Warden and Weinberger, see Col. Larry D. New, "Clausewitz's Theory: On War and Its Application Today," *Airpower Journal* (Fall 1996): 78–86.

49. Yet morale is hardly irrelevant. In the three-week Falkland Islands/Malvinas campaign of 1982, in cold, sodden conditions some 14,000 mostly conscripted Argentine troops—poorly trained, poorly led, and inadequately fed—abandoned their weapons and ran from a single brigade of lightly armed British professional troops, virtually bereft of ammunition and adequate tactical air or light tank support. Combat cohesion, not technology, made the critical difference. The British forces were better trained, better indoctrinated, and more convinced as to the legitimacy of their mission. For a fine eyewitness account of the British troops, see Max Hastings and Simon Jenkins, *The Battle for the Falklands* (New York: Norton, 1983); for a carefully judged account of the second battalion British parachute regiment by its former leader, see Maj. Gen. John Frost, *2 Para in the Falklands: The Battalion at War* (London: Buchan & Enright, 1983).

50. See, on these points, the issues raised in the essays collected by Vincent Davis, *Civil Military Relations and the Wars of the Present and Future* (Carlisle Barracks, Pa.: Strategic Studies Institute of the U.S. Army War College, 1995). For Clausewitz's notions, see the essays in Clausewitz, *On War*, pp. 595–596; Col. John A. Warden III, who designed modern air campaigns, wrote presciently about them in *The Air Campaign: Planning for Combat* (Washington, D.C.: National Defense University Press, 1988). Warden's renunciation of Clausewitz became somewhat bolder as he neared retirement. See Col. John Warden III, "The Enemy as a System," *Airpower Journal* (Spring 1995): 40–55.

Clausewitz had many battlefield admonitions, some of them lasting; some of them, necessarily, tied to the technology of his time. His most fundamental lesson, as his translators and students Michael Howard, Peter Paret, Raymond Aron, and James King have insisted, is the overriding significance of policy.

51. See A. K. Baceivich, "Tradition Abandoned: America's Military in a New Era," *The National Interest* 48 (Summer 1997): 16–26.

52. Robert E. Osgood and Robert W. Tucker, *Force, Order and Justice* (Baltimore, Md.: Johns Hopkins University Press, 1967), p. 49 n.13. Osgood notes that Frederick funded four armies that were, in aggregate, five times larger than any conceivable adversary. The United States supports an army of comparable prepon-

derance. The difference, of course, is one of the comparative effects of weapons and geography. Frederick had reason to worry about his neighbors. The United States is not concerned about its neighbors. Rather, it has taken on the whole question of global order.

53. Frederick's comments in Frederick the Great, *Posthumous Works*, "History of My Own Times," Vol. I (London: C.G.J. and J. Robinson, 1789), Letter XXXI to Jordan, 3 March 1741, "Correspondence," Vol. IX, p. 63.

54. NBER Business Cycle Dating Committee Determines that Recession Ended in March 1991, http://www.nber.org/March91.html.

55. According to Alan Greenspan, chairman of the U.S. Federal Reserve. Quoted by Mitchell Martin, "Fed Chief Predicts Low Inflation," *International Herald Tribune*, July 23, 1997, p. 1. In reality, the stunning growth of the U.S. economy continued until December 2000, for a total sustained growth period of nearly nine years.

56. Cited by William Diamond, *The Economic Thought of Woodrow Wilson* (Baltimore, Md.: Johns Hopkins University Press, 1943) p. 168 n.24.

57. "Address to the People of Detroit," Fisher Theater, Detroit, Mich., October 22, 1996.

58. Henry S. Farber and Joanne S. Gowa, "Common Interests or Common Polities? Reinterpreting the Democratic Peace," Working Paper Series No. 5005 (Cambridge, Mass.: National Bureau of Economic Research, 1995); Zeev Maoz, "The Controversy over the Democratic Peace: Rearguard Action or Cracks in the Wall," *International Security* 22(1) (Summer 1997): 162–198; and Bruce M. Russett, *Grasping the Democratic Peace: Principles for the Post–Cold War World* (Princeton, N.J.: Princeton University Press, 1993). Some of the caveats can be found in Christopher Layne, "Kant or Can't: The Myth of the Democratic Peace," David Spiro, "The Insignificance of the Liberal Peace," and John M. Owens, "How Liberalism Produces Democratic Peace," *International Security* 19(2) (Fall 1994): 5–49, 50–86, and 87–125; Edward D. Mansfield and Jack Snyder, "Democratization and the Danger of War," *International Security* 20(1) (Summer 1995): 5–38; and Bruce M. Russett, "Correspondence: 'And Yet It Moves'," Christopher Layne, "Correspondence: The Democratic Peace: The Author Replies," David E. Spiro, "Correspondence: The Liberal Peace 'And Yet It Squirms': The Author Replies," and Michael Doyle, "Correspondence: The Democratic Peace," *International Security* 19(4) (Spring 1995): 164–175, 175–177, 177–180, and 180–184. Also see Andrew Wyatt-Walter, "Adam Smith and the Liberal Tradition in International Relations," *Review of International Studies* 22(1) (1996): 15–28. See also Elihu Root, *The Effect of Democracy on International Law* (Washington, D.C.: Carnegie Endowment for International Peace, Division of International Law, 1917). One is surprised continually at the degree to which Jefferson, the philosophes, and the French Revolutionaries are passed over in these discussions. Immanuel Kant fares somewhat better, even if in passing.

59. See Susan Peterson, "How Democracies Differ: Public Opinion, State Structure, and the Lessons of the Fashoda Crisis," *Security Studies* 5(1) (Autumn 1995): 3–37.

60. Thomas A. Bailey, *A Diplomatic History of the American People*, 4th ed. (New York: Appleton-Century-Crofts, 1950), p. 540, passim.

61. McGeorge Bundy, *Danger and Survival* (New York: Random House, 1988),

p. 254. Other worrying examples abound: Curtis LeMay, during his tenure at Strategic Command, was a firm believer in striking first if there was evidence that the Soviets were preparing for war; and in the Cuban Missile Crisis, LeMay actually advised the president to bomb Cuba after the Soviets had agreed to withdraw their missiles on the island. The Joint Chiefs proposed war against China in the late 1960s when there was considered talk of seizing the Arabian oil fields in response to the first OPEC boycott; and in the first year of the Reagan administration, Secretary of State Alexander Haig suggested the United States "go to the source" of regional instability and bring the Castro government down by force of arms.

62. Ido Oren, "The Subjectivity of the 'Democratic Peace,' " *International Security* 20(2) (Fall 1995): 147–184.

63. Ethan B. Kapstein, "Workers and the World Economy," *Foreign Affairs* 75(2) (May/June 1966): 5. I am indebted to the prescient review essay by Thomas J. McCormick, "Troubled Triumphalism: Cold War Veterans Confront a Post–Cold War World, a review of Tony Smith's American Mission," *Diplomatic History* 21(3) (Summer 1997): 481–492.

64. Otto von Bismarck, 1862. The full quote refers to the struggle to unify Germany, when Bismarck informed the liberals in Parliament, "the great question of the day will not be settled by speeches and majority decisions—that was the great mistake of 1848 and 1849—but by blood and iron." For the meld of material and coercive power in Bismarck's foreign policy, see Fritz Stern, *Gold and Iron: Bismarck and Bleichröder and the Building of the German Empire* (London: George Allen & Unwin, 1977), pp. 26–47.

65. The literature on the "democratic peace" is now immense. For a good start in reviewing the literature, one profits from the important cautions offered by Edward Mansfield and Jack Snyder, in their "Democratization and War," *Foreign Affairs* 74(3) (May/June 1995): 79–98.

66. On these points see Edward Luttwak, "Post-Heroic Warfare," *Foreign Affairs* 74(3) (May/June 1995): 109–122; and General Eugene Habiger, Commander in Chief, U.S. Strategic Command, in a speech to the Atlantic Council, February 10, 1997, reprinted as "Deterrence in a New Security Environment," *Strategic Forum* (Washington, D.C.: The National Defense University, Institute for National Strategic Studies) 109 (April 1997).

67. See Walter Laquer, *Fascism, Past, Present, Future* (New York: Oxford University Press, 1996).

SOLDIERS, STATECRAFT, AND HISTORY

Chapter 1

Westphalia and the Rise of Modern Diplomacy

INTRODUCTION

The emergent post–Cold War international order is unique: For the first time since the invention of the diplomatic method, an international architecture is materializing without any postwar diplomatic charter. Moreover, order is now conditioned not on a Germany divided and distracted; on the contrary, if it is to be sustained, order requires Germany to be geopolitically coherent and competent—the reverse of the Cold War reality that the fragmentation of German power was an essential element of stability. Still, this radically new international structure, if it is to sustain itself and prosper, will have to reconcile those contradictory supports of order that were first adumbrated in the Westphalia Treaty of 1648: collective security on the one hand, and the balance of power on the other.* Like those well-fed mid-seventeenth-century congregants who met in a bereft corner of Germany, we have come to the crossroads of choice.

Let us recall first the origins of Westphalian order. By the mid-seventeenth century, the flames of the Thirty Years War scorched the steppes of Transylvania, darkened Ireland, passed the Americas, touched the Cape of Good Hope, and licked at the Straits of Malacca. By 1648, Germans found their numbers reduced by a third. Much of the German

---

*Swedish diplomat Johan Adler Salvius wrote back to Stockholm that a primary Swedish interest was a balance of power as opposed to other mechanisms for maintaining international order: "The first rule of politics is that the security of all depends on the equilibrium of the individuals. When one begins to become powerful . . . the others place themselves, through unions or alliances, into the opposite balance in order to maintain the equipoise." Cited by Geoffrey Parker (ed.), *The Thirty Years' War*, 2nd ed. (New York: Routledge, 1997), p. 164.

countryside had been turned into a howling wilderness, and travelers reported vast stretches populated only by wolves.

THE ONSET OF DIPLOMACY AND MODERN INTERNATIONAL RELATIONS

The animus that characterized international politics prior to the mid-seventeenth century contradicted civility and denied diplomacy. In an age when religion defined politics, the purpose of war was largely the extirpation of wickedness. In such a moral environment, peace treaties were not just impracticable, they were impermissible. The princes and potentates of the seventeenth century, fired with chiliastic certainty, held compromise to be not merely wrong-headed, but godless and malign. This worldview admitted no middle position: If one side fought with God, it followed that the other had sided with evil. For the hundred years that preceded the treaties of Westphalia, only truces were permissible. It was allowable to truck with heresy only to regroup and fight anew. The very essence of diplomacy—the peaceful adjustment of conflicting interests by dint of reason and tact—was perforce banished to the shores of a rising ocean of blood that would, it was believed, wash away misbelief, or, quite simply, end the world in a final sanguinary flood.

Sometime in its third decade, it became clear that the Thirty Years War had become a struggle between contending visions of international order: The first might be based on sovereign, independent dominions; the second would be based along medieval lines on religious faith and universal authority. In the general defeat of the Hapsburgs, the latter theory was demolished.* The formal settlement of the Thirty Years War at the Congress of Westphalia heralded the onset of what we now call the "classic" period of international diplomacy.

The Congress of Westphalia was the first such meeting of its kind: Great numbers of "accredited" diplomatic representatives, plenipotentiaries, and clerics from over 96 entities assembled in two cities thirty miles apart— Osnabrück and Münster. The whole area of Westphalia was a kind of demilitarized zone, surrounded by a hunger so pervasive that criminals feared their famished warders more than any jail. The envoys met continuously from 1642 to 1648. Years were consumed by squabbles over abstruse claims which served to befog their hope that ongoing battles, raging

---

*As Derek Croxton points out, the division, like any episode in history, is not a divide but is, on closer inspection, not as clear-cut as commentators would have it in retrospect, especially as to the issue of "sovereignty" which, in the English, French, and Swedish instances, was more developed than it was in Germanic signatories of the Westphalia Accords. "The Peace of Westphalia and the Origins of Sovereignty," paper delivered on the occasion of the 350th anniversary of the Peace of Westphalia, Enschede, 1998.

on fronts as near as three days' hard ride and as distant as the coast of Ceylon, would compel terms which the negotiators would not otherwise concede.

Time was required to fashion what would be, in their words, a "once and for all" settlement. Diplomats seeking protocol stumbled over conflicting claims of precedent; this formality of the future validation of power was a threatening matter in an age where even "reputation" was valued as life itself.

There were two pillars to the Westphalia settlement: one procedural, the other geographic. The first prerequisite of the post-Westphalian order was the legitimation of the diplomatic enterprise. But the more palpable element of the Westphalia settlement was the fragmentation of German power. The congregants at Westphalia knew they were preparing for a new kind of politics predicated on the evident geopolitical reality of a Germany first enervated by war and then divided by design.

Most of the delegates' time and energy at the Westphalia Congress were consumed in devising what we would now call "collective security" arrangements for the 300-odd polities: principalities, bishoprics, leagues, duchies, and city-states of Germany.* However, the more lasting mechanism for sustaining international order advanced at Westphalia was a rudimentary pan-European balance of power "system." Indeed, its broad outlines remained at the core of "international society" until the summer of 1914; the Westphalia settlement was truly a stunning success.

The Westphalia methodology seemed so successful that within 80 years Europeans believed they had once again become bound up in a wholly new, and now palpably *secular,* "international society." After 1648, Europeans started to become accustomed to dealing with large issues at major gatherings. Congresses composed of ambassadors would meet after wars to frame a peace based on an assumption of the legal "sovereign" equality of victors and vanquished alike. Indeed, the whole of the diplomatic history of Europe, as Sir George Clark once said, can be seen as the stride from one congress to the next. At each new conclave, diplomats assembled to beat out new permutations in the classic Westphalia formula. So common had this process become that, by Rousseau's time, Westphalia seemed to him to have become "the constitution of Europe."

*This was clearly the idea of Salvius, the Swedish negotiator, who wrote: "The crown of Sweden had to pay close attention to Germany and protect itself, because it was a temperate and populous part of the world and a warlike people, . . . there is not a country under the sun in a better position to establish universal monarchy and absolute dominion in Europe than Germany; . . . now, if one potentate wielded absolute power in this realm, all the neighboring realism would have to apprehend being subjugated." Cited by Andreas Osiander, *The States of Europe, 1640–1990: Peacemaking and the Conditions of International Order* (Oxford: Clarendon Press, 1994), p. 79.

HAPSBURGS WEST: SPAIN'S RECESSIONAL AND DUTCH ASCENDANCE

Much of the Thirty Years War parallels the Cold War. Both had their geostrategic loci centered, ultimately, on the issue of the disposition of German power. Both were waged at a time when diplomacy was depreciated or nearly absent. Both were heated ideological contests. Both were waged by powers worried that concessions, although not significant unto themselves, might lead to a further unraveling of position; so it was better not to concede the paltry lest the critical be put into play. And both contests were fought with such bitterness that domestic well-being had to be placed behind the necessity of what many felt was becoming virtually a perpetual struggle.

By 1609, at the time of the signing of the Truce of Antwerp, Spain had spent five times the revenues of France, England, and the United Provinces put together in trying to put down the 50-year Dutch rebellion. To the pretenses of a substantially theocratic Hapsburg imperium that claimed much of Christendom and beyond as its own, the Protestant Dutch republic was itself a challenge.[1] In the Truce of Antwerp, Spain "recognized" the Dutch Republic as if it were a sovereign power, and conceded the closure of the once great city of Antwerp; but the Truce hardly touched any of Spain's continuing irritants, for the Dutch combined a ruthless commercial talent with a penchant for provoking their one-time overlords.

The Dutch seemed to feel they were free to smuggle whatever they wanted into Spain, including enormous quantities of counterfeit coins, minted to a higher standard than the Spanish seemed capable of themselves. The practice made the Dutch the arbiters of Spain's money supply while reversing Gresham's Law—driving the Crown's bad money out of the market with the "good," but counterfeit, coin of the cheeky Protestant rebels.[2] The Dutch also claimed that they had discovered a legal loophole that allowed them to continue to prey on Spanish trade out of European waters. As a result, 10 years into the Truce, Spain had nearly lost its entire trade in spices—a commerce so valuable that one successful delivery could retire a whole ship's company for life.[3] A more vexing activity, which even the most ingenious Dutch lawyering could not explain away, was the Dutch raids on Spanish ships within European waters. Virtually the whole supply of Baltic war stores, amounting to a third of Dutch wealth, was captured by armed Dutch merchantmen.

"The Truce," concluded Count Olivares, the principal adviser to Philip IV, had become "an abomination." It was the view of Carlos Colima, the governor of the Flemish city of Cambrai, that "[i]f the truce is continued, we shall condemn ourselves to suffer all the evils of peace and all the dangers of war."[4]

When the rebellion of 1618 in Bohemia came to be known to Madrid, the king's advisers viewed the revolt as inseparable from Spain's position in the Low Countries. Philip IV was told that if he did not aid his Hapsburg brethren in Bohemia, Spain would lose its position in the Low Countries; and then, soon, Spain itself would be lost to heresy and rapacious foreigners. A dramatic erosion in the impression of Spain's influence—even if it occurred at the remote corners of an Empire controlled by an impoverished relative—was posited as inextricably linked to Spain's overall position. Those who were for war knew that it would expand, that the Dutch were likely to aid their Protestant co-religionists, and that war could not be confined since the Dutch would probably be abetted by the French and perhaps England as well. A far-flung war was, then, quite deliberately chosen by Spain not because the balance of power favored Spain—the new king commanded, by his own reckoning, only seven battle-worthy ships— but because Spain had been losing the peace and hoped to recoup by a great roll of the iron dice.[5]

HAPSBURGS EAST: THE DEFENESTRATION OF PRAGUE

Even before the time of the Bohemian rebellion, the Holy Roman Empire was something of an anachronism. Imperial claims on the spiritual and temporal life of the whole of Christendom had been unreal since the death of Charlemagne. Outside Germany, the universal claims of the Holy Roman Empire were contradicted by the fact of Protestant states. Within Germany, the Empire was even more bedeviled by the reality of Protestant electorates, Protestant princes, and a rising class of Protestant worshippers.

By the end of the sixteenth century, most Bohemian nobility had turned Protestant. Catholic emperors were largely content that their Protestant Bohemian subjects served up enormous revenues to the emperor, who, by custom, had been a Hapsburg since the fifteenth century. But imperial elections were genuine and by no means was any one candidate a shoo-in. Yet, in 1617, the Bohemian nobles, more or less reflexively, deferred to tradition and accepted Ferdinand, the Catholic Hapsburg, as their King of Bohemia. For Ferdinand, it was to be a time of apprenticeship, since he was also slated as the next emperor.

Ferdinand, a profound bigot, felt no obligation to those who had given him a lock on the emperor's throne. For unbeknownst to the Bohemian nobles, Ferdinand had vowed that he would rather "be cut to pieces, or beg my bread outside the gates of my palace, than suffer their heresy." It was a conviction held not out of malice, for this strange fanatic was said to be of a kindly disposition. "[I]t is because I love heretics," the new Bohemian king explained with unfeigned, but peculiar, sweetness, "that I wish to convert them from the path of evil."[6]

Hardly a year past Ferdinand's accession to the Bohemian throne, Protestant churches in Bohemia were boarded up. Permits for new churches

were denied; and the Protestant leadership of Bohemia began to have second thoughts about their new king. On May 21, 1618, Bohemian nobles
and gentry pushed their way into the Hapsburg castle of Hradshin. Upon
finding two senior officers and an inoffensive secretary, the Protestant leaders conducted a kangaroo court. "Were these Hapsburg officials guilty of
treason against Bohemia?" The crowd shouted its affirmation, whereupon
the three unfortunates were hurled from a window. Catholics maintained
that the trio was borne safely to ground—some 75 feet—upon the wings
of angels. Skeptics and Protestants pointed to the moldering dung heap in
which all three came to rest.

From death's door in Vienna, Mathias, the depleted and half-crazed emperor, sent offers of amnesty, but the Bohemian rebels showed no interest
in further Hapsburg rule. Within days, the senior Spanish representative to
Vienna mustered an army for the emperor's use in repressing rebellion.[7]

FERDINAND LOSES HIS CROWN TO FREDERICK, ALONG
WITH THE PEACE OF EUROPE

Meanwhile, the Bohemian nobles met to strip Ferdinand of his recent
crown and offer it to a fellow Protestant: Frederick of Palatine. Frederick
appeared to be a logical candidate. The Protestant son-in-law of King James
of England, Frederick was also related to William of Orange, the House of
Denmark, and Sweden's Gustavus Adolphus. In sum, young Frederick was
one of the best-connected princes in Protestant Europe.[8] If he were King of
Bohemia as well as Elector of the Palatinate, Frederick would have immense
power, for he could then dominate the upper waters of the Elbe, the Oder,
and the middle of the Rhine. Moreover, if Frederick accepted the invitation
of the Bohemians, he would have two votes out of seven in the Imperial
Diet.

Frederick found little support among his new fraternity of kings. England's James I was too troubled by rebellion and plots himself to be pleased
by his son-in-law's exploitation of a Bohemian rebellion. James even for-
bade public prayer to be said on Frederick's behalf. In fact, no crowned
government in Europe encouraged Frederick's accession to the Crown of
St. Stephan. If Frederick accepted the Bohemian offer, he could reason that
he would become one of the great princes of Europe. But when he contemplated the opposition, the 21-year-old Frederick mused with uncharacter-
istic perspicacity: "This is risky business."[9]

If Frederick was given to some hesitation, Frederick's wife was not. As
the daughter of England's king, Elizabeth figured she and her husband were
meant for grander things: "I would rather eat sauerkraut with a King than
roast meat with an elector."[10] Emboldened by his wife's ambitions, buoyed
by his astrologer, and steeled with a substantial Dutch pledge, Frederick
rode defiantly from Heidelberg. Frederick's party left for Prague, taking

with them 153 baggage carriages, a thousand soldiers, and the peace of Europe.[11]

A year and a half later, on the outskirts of Prague, Frederick's army found itself trapped by Hapsburg forces. At the gates of the city, readying himself to visit his forces at what was to be the scene of the "Battle of White Mountain," Frederick and an English ambassador found themselves nearly bowled over by the first wave of fugitive Protestant forces. The panicked Bohemians shouted at the young king to flee for his life as they were most certainly fleeing for theirs. Frederick V and his queen heeded the advice of the mob.

Making their way to Holland, the exiles were sustained only by the jewels the queen was able to carry on her person. In one broadside after another, Frederick's departure was mocked. In Berlin, one wall poster read:

> . . . His men and horses were quickly
> Struck down on the White Hill.
> . . . He was very much frightened
> He applied this magical spell to his feet,
> And with his wife he hastily took to his heels.[12]

A HAPSBURG INDIAN SUMMER AND WIDENING WAR

The emperor offered Frederick the status quo ante bellum. If he had accepted, the matter would have ended. But the Dutch would not let the issue go; nor, by then, could Frederick's father-in-law. Although one of England's least bellicose kings, James I was forced by militant Puritan pressure to offer a modest stipend for the restitution of his son-in-law's Palatine estates. Meanwhile, among the advisors to both Hapsburg branches, but especially in Madrid, there was the hope that the moment had arrived to finally extirpate heresy from Hapsburg lands: Fortune's top was set in motion. The Spanish army, only awaiting the end of the 12 Years' Truce of Antwerp, occupied the whole of Frederick's lands; the Palatinate suffered frightfully; and the city of Frankenthal was besieged for more than a year. The fortress capital of Heidelberg finally fell in the spring of 1623: Much of the old city, including universities and libraries, was set to flames.[13]*

Ferdinand, the zealous Hapsburg Emperor, personally visited Bohemia to oversee a long night of Inquisitional terror. In the rooting out of heresy, a famed Bohemian named Debis was nailed by the tongue to the gibbet.

---

*Seven years later, upon returning to his hereditary lands escorted by Swedish troops, Frederick found the Palatinate "in ruins." Separated from his guards by battle, weary from wandering, Frederick picked his way up the road to the Hague, where his exiled queen awaited him. Taking uninvited refuge from a storm, in the cellar of a merchant, Frederick died as unwelcome as the pest that felled him.[14]

Another, Count Schlick, 80, a leader of the rebellion, had his right hand cut off—and only then beheaded. Protestant school masters were ordered to leave Bohemia in eight days. To make the point, the chancellor of the university had his tongue torn out before he was executed. University life ceased. One-half of the property of Bohemia changed title. Protestant landowning virtually disappeared. The mint was contracted to a foundry that produced coins so light and manifestly worthless that disgusted imperial soldiers flipped their pay back at their officers. Protestants were denied wills, testaments, and marriages. When the citizens of Bohemia were given 18 months to accept Catholicism or leave, 180,000 people fled. In little more than two years, one of the brightest cultures of Europe had been eclipsed.[15]

By 1624, the Bohemian rebellion had been resolved to the immediate satisfaction of both Hapsburg houses. It could have ended then: Spanish troops had been confirmed again as the most formidable force in Europe; "The Spanish Roads," the passages from Italy to Flanders, were more secure than they had been in a hundred years; and France, the greatest potential continental adversary of Spain, was surrounded north and west by Spanish redoubts.

For Spain, however, the most serious irritation was not the Bohemian provocation, but the Dutch Republic: The Dutch would not turn away from the issue of the future of the Palatinate. When the Emperor Ferdinand decided to transfer Frederick's lands to Catholic-led Bavaria, it became certain that Holland and whatever allies the merchant republic might muster would stand in opposition to Spain.

ENGLAND'S ODD MAN OUT

King James I's general desire had been for peace. The king knew that Parliament's continuing demands to help Frederick's cause were in contradiction to any dispassionate understanding of English interests. Any Machiavellian could have easily understood that England would only benefit if the Spanish and the Dutch exhausted themselves in war. After all, the Spanish were England's rivals in the Americas. In the Indies, English merchant ships involved in the pepper trade were subject to Dutch plunder. In more than a few oceans, armed Dutch merchantmen captured English crews, and even sold some of them into slavery. Finally, the king agreed to let the redoubtable Mansfield, Frederick's generally luckless commander, empty London's poor houses of a few thousand reluctant warriors, some of whom, anticipating the rigors of service, committed suicide.

So disreputable had Mansfield become, the Dutch did not even want his English forces to transit their soil. As a result, the English army was confined to its ships. Without water or provision, 75 percent of the English troops, some 8,000 men, were lost at anchor in Dutch harbors. News of

Mansfield's failure drifted back to London as James fell mortally ill, leaving the final determination for peace or war to his son, Charles I.[16]

Since the days of Drake, raiding Spanish ports had a certain cachet. Hence profit, along with Parliament's Catholic phobia, explains much of Parliament's desire for a war with Spain; but the Commons had not wanted to provide for it or much else in the way of royal income. Charles decided to provide the war, hoping that a great victory would make Parliament more compliant in confirming the king's revenues. A victory at sea, Charles I was persuaded, would establish his position with the Commons—although it was not clear what this would do for his long-suffering sister, Elizabeth, the wife of Frederick.[17]

Charles sent the navy to Cadiz, where 15,000 English sailors managed only to secure the Spanish wine store. Blamed for the Cadiz disaster, the organizer of the Cadiz raid, Charles' handsome "favorite," Buckingham, was impeached in the Commons. But Charles sided with his companion and dismissed the House. Two years later, the Duke of Buckingham still held the king's commission—but Buckingham failed again, most disastrously, in a naval expedition. Less than a third of the expeditionary forces returned to English ports. "That slime" Buckingham became a common epithet:

> And now, Just God! I humble pray
> That thou wilt take that slime away
> That keeps my sovereign's eyes from viewing
> The things that will be our undoing.[18]

Charles was now without any more disposition for war: He paid off the army from his own purse and had his forces stand down. As Thomas Crew wrote, in 1630, of England's temper,

> . . . What thought the German drum
> Bellow for freedom and revenge, the noise
> Concerns not us, nor should divert our joys;
> Nor ought the thunder or carbines
> Drown the sweet air of our tun'd violins.[19]

But Parliament's long recess made Charles susceptible to Spanish silver. In 1639, Charles enabled Spain, for a fee, to ship Spanish troops to Flanders by way of Dover, sometimes even transporting Spanish terceros in English ships. When, in 1640, the Irish revolt broke out (abetted, it was rumored, by Spanish priests and Spanish soldiers), the just-reconvened Parliament would insist that any English forces raised to quell rebellious Catholics ought to be controlled by the Commons. Charles was forced into a compromise that soon broke down. Following a lengthy and destructive civil war, Charles was captured by parliamentary forces. A rump Parliament brought the unfortunate king to a drumhead trial, where it was resolved that Charles was a "tyrant, traitor, murderer and public enemy."[20] Three days later, Charles' head was detached from his body in a stroke. News of Charles' death reached the Hague as the just-ratified Peace of Westphalia restored the long-suffering Palatinate to the descendants of Charles' sister, Elizabeth.

THE FRENCH PHASE: SPAIN BROUGHT LOW

France had prepared for war against its old Hapsburg rivals for years, and in the last days of 1634, French forces moved across the Rhine to take the much-abused fortress city of Heidelberg. Not much later, Richelieu sent his heralds to Brussels to deliver to the Spanish viceroys a copy of his after-the-fact declaration of war.[21] Catholic France had to align itself with its Protestant neighbors, Richelieu explained, since Spanish power had "for its goal to augment its dominions and extend its frontiers" at French expense.[22] Richelieu justified France's alliance with Protestants to his king, Louis XIII, advancing as an argument the "necessity of state." To hedge his theological bets, Richelieu meanwhile employed an army of lawyers to argue that the Pope would have approved of his policies if he had been aware of the true facts.

In contrast to the national egoism suggested, however it was dressed, by Richelieu, Spain's Philip IV and his advisors saw themselves as pure Paladins of Catholic rectitude. The Spanish king had, after all, helped his brother-in-law, Louis XIII, against the Huguenot challenge; indeed, Spain had extended herself beyond all proportion on behalf of France and the cause of Catholic princes. Richelieu, Philip despaired, had repaid the Spanish badly.

Soon the French and Dutch were working in close cooperation: The Spanish lost huge numbers of men and ships in engagements with the Dutch that extended from Brazil to Sicily. By land, French troops occupied key points astride the old Spanish Road. By the end of the 1630s, Spain, in its attempt to eliminate the Carthage of the Zuider Zee, had begun to come apart; in 1640, Catalonia and Portugal rebelled and went over to the French.

From their Flanders redoubt, the Spanish, in a last desperate effort to reverse their fortunes, tried to move on Paris with all their available strength, some 32,000 battle-hardened veterans. But because horses had become too expensive, the Spanish marched without adequate cavalry. At the frontier fortress of Rocroi, in a single morning in February 1643, French cavalry and cannon tore into the Spanish positions. At the end of the day, Spain's military treasury had been captured and half the Spanish army lay dead or had been made prisoner. A French officer asked one tired

Spanish officer, "How many of there are you?" "Count the dead and the prisoners, that is all," came the weary reply.[23] The great battle marked all but the formal end of Spain's position and its displacement by France. As Philip IV's new minister, Don Louis De Haro, put it later: Rocroi was "a defeat that gives rise in all parts to the consequences we feared."[24]

PEACE

The old war hawk, Olivares, Philip IV's principal advisor, finding neither army fit to serve nor generals fit to lead, relented: "I propose peace, and more peace, . . . we must certainly beg God to give us general peace, which even if it is not good, or even average, would be better than the most advantageous war."[25] In fact, Spain and Holland were able to agree on a peace on January 30, 1648, as Spain and France could not. All through Spain's negotiation with Holland, the Dutch refused to lift the siege of Antwerp. In the end, Spain was forced to concede much of its critical trade in the Indies. It was the greatest loss of all. As Queen Elizabeth had noted 100 years earlier, if "you touch" the King of Spain "in the Indies, you touch him in the apple of his eye, for you take away the treasure . . . his . . . bands of soldiers will soon dissolve, his purposes defeated, his power and strength diminished, his pride abated and his tyranny utterly suppressed."[26]

But France paid heavily as well. Within France itself, with interest rates exceeding 24 percent and Crown revenues pledged years in advance, there were hints of civil war. The French Advocate General wrote his young king, Louis XIV, and the king's regent, Jules Mazarin (who had succeeded Richelieu as prime minister in 1642):

We are told that it is not easy to conclude peace, that it is to the state's advantage not to neglect the King's victories. . . . Whether or not it is true . . . there are whole provinces where they live on nothing. . . . Taxes and duties are put on every imaginable thing. The only thing your subjects have left, Sire, is their souls, and if they had any market value they would have been put up for sale long ago.[27]

With a shudder of horror at the door opened in England by the arrest of Charles I, Mazarin sped to make "peace at the earliest opportunity," if not with all the Spanish Hapsburgs, then at least with its Austrian branch. France was in danger of becoming undone.*

The new Austrian emperor's honest loyalty to Spain (Ferdinand III had been elected emperor in 1637) could only seem lopsided when he learned of Spain's eagerness to make a separate peace with the Dutch. Abandoned by his Spanish cousins, his armies broken, the cannon of his enemies within

---

*Boris Porshnev, "Angliskaia respublika, frantsuskaia Fronda i Vestfalsky mir," *Sredniie veka* 3 (1951): 180–216; and Croxton, n. 835, op. cit.

earshot, the son of Ferdinand III had no choice but to yield to the logic of peace.

For the rest of Europe, there was the hope of repose, signaled on Saturday, October 24, 1648, by sounds of cannons and bells, and endless Te Deums sung from the Russian Steppes to the Americas. As the Treaty of Münster put it: "The mishaps, destruction and disorders which the heavy plague of war has made men suffer for so long and so heavily" had ended.[28]

THE MEANING OF THE WESTPHALIA SETTLEMENT

The geographic division of the conferences between Münster and Osnabrück was the empirical affirmation that international order was to be newly undergirded by an assumption that Germany, from then on, was not whole. Instead, Germany was defined as a congeries of autonomous and semi-autonomous states. A new organizing principle was offered to replace Hapsburg religious and political hegemony in Germany: Each signatory to the Westphalia settlement would have the right to determine the faith of the realm. The prince of a region, "the sovereign," was to make the rules. Once the emperor acknowledged this formula, he recognized the Protestant states of Germany as morally valid objects of diplomacy and not secular subjects of a vast Christian realm.

Political relations from the periphery to the center are different from those politics that proceed along a horizontal plane of moral equality. Although both types of interactions may be called "diplomacy," one implies the politics of submission, the other the politics of compromise. One requires deference, and works best with orthodoxy, while the other specifies noninterference, and allows for pluralism and autonomy. In conferring a moral equality on hundreds of entities, the Westphalia settlement detailed the undoing of the Hapsburg-maintained medieval hierarchy, and began to put in its place a new organizing principle based on the sovereign equality of states.

At a time of civil disorder that ranged from the Irish Sea to Turkey (and according to one diplomat at the conference, Salvius, even to China), the Westphalia settlement was a self-conscious effort to buttress domestic authority. By granting the right of each state to give the law and maintain order in its own realm without interference, the conference of Westphalia aimed to solve the problem of internal legitimacy and order while mitigating the animus that characterized the relations of warring states. The troublesome problem of domestic authority was eased by making religion an exclusively internal matter at the determination of the realm's ruling house.

ANTINOMIES OF ORDER: THE BALANCE OF POWER
VERSUS COLLECTIVE SECURITY

Although the Westphalia treaties allowed the signatories to be "free perpetually . . . to make alliances with strangers for their preservation and safety," an alternative was presented in the form of a rudimentary "collective security" system. Article XVII of the Treaty of Osnabrück declared: "All and each of the contracting parties of this treaty shall be held to defend and maintain all and each of the dispositions of this peace, against whomsoever it may be, without distinction of religion."

Like the League of Nations and the Charter of the United Nations, the Münster treaty "outlawed" a recourse to arms: "It shall not be permitted to any State of the Empire to pursue his Right by Force and Arms; but if any difference . . . happens for the future . . . the Contravener shall be regarded as an Infringer of the Peace."[29]

Within Germany, the Westphalia treaties sketched out the antinomies of a system based on armed self-help on the one hand and, on the other, on mutual interests and diplomacy. States could either go their own way, secured by their own means and those of their allies, or they could arrange for their collective defense, perhaps as Grotius had suggested (and the Westphalia treaty called for) in the context of great conferences.

Outside the Holy Roman Empire, the Westphalia treaty pointed down a similar divide. The first led to a society of states that might compose their difficulties by negotiations and tribunals. The other way led to a self-centered system undergirded by the now undisputed right of each state to make alliances with foreigners and manage their own defense.*

But collective security would prove the weaker thread with which to weave a fabric of stability. For any collective security would require the habit of subordination of conflicting interests to the common good. The problem with the notion of a common good is that it usually proves either quite elastic or ethereal—or both. Even if the common good were knowable and fixed, it might require self-sacrifice. Nations without any higher authority to compel them to do otherwise would not prove themselves ready candidates for martyrdom. The Westphalia settlement thus resulted in a system predicated on a sovereign self-help. It limited war by dispersing power among a great number of states so that no single state, nor any combination of states, might gain more than limited objectives against adversaries.

Almost every study of the balance of power argues that it emerged as a self-conscious European strategy of order in the crucible of the Thirty Years

*The Consolidated Treaty Series, ed. Clive Parry, Vol. 1 (1648–1649) (Dobbs Ferry, N.Y.: Oceana Publications, 1969), Vol. 22 (1697–1700), viii, 344.

War. Indeed, as Cornelis Peiterszoom Hooft wrote at the time of West-phalia, "Everything, indeed, has been due to the jealousy of Spain, France and England."[30] But the balance of power system was not just a matter of power unconstrained except by the counterweight of equivalent power, a kind of physics reified to the level of statecraft. The post-Westphalia system embraced, on the one hand, the emergence of a new community of interests and, on the other, a new restraint borne from universal revulsion at the inhumane excesses—and cost—of war.

A REPELLING WALL OF DISGUST

By 1635, hordes of plague-infested refugees were trampling crops. De-pleted pastures were called on to support ever larger armies (Wallenstein and Gustavus fought with over 100,000 at their command; the French mustered over 180,000.)[31] While armies were forced to circulate ever faster to find their daily requirements, plague increased as a function of the ve-locity of armies on the move. Discipline broke: By 1640, war had achieved a general barbarity. Peasants were sawed, pierced, burned, and boiled. "He who had money," a contemporary saying went, "was the enemy. He who had none was tortured because he had it not."[32]

A sport was made from wagering how many peasants or prisoners could be felled by a single bullet. Soldiers sprinkled gunpowder on the clothes of prisoners and set their garments alight. Children were kidnapped and held for ransom. Priests and burghers were tied under wagons and made to crawl until they dropped. Hunger was everywhere, and there were reports that criminals were cut down from the gallows to be devoured, and graves opened so that the newly buried could nourish the still living.[33]

Formerly verdant, Germany itself was in ruins. When Robert Monroe, a Scottish mercenary, made his way to the Rhine Valley with Gustavus Adol-phus, he had written: "No country in Europe is comparable unto Germany, for fertility, riches, corn, and wine, traffic by land, pleasant sites, fair build-ings, rare orchards, woods and planting, civility as well in the country as in the cities." Four years later, a secretary to an English ambassador trav-eling from Cologne up the Rhine came by "many villages pillaged and shot down." In Bacharach, "the poor people are found dead with grass in their mouths." In Metz, the party had to stay aboard ship and hurry away from the starving, who swam out to beseech the travelers for a scrap. From Cologne to Frankfurt, "all the towns, villages and castles be battered, pil-laged or burned." At Neustadt, "a fair city . . . now burned miserably." One village in the Upper Palatinate had "been pillaged eight and twenty times in two years and twice in one day."[34]

The Thirty Years War itself had created a repelling wall of disgust. The percentage of people lost in Germany—some 7 million out of a population of 21 million—was far greater than the numbers lost even in World War

II; and the material devastation was probably worse. On nearly every measure—duration, number of participants, severity of damage to the population, and battlefield deaths as a percentage of the population—the Thirty Years War was the most destructive in history. During the period of continuous warfare between 1621 and 1639, out of a population of a million in Sweden and Finland, 100,000 were in the army, and of these, nearly half were killed or wounded. Between 1618 and 1659, about 300,000 men were lost from Castille out of a population of 6 million.[35]

For ordinary people, peace had become a mirage, long promised but seemingly extinguished by each near approach. So bad were conditions for the ordinary people of Germany that many thought the Thirty Years War was but apiece with the imminent arrival of the end of the world; and when, at long last, the news of the peace came, it was hard to believe. A Nuremberg poet, Johann Vogel, wrote:

> Something you never believed
> Has come to pass. What?
> Will the camel pass through the Needle's Eye
> Now that peace has returned to Germany?[36]

NOVEL PREMISES: NATIONALISM, *RAISON D'ÉTAT*, THE REGULARIZATION OF DIPLOMACY, AND THE MANAGEMENT OF FORCE

The Thirty Years War gave a great fillip to national consciousness, provoking Englishmen to hate Spaniards and Swedish antipathy to Russians. Brandenberg's chief religious authority, John Bergius, thundered: "Is there anyone with German blood in his veins whose heart does not ache when he sees and hears how our fatherland is plundered and ravaged by foreign invaders worse than the Turks and the Tartars?" Religion had become the bridge on which nationalism passed and prospered. In England, "Protestant" and "English" gradually became coterminous. The feelings in England expressed for James' exiled daughter, Elizabeth "the Winter Queen," could best be described as a patriotic sense of outrage. A kind of jingoism even infiltrated the law courts where, notwithstanding their age or position, those who made light of Frederick's precipitous exit from Prague found themselves branded, fined, imprisoned, or worse. Some of Elizabeth's detractors were nailed by their ears, and others were recorded to have been nearly torn to pieces by angry mobs.[37]

Much later, nationalism would become a constant in the life of states and even be married to state power. But for 150 years, patriotic feeling remained tamed and subservient to reason of state. In the absence of debilitating religious or national passions, a genuine diplomacy could develop that ascertained "the balance of interests" as well as the balance of forces

available to support them. Those agreements that proceeded from this process went on to create their own constituencies, and the elaborate process
of negotiation and treaty-making would endow some Europeans with more
than the pious hope that international "society" might become a permanent
feature of international relations.

In the 100 years before Westphalia, the gulf between Catholics and Protestants contradicted civility, obstructed diplomacy, and defined the purpose
of war as the extirpation of wickedness. If one fights with God, it follows
that one's opponents are fighting iniquitously. The argument admitted no
middle positions. Fired with chiliastic certainty, contestants denied compromises and adjustments short of war as being not merely wrong-headed,
or injurious, but evil. In this kind of moral environment, the very essence
of diplomacy—adjudication of conflicting interests by dint of reason, persuasion, and tact—was, perforce, banished.

But Westphalia was the summary diplomatic experience, a great conference which adjudicated what was hoped to be a lasting settlement predicated on reason and interests. Now that "reason of state" has prevailed,
one wag observed after the Westphalia Congress, it seems to be "a wonderful beast for it chases away all other reasons."[38] The Westphalia settlement advanced reason of state, depriving the notion of its religious garb.
As Richelieu's confidant, Rohan, wrote (somewhat optimistically), "Princes
rule the people and interests rule the prince." But if interests are to be
rationally pursued they must be detached from zeal. As Rohan put it:

In matters of state one must not let oneself be guided by disorderly appetites, which
make us often undertake tasks beyond our strength; nor by violent passions which
agitate us in various ways as soon as they possess us; . . . but by our own interests
guided by reason alone, which must be the rule of our action.[39]

"State interests" suggests proximate goals of a definable group that neither extend to the whole of humanity nor are confined to any slim section
of a community. Interests implies a collectivity whose well-being can be
advanced by specific measures. Yet, interests admits compromise, whereas
passionate truths obviate middle measures. Interests can be approximated.
One does not have to achieve them at one fell swoop or risk damnation.
A statecraft infused by interests necessarily places a premium on the tangible rather than the theological. An emphasis on interests hoists calculable
advantage over transcendent purposes. Interests imply predictability, prudence, reason, and mutual gain. In itself, the notion of interests is a moderating idea. Passions are inconsistent or, as Hobbes put it, they are
"insatiable." But in the mid-seventeenth century, the concept of interests
became the means to exorcise caprice, instability, and unmitigated zealotry
in human affairs. Therein lay the burden of virtue in the mid-seventeenth
century maxim, "Interests do not lie."[40] If interests were as "actual" and

"true," then interests might have a claim equal to and perhaps beyond religion. With the rise of the notion of *raison d'état*, states could find a mechanism for tolerating and even accommodating one another.

A NEW CLASS OF DIPLOMATS AND STATECRAFT

The Westphalia settlement marked the start of a novel premise in international affairs: Armed struggle did not any longer have to be defined as a contest between varieties of confessional truths; rather, they could be disputes among secular "sovereigns."[41] The final settlement of armed disputes, after Westphalia, was no longer left to the province of military contractors and theologians. Instead, the termination of war fell within the purview of a new and identifiable coterie: a class of professional diplomats and warriors sworn to the service of a state.

Before the Westphalia settlement, there was no recognizable diplomatic profession. Spies, irregular envoys, and heralds citing scripture or handing out ringing declamations were the usual route that princes chose to alert one another to each other's demands and to sound the start of war. After Westphalia, the diplomatic craft was practiced by a kind of well-born guild, with members who were adept at melding reason, precedent, and law with quiet allusion to the implication of armed compunction.

Before Westphalia, soldiers were frequently led by contractors, private entrepreneurs who garnered pay from their won estates or from the lands they plundered. After Westphalia, soldiers were more commonly led by military bureaucrats who raised armies year-round and paid for their keep through levies and taxes. After Westphalia, diplomats and warriors began to share a kind of regulatory synergy. Both diplomat and warrior sought "victory" less, and the achievement of a favorable peace more. War, after Westphalia, as the great observer Clausewitz put it, came to be a "stronger form of diplomacy," and the battlefield an extension of the conference chamber.[42]

War itself was, to a degree, more tame as a result of the great mêlée. Gustavus Adolphus, the principal champion of Protestants during the Thirty Years War, took to carrying a copy of Grotius' massive work on the rules of war and peace with him to battle.[43] To Gustavus, the model of the enlightened prince, moderating the savagery of battle was part self-interest and Calvinist piety. But after the Thirty Years War, armies throughout Europe started to review and publicize codes of conduct. The notion spread that there was a lawful way to conduct war and that it was a palpable interest of states to heed legal restriction.[44]

THE CONTEMPORARY MEANING OF THE THIRTY YEARS WAR AND THE WESTPHALIA SETTLEMENT

The Thirty Years War had a lasting effect. In Germany, neither religion nor Hapsburg imperialism ever produced another war.[45] In the 100 years after Westphalia, war had achieved a certain "regulatory function" in delimiting change and state ambition. But as the technology of violence available to combatants expanded war's potential violence, war's "legitimacy" as an instrument of statecraft began to erode. In the end, the great success of the Thirty Years War was that it had impeached Europe's medieval order, making way for the possibility of the reintroduction of a more constrained kind of warfare and international politics. Finally, in the twentieth century, war began to again approach its terrible and absolute form, and the most compelling rationale for its employment came to be once again absolute: this time it was the defeat of the causes of war itself. As Raymond Aron put it, "As operations mounted . . . it was essential to inflate the purposes of victory . . . [P]eace would be durable only if dictated unconditionally after crushing the enemy. The demand for total victory was not so much the expression of politics as a reflex reaction to total war."[46]

In the present century, at the same time the expansion of violence tended to take "absolute" and "absurd" form (in Clausewitz's words), diplomacy abutted another zealous nemesis: the recrudescence of fervent, apocalyptic belief. Illustrative was Harry Truman's famous address to Congress in March 1947, when he argued that the West's struggle with the Soviets was over "two ways of life": "One . . . based upon the will of the majority, and . . . distinguished by free institutions . . . free speech . . . and freedom from oppression. . . . The second . . . based upon the will for a minority . . . rel[ying] upon terror and oppression."[47]

To the extent that Truman's analysis obtained, negotiation would be little valued. To be sure, conferences would still be staged; diplomats would meet; and communiqués could be issued. But meetings, in this kind of highly charged ideological atmosphere, would necessarily be little more than venues for mean-spirited propaganda, or complex traps to lure Western innocents. In 1954, for instance, Secretary of State John Foster Dulles asked an aide if he would be satisfied if the Soviets accepted free elections and the reunification of Germany. "Why, yes," his aide acknowledged brightly. "Well, that's where you and I part company," Dulles retorted. "I wouldn't. There'd be a catch in it."[48]

Associated with appeasement and grisly calamities for most of the twentieth century, ancient practices of European diplomacy fell into a swamp of disgrace. Diplomacy, especially in the Cold War, came to be known not so much as a method of ameliorating the clash of interests but, at best, as a self-defeating vestige of an ancient and irrelevant civility. Now, however, with the passing of Cold War passions, prospects for a renaissance of the Westphalian diplomatic patrimony brighten anew. The settlement of the Thirty Years War at Westphalia marks the start of the new professionalization of diplomacy. And if, in fact, diplomacy has now been given a reprieve, it behooves us, then, to recall its painful beginnings and its achievements, and to explore its relevance to our collective future.

NOTES

1. By the early seventeenth century, there was a widespread sense that Spain was in a state of precipitous decline. "Never," in nearly 800 years of continuous war, "has Spain been as poor as it is now." Louis Valle de la Cerda, cited by J. H. Elliot, " 'Self Perception and Decline' " in Spain," *Past and Present* (74): 53.

2. Charles Howard Carter, *The Secret Diplomacy of the Hapsburgs: 1598–1625* (New York: Columbia University Press, 1964), p. 31.

3. John Lynch, *Spain under the Hapsburgs*, Vol. 2, *1598–1700*, 2nd ed. (Oxford: Basil Blackwell, 1981), p. 65; and Carter, *The Secret Diplomacy of the Hapsburgs: 1598–1625*, p. 30ff.

4. In a letter written in 1629, cited by John Elliot, *The Count Duke Olivares, the Statesman of an Age of Decline* (New Haven, Conn.: Yale University Press, 1986), p. 66 n.57. See also Peter Brightwell, various articles: "The Spanish Origins of the Thirty Years War," *European Studies Review* 9 (1979); and "Spain and Bohemia, 1619–1621," *European Studies Review* 12 (1982); "The Spanish System and the Twelve Years Truce," *English Historical Review* 12 (1982): 270–292.

5. Hugh-Trevor Roper, "The Outbreak of the Thirty Years War," in Hugh Trevor-Roper (ed.), *Renaissance Essays* (Chicago: University of Chicago Press, 1985), p. 293; Peter Brightwell, "The Spanish Origins of the Thirty Years War," *European Studies Review* 9(4) (October 1979): 409–431; and H. R. Trevor-Roper, "Spain and Europe: 1598–1621," in J. P. Cooper (ed.), *The New Cambridge Modern History*, Vol. 4: *The Decline of Spain and the Thirty Years War: 1609–48/59* (Cambridge: Cambridge University Press, 1970), p. 281.

6. Cited by Lt. Col. J. Mitchell, *The Life of Wallenstein: Duke of Friedland* (Westport, Conn.: Greenwood Press, 1968), p. 21. The defenestration of 1618 was, in fact, a well-planned imitation of a famous defenestration 200 years earlier that had started the Hussite revolution.

7. David Maland, *Europe at War: 1600–1650* (Totowa, N.J.: Rowan and Littlefield, 1980), p. 64ff.

8. Geoffrey Parker and Simon Adams, "The Indecisive War, 1618–1629," in Geoffrey Parker (ed.), *The Thirty Years' War*, 2nd ed. (London: Routledge, 1997).

9. Elmer A. Beller, "The Thirty Years War," in Cooper (ed.), *The New Cambridge Modern History*, Vol. 4, p. 311.

10. C. V. Wedgwood, *The Thirty Years War* (New Haven, Conn.: Yale University Press, 1939), p. 100; also Mary Anne Everett Green, *Elizabeth: Electress of Palatine and Queen of Bohemia*, rev. ed. (London: Methuen & Co., 1909), pp. 129–130, for Frederick's hesitations.

11. Wedgwood, *The Thirty Years War*, p. 85ff.

12. Elmer Beller, *Propaganda in Germany during the Thirty Years War* (Princeton, N.J.: Princeton University Press, 1940), p. 24.

13. Traveling south to the Rhine, disguised as a merchant, Frederick caught up with his commander, General Mansfield who, at the moment of his encounter with Frederick, was actually engaged in talks about switching sides with a Spanish diplomat. Frederick would have been advised to release his mercenary to Spain; for

Mansfield's record in the field was one of almost perfect failure. As for the army, Frederick wrote his queen as he fled from the battlefield, "I think there are men in it who are possessed of the devil, and who take a pleasure in setting fire to everything." Green, *Elizabeth*, p. 93; and Elmer A. Beller, "The Thirty Years War," in Cooper (ed.), *The New Cambridge Modern History*, Vol. 4, p. 317.

14. On November 19, 1632. Green, *Elizabeth*, p. 299; Wedgwood, *The Thirty Years War*, p. 332.

15. Mitchell, *The Life of Wallenstein*, p. 74; and Wedgwood, *The Thirty Years War*, pp. 143–169.

16. See Leopold Von Ranke, *A History of England, Principally in the Seventeenth Century*, Vol. 1 (Oxford: Clarendon Press, 1875), p. 562ff.

17. C. V. Wedgwood, *Richelieu and the French Monarchy* (New York: Collier Books, 1962), pp. 50–52.

18. Charles Carlton, *Charles I: The Personal Monarch* (London: Routledge and Kegan Paul, 1983), p. 96.

19. C. V. Wedgwood, *History and Hope: The Collected Essays of C. V. Wedgwood* (London: Collins, 1987), p. 72.

20. Ibid., p. 87.

21. Even his declaration was novel for a medievally trained man of the Canon. Indeed, Richelieu's policy would be recognized by any of the American "realist" architects of "containment."

22. Wedgwood, *Richelieu and the French Monarchy*, p. 63; and J. H. Elliot, *Richelieu and Olivares* (Cambridge: Cambridge University Press, 1984), p. 67. But the calculations and techniques of Richelieu were only partly modern. On the one hand, Richelieu's view that France was divinely sanctioned to find lasting peace for Christendom was decidedly medieval. But Richelieu's view of political authority was distinctly modern. Papal authority was moral only; the Pope had no temporal rights in Richelieu's cosmos: "[T]he King," wrote Richelieu, "is the recognized sovereign in his state, not holding his crown but from God alone, there exists no power on earth whatever it might be . . . which has any right over his kingdom." J.A.W. Gunn, "Interests Will Not Lie: A Seventeenth Century Political Maxim," *Journal of the History of Ideas* (October–December 1968): 551–564; and J.A.W. Gunn, *Politics and the Public Interests in the Seventeenth Century* (London: Routledge and Kegan Paul, 1969), p. 36ff. Richelieu's argument for fidelity to treaties was also modern. As he told his king, even though "many political thinkers teach the contrary," treaties should be "religiously" observed. But to the cardinal, the rationale for solemnly honoring contracts with other princes was less the cause of international order and more the Baroque-age issue of his sovereign's "reputation." "A great prince," the cardinal wrote, "should risk even his person and the interests of state rather than break his word." C. R. Fredericks, "The War and Politics," in Geoffrey Parker (ed.), *The Thirty Years' War*, 2nd ed. (London: Routledge, 1997), p. 199. In the end, Richelieu's insistence on talks with adversaries, no matter how remote the chance of settlement or hostile the confessional claims of one's adversaries, became the basis of modern diplomacy.

23. Archer Jones, *The Art of War in the Western World* (Urbana: University of Illinois Press, 1987), p. 293ff.

24. Robert Stadling, "Catastrophe and Recovery: The Defeat of Spain, 1639–1643," *History* 64(211) (June 1979): 217ff.

25. Cited by Elliot, *Olivares*, p. 601.

26. Geoffrey Parker, "The Dutch Revolt," in Geoffrey Parker and Leslie M. Smith (eds.), *The General Crisis of the Seventeenth Century* (London: Routledge and Kegan Paul, 1978), p. 69.

27. Georges Pages (David Maland and John Hooper, trans.), *The Thirty Years' War* (New York: Harper and Row, 1939), p. 226.

28. Geoffrey Parker, *Spain and the Netherlands: The Military Revolution, 1560–1660* (Short Hills, N.J.: Enslow Publishers, 1979), p. 203. The list of contemporary disorders is impressive: England, Ireland and Scotland, Sicily, Naples, Paris, Catalonia, and Portugal. There were peasant uprisings in Sweden and rumors of revolt in Poland. See Herbert Langer, *The Thirty Years' War* (Poole, U.K.: Blandford Press, 1978), p. 260. One well-informed diplomat, Savius, wrote that people everywhere had risen up, even in Turkey and China.

29. A complete text is available in Clive Perry (ed.), *The Consolidated Treaty Series* (Dobbs Ferry, N.Y.: Oceana Publications, 1969–1981. See also R. B. Mowat, *The European States System: A Study of International Relations* (London: Oxford University Press, 1923), p. 16. As a function of the sheer cost of power, there was a drastic reduction in the number of states in the first rank. A standing army exacted an enormous price, and only well-organized and prosperous states could afford the expense of big battalions for long.

30. Parker, "The Dutch Revolt," in Parker and Smith (eds.), *The General Crisis of the Seventeenth Century*, pp. 68–69, 72.

31. It is hard to find parallels with the armies of this period. The Mongol army that stormed Samarkand in 1219 may have exceeded 200,000, but did not have the extensive support system of Wallenstein's armies. See James Chambers, *The Devil's Horsemen: The Mongol Invasion of Europe* (New York: Athenaeum, 1985), p. 9. Rome's regular legions are usually put at 160,000 to 175,000, although they may have had as many as 360,00 men under arms throughout the Empire. See Edward Luttwak, *The Grand Strategy of the Roman Empire* (Baltimore, Md.: Johns Hopkins University Press, 1976), p. 16; Robert L. O'Connell, *Of Arms and Men: A History of War, Weapons, and Aggression* (New York: Oxford University Press, 1989), p. 75; and Philippe Contamine (Michael Jones, trans.), *War in the Middle Ages* (London: Basil Blackwell, 1984), p. 306.

32. Charles Petrie, *Earlier Diplomatic History, 1492–1713* (London: Hollis and Charter, 1949), p. 147.

33. Wedgwood, *The Thirty Years War*, pp. 257, 410–411, 419; David Ogg, *Europe in the Seventeenth Century*, 8th rev. ed. (London: Adam and Charles Black, 1961), p. 168.

34. William Crowne, *A True Relation of All the Remarkable Places and Passages Observed in Travels of the Right Honorable Thomas Lord Howard, Earl of Arundel and Surrey, 1636* (London, 1637), pp. 5–17. Cited by Elmer A. Beller, "The Thirty Years War," in *The New Cambridge Modern History*, Vol. 4, pp. 345–346.

35. Evan Luard, *War in International Society: A Study in International Sociology* (London: I. B. Taurus, 1986); and H. R. Trevor-Roper, "The General Crisis of the Seventeenth Century," *Past and Present* 16 (November 1959): 31–64.

36. Cited by Parker, *The Thirty Years' War*, p. 189.

37. Joycelyne G. Russell, *Peacemaking in the Renaissance* (London: Duckworth, 1986), pp. 228–229; Bodo Nischan, "Calvinism, the Thirty Years' War, and the

Beginning of Absolutism in Brandenburg: The Political Thought of John Bergius," *Central European History* 15(3) (September 1982): 216.

38. C. R. Fredericks, "The War and Politics," in Parker (ed.), *The Thirty Years' War*, p. 219.

39. "On the Interests of Princes and States of Christendom," cited by Albert I. Hirschman, *The Passions of the Interests: Political Arguments for Capitalism before Its Triumph* (Princeton, N.J.: Princeton University Press, 1977), p. 34.

40. See also Gunn, "Interests Will Not Lie," pp. 551–564; and Gunn, *Politics and the Public Interests*, p. 36ff.

41. The French idea of sovereignty was, as one diplomat at Westphalia, Abel Servien, noted, a notion with no equal. Cited by Croxton, draft, p. 430. Westphalia, as Croxton points out, marked the last of a series of papal retreats and defeats on the issue of exclusive claims to the Holy Roman Empire. See Michel Zimmerman, "La Crise de l'organisation internationale: La fin du moyen ge," *Académie de droit international: Recueil des cours* 44 (1933, part 2): 315–438, cited by Derek Croxton, "The Peace of Westphalia and the Origins of Sovereignty," paper given on the occasion of the 350th Anniversary of the Peace of Westphalia, Enschede, July 18–21, 1998. And Croxton's work, *Mazarin and French Foreign Policy* (Susquehanna University Press, forthcoming).

As Croxton puts it: "like all such historical benchmarks, Westphalia is in some respects more a convenient reference point than the source of a fully formed new normative system. Some elements that characterize the modern world, separating us from the Middle Ages, were well established long before 1648; others did not emerge until many years after. Still, the Peace of Westphalia created at least the foundations of a new European system."

42. Carl von Clausewitz, *On War* (Michael Howard and Peter Paret, eds. and trans.) (Princeton, N.J.: Princeton University Press, 1984), Book Eight, chapter 3B, p. 590. The divorce armies and policy at the end of the Thirty Years War, however, were never total. Were the contractors and commanders unconcerned with state policy? If they were, like Wallenstein and Mansfield, they were fired. On this point see Derek Croxton, "A Territorial Imperative? The Military Revolution, Strategy, and Peace Making in the Thirty Years War," *War in History* 5(3) (1988): 253–279. I am grateful for the close reading of this manuscript and generous time and ideas Dr. Croxton has shared with me on some of these matters.

43. G. Teitler (C. N. Ter Heide-Lopy, trans.), *The Genesis of the Professional Officers Corps* (Beverly Hills, Calif.: Sage, 1977), pp. 181–188.

44. Sir George Clark, *War and Society in the Seventeenth Century* (Cambridge: Cambridge University Press, 1985), p. 84.

45. The Westphalia settlement also helped to limit war by dispersing power among a great number of states so that no single state, nor any combination of states, might gain more than limited objectives against adversaries. The drastic reduction in the number of states to the first rank occurred as a function of the sheer cost of power. The first sign of this winnowing process was the Westphalia settlement itself, which reduced the number of sovereign entities within the German Empire from 900 to about 234. The figure varies from 355 to 234. Geoffrey Barraclough's figures are at the low end but probably more accurate: see *The Origins of Modern Germany* (New York: Capricorn, 1963), p. 385.

46. Raymond Aron, *The Century of Total War* (Boston: Beacon Press, 1954), p. 28.

47. Harry S. Truman, "The Truman Doctrine: Special Message to the Congress on Greece and Turkey," March 12, 1947, 180th Congress, 1st Sess., March 24, 1947.

48. Richard Gould Adams, *John Foster Dulles: A Reappraisal* (New York: Appleton-Century-Crofts, 1962), p. 293.

Chapter 2

Force, Order, and Diplomacy in the Age of Louis XIV

The great chronicler of the diplomatic method, Harold Nicolson, once wrote that the origins of modern diplomacy can be traced to the "determinant influence of Cardinal Richelieu. Richelieu's achievement was the development of a coterie of trained "creatures" dedicated to promoting state interests through "ceaseless negotiation."[1] By the time Richelieu died, in 1642, France had fostered a new class of diplomatists, and thus somewhat inadvertently had helped to pave the way for the great settlement of the Thirty Years War signed at Westphalia in 1648.

Richelieu's last devoted servant, Mazarin, died in 1661, leaving a stepson, the 23-year-old Louis XIV, and a group of experienced advisors to direct a vast and far-flung foreign policy apparatus. After 24 hours of seclusion and weeping for the passing of his guardian, Louis commenced his 63 years of personal rule—the longest in European history—with, in his words, a "request and order" that you not "sign anything, not even a passport . . . without my command."[2] Within days, each French ambassador had received a letter which began, "I have decided to reply myself to all letters which I order my ambassadors to write me."[3]

Louis' single-minded search for advantage was so raw, unencumbered, and bellicose that, even in the ethos of the times, it was unique. From the onset of his reign, Louis XIV was intent on ensuring that French diplomatic hegemony ceased serving any abstract international order which may have emerged, in part, as a result of Richelieu's ministry. Instead, with a great system of well-provisioned clerks, residents, heralds, ambassadors, and spies, French statecraft was to become Louis' own instrument: a great narcissistic engine—fueled and sated only by war. Backed by a colossal army (some 450,000 troops at its height), and a treasury never too depleted to find huge sums to subsidize and suborn, Louis' agents worked tirelessly for his advance.

Like nearly all his contemporaries, Louis had held that the "craft of kingship" consisted in attending to the "true maxims" of states.[4] But Louis did not study the interests of others to harmonize French purposes with those of his neighbors (the dictionary definition of diplomacy). Instead, Louis considered the "science of interests" a kind of late-seventeenth-century jujitsu, the object of which was to secure a pivot by which his neighbors' undoing could be leveraged.

A real constraint to arbitrary and unanticipated state action was Richelieu's emphasis on a modicum of good faith—or in the language of the day, the sanctity of the "pledged word" of a sovereign. To Louis XIV, however, diplomacy was a species of rarefied dust, mined only to be used in the eyes of his enemies. The king's envoys were, as he put it, "good for keeping [potential adversaries] occupied while I made my preparations . . . so that . . . when they heard the truth in those vague rumors . . . they took them as an artifice."[5] "[E]veryone," Louis advised his son, "arranges treaties according to his present interests."[6] Treaties, said Louis, were more like compliments; on the one hand "absolutely necessary" for coexistence; on the other, "of little significance beyond their sound."[7] In his early negotiations with the Dutch, the king wrote his ambassador that "there are hardly any [words] in the world so clear, in any dispute whatsoever, that do not have some exceptions and contrary reasons."[8]

Louis' disregard for his own undertakings turned out, in the short run, to yield the intended surprise. The success of the tactic bespoke the heed accorded by others in the second half of the seventeenth century to a sovereign's "pledged word," even when there was abundant evidence of dubious intent. For worn and sour William of Orange, then King of England, who had already spent some 30 years combating Louis' ever-keen avidity, there was unfeigned astonishment at Louis' ability to bend and break his undertakings. As William III wrote to his Dutch confederates on the eve of a war over the Spanish succession, "I never relied much on engagements with France; but I must confess, I did not think they would have broken, on this occasion, in the face of the whole world, a solemn treaty before it was well accomplished."[9]

"L'ESTAT A MOI"?

Louis' demands and incessant wars seemed to demonstrate the truth that power creates its own interests, limited in turn only by the power. Louis' own morality was grounded, as he tutored his son, on "reason of state," a judgment inspired and given, he wrote, only to kings "over whom God alone is judge."[10] But the ever-plastic ground of "reason of state" rarely supported the interests of his countrymen. To those who implored some favor or another, his customarily withering comment was, "we do know them." His disinterest applied to courtiers and commoners alike. In 1709, after seven years of war and the "little Ice Age" had ravaged Europe, food disappeared, and whole families froze in doorways. Louis turned to his brother and said "what if four or five thousand of those scoundrels die . . . would France be any less France?"[11]

Although he probably never said "L'estat c'est moi," clearly Louis felt that the state was his patrimony ("L'estat a moi"). Late in his life, Louis may have recognized the distinction between the state and himself. On his death bed, he had breathed: "I depart, but the state remains."[12] But for most of his life, the identity between France and Louis' own person was nearly complete. "A king works for himself, when he has the state in mind," he wrote his son, and "the welfare of the one enhances the glory of the other: when the state is prosperous, exalted and powerful, he who is the cause of it is rendered glorious by it and no consideration should prevent him from doing so, not even for the sake of doing a kindness."[13]

GLORY

It is easy to read Louis' tireless self-promotion as a massive exercise in appeasing an abundant vanity. Louis' "house at Versailles," one English visitor wrote, "is something the foolishest in the world, he is strutting in every panel and galloping over one's head in every ceiling, and if he turns to spit he must see himself in person or his Vicegerent, the sun."[14] Built with a great hemorrhage of money, Louis' palace outside of Paris was named after Helios, the resting place of the sun. The king also had a plethora of monuments erected, medals struck, walls decorated, plays written, poems read. But Louis' quest for reputation—for fame and "gloire"—was informed by a larger compass than his own ego. At the broadest level, Versailles' function was to advance the notion that Louis himself was a kind of sun, giving radiance to all his people in his divinely ordered mission on earth. More narrowly, it served to keep some 2,000 troublesome nobles—the bane of Louis' childhood—in an elegant detention camp. It was also an enormous public works project, employing artisans, weavers, carpenters, glass blowers, furniture makers, and architects, making French crafts competitive with any in Europe. Versailles was also an effective instrument of administration.

As Saint-Simon, no great admirer of Louis, observed, the

constant residence at Versailles caused a continual coming together of officials and persons employed, which kept everything going, [getting] through much more business in one day than would have been possible in a fortnight had the court been in Paris. The benefit to his service . . . was incredible. It imposed orderliness on everybody and secured dispatch and facility to his affairs.[15]

To Louis, Versailles, his promotion of the arts, his medals, were a kind of very expensive and pervasive propaganda, useful in assuaging the people of his realm with the balm of realization that they were led by a man who truly was "like a god." And, abroad, it made it appear that France's eminence was a fact of life.

When foreigners came to present credentials, Versailles was constructed to convey a sense of secular awe. The message was to be clear, that Louis' power, taste, magnificence, wealth, and martial prowess were without peer. The Hall of Mirrors, the place where ambassadors were received, forced diplomats to walk under ceilings that trumpeted Louis' military genius, showing Louis transported across the Rhine as Apollo on a triumphal chariot, holding Jupiter's quiver of thunderbolts. Behind Louis, "Hercules swings his club while Holland prepares to give the keys to the Republic to the King."[16] Previously, great structures were for the glory of God. Even Philip II's Escorial was more, at its heart, a grand ossuary and swollen chapel than an administrative center. Soon, however, Louis' point—made at the cost of perhaps eight years of state revenues—had been driven home to governments and city planners from Dresden to St. Petersburg.*

> So that in the first place, I put a general inclination of all mankind, a perpetual and restless desire of Powere after Powere that ceaseath only in Death.
>
> Thomas Hobbes, 1661

Thomas Hobbes lived in the "recovery of hope" that his writing would "fall into the hands of a sovereign." As a little-read Oxford curmudgeon, Hobbes would have found great satisfaction if he had known how well his words were echoed in Louis' and his advisors' musings on the "*métier du roi*"(the job of being king). "[G]lory," Hobbes insisted, "is like honor, if all men have it, none hath it, for they consist in comparison and precellence."[17] *Gloire*, Louis wrote, is "my aspiration in all things, . . . the principal object of my actions." A king, Louis wrote, "need never be ashamed of seeking fame, for it is a good that must be ceaselessly and avidly desired, and which alone is better able to secure success of our aims than any other

---

*When the Princess Sophie, the mother of the future George I, came to visit Versailles, Louis' queen offered her the hem of her robe to kiss. This practice was in keeping with a series of *peties affaires*, by which Louis sought to ensure that others would yield to the logic of the hoary predicate of Bourbon blood. In the spring of 1661, the French ambassador to Spain demanded, and succeeded in, gaining the right—previously denied to France—to make a public entrance into Madrid. In the fall of 1661, at a funeral procession held in London, the Spanish ambassador ordered the horses drawing the French ambassador's carriage killed, so that the Spanish ambassador's entourage could pass first. Louis' response was to threaten a renewal of war, and Spain was forced to apologize. France's precedence before Spain, at all occasions of state and ceremony, was not just acknowledged, but, as Louis demanded, read aloud by the Spanish ambassador resident at every capitol and court of Europe.

thing." Similarly, Hobbes held that "Riches, Knowledge, and Honour are but several forms of powere," and that when men share an "appetite to the same thing . . . [and] neither [can] enjoy it in common, nor . . . divide it, it follows that the strongest must have it, and who is strongest must be decided by the sword."[18]

Louis and his mercantilist advisors, especially Colbert, his Minister of Commerce, were certain that glory, gold, security, and power were finite commodities. If one party shared similar stature or wealth, the wherewithal of others would be diminished. If one party had it all, others would have none. Therefore, as Colbert wrote to Louis, "commerce" was merely "perpetual . . . war . . . of intelligence and industry."[19]

A MEASURE OF WAR

Louis had always been a war-lover. As a child, he set up toy fortifications in his garden. Before adolescence, the king had learned to drill, master the manual of arms, and practice long hours with pike, musket, lance, and saber from horseback.[20] At the age of 13, Louis had already seen battles close up enough to have tasted the tartness of gunpowder. When he came of age, Louis lamented the "unfortunate" peace he had inherited from Richelieu and Mazarin. Finding a "peace more profound than anyone had seen in centuries," he told his son, was distressing. "[A]t my age," he confessed, the thought of "the pleasure of my being at the head of my armies" provoked in him the "desire for a little more action abroad."[21]

Ultimately, Louis measured himself only with the iron gauge of war. An almost audible shadow of buoyancy and relief appears in his memoirs when the king revisits "the prospect of . . . two wars [providing] as a vast field that could create opportunities for me to distinguish myself."[22] War on land in Europe was Louis XIV's real self-validation. Colbert had spent huge sums on a competent navy, overseas exploration, and the development of an autonomous marine branch of arms. But the king's priorities were reflected in his activity. He visited no ship or shipyard until 1681, and that appears as an effort to mollify his aging minister. Colbert's attention to cartography, hydrography, and marines was generally dismissed as an infatuation. As Louis advised his son, the "caprice of the sea" never gives real greatness. "Warfare on land is a more advantageous business than naval war, in which the most valiant almost never have occasion to distinguish themselves from the weakest."[23] Other kinds of competition counted to Louis, but not as much as that which could be tested by armed infantry.

War was the primary means, Louis felt, to define his greatness. To Louis, a state without a competence at arms lacked "gloire," and was incomplete and contemptible. Louis thought "of war ten times more than he thinks of finances," Colbert complained.[24] Reform of the antiquated and ultimately ruinous tax system languished. The problem was that, as Colbert observed, the king considered "finances only when extreme need obliges him to do so."[25] In the end, even though revenues decreased radically, it was still easier to sell tax privileges and tax immunities than change the whole complicated and corrupt tax collection process. The war against the Grand Coalition would be determined, Louis lamented, by he who held the last gold coin, after the coin of all others had been depleted. But for most of Louis' life, wealth, reputation, glory, and status were but the residuum of military success. For Louis, like Frederick the Great a century later, real power could come only from big battalions and big guns.

INSTITUTIONALIZING COUNTERVAILING POWER

For Louis, especially in his early years, the only legitimate object of peace could be the gift of time in which France would prepare for war. The king yearned for what he was sure would be a lopsided romp through the Dutch countryside. Holland had affronted Louis' gloire. It was too rich, too Protestant, and too independent. Shielded from France by the Spanish Netherlands and the Rhine, the Dutch "herring merchants," observed Louis, desired "only to maintain their commerce." The contentious amalgam of merchant factions that constituted the Dutch government was, to Louis, a pitiable, a "shattered and divided thing."[26] With no real army, the Dutch Republic's foreign policy, Louis recalled, had to be based on mere "utility," a base sort of reasoning that would not support the kind of "gloire" that Louis sedulously pursued.

Louis' meticulously prepared war with Holland began in 1672. When, initially, things appeared to go well for the French, Colbert asked his king, with no irony intended, "What was to be done with Holland?" when final victory was delivered.[27] The question must have puzzled Louis. "Kings made war"; that is what they did; and that is how Louis planned to "fulfill the great expectations" that he had "for some time inspired in the public."[28] The Dutch Republic was an ideological and commercial irritant. Holland, moreover, rivaled Louis' vision of domestic political and religious order. If Holland were humbled, it might no longer deny its more numerous Catholics the right to worship; it might loosen its monopoly on the Baltic trade, as well as nearly all of Western Europe's interstate waterways, save the Danube. If France took the Belgium borderlands and reopened Rotterdam, Amsterdam's trade would wither. A broken Holland would hardly find its institutions or "freedoms" admired by many. If Louis had his way the Dutch Republic, brought low and poor, would not ever even be in a position to abet another anti-French coalition.

Holland had supported Spain, indirectly, after 1635, and had signed a separate peace at Westphalia with Spain in 1648, and then again made a separate arrangement with England in 1668.* But the Dutch Republic presented much more of an affront to Louis than a threat. Holland's allies were easily detached, and as Colbert's tariffs began to bite after 1670, it became clear that Louis could have the ruin of Holland without firing a shot. But the winning argument for war was that though Holland appeared commercially strong, it was vulnerable, and hence the perfect target of opportunity. As Louis wrote, "[E]ven a little war would endanger one or the other of their interests" and reaffirm French preeminence in the coin that counted: prowess at arms.[29] He would lead the troops himself.

In the end, the Dutch opened the dikes and flooded the countryside. French forces we obliged to retreat. By the end of the war, Louis' gains were extracted not from Holland, but from the first "sick-man" of Europe, Spain. Franche-Comte, now Eastern France, some positions in the Spanish Netherlands, and the lasting animus of William of Orange were Louis's prizes. William brooked no particular affection for Spain but as Stadholder of Holland, and then King of England, William was determined to tame Louis' hauteur. By the second decade of the next century, it was William who proved more resourceful. Although Louis' glamour and style pervaded European courts, the tax efficiency and prosperity of the Dutch and the English helped William establish European leadership. Although the threat of French hegemony was to remain for 200 years, European politics, in adopting William's remedies of coalition building and coalition management, came to rest on the pinion of the balance of power as the first principle of European statecraft and public law.

FAITH, TERRITORY, AND THE RULES OF THE GAME

When Colbert died (1683), Louis' instincts for domestic as well as international hegemony deepened and coarsened.[30] At home, he began a species of inquisition to solidify the Catholic faith in his realm. With fire and his notorious dragonnades, recalcitrant Huguenots were coerced into an embrace of Catholicism. Although flight was forbidden, hundreds of thousands nonetheless made their way to Holland, Prussia, and England, where they joined the ranks of the anti-Louis coalition that emerged at the end of the 1680s. When Louis revoked the Edict of Nantes, Frederick William invited the Huguenots to come to Brandenburg. Other German princes followed suit. Soon tens of thousands of Louis' best soldiers, sappers, and engineers had dispersed throughout Protestant Europe.†

---

*France assisted, albeit desultorily, the Dutch Republic in the Second Anglo-Dutch war. The war was soon ended at Aix-La-Chapelle, where the Dutch arranged the Triple Alliance of the Hague with England and Sweden, ostensibly to assist the end of hostilities between France and Spain, but really to limit the gains of France in the Spanish Netherlands and Franche-Comte.
†He later fought against Louis' protégé, James II.

Louis' neighbors were hardly made more secure by the rivulets of Huguenot immigration, since Louis reckoned his success in war as well as his peacetime diplomacy in terms of French expansion. Part of the king's reasoning, after some of his earlier preoccupation with *gloire* faded, was "security"; hence, his demands on his neighbors were directed to creating a kind of seventeenth-century "free-fire zone," a vast "dueling field"—as his Minister of War, Vauban, put it—where the overwhelming number and competence of French infantry could prevail as supporting fire poured down from the finest fortifications in Europe.[31]

By the mid-1680s, Louis' appetite for territory had achieved a kind of autistic autonomy and momentum of its own. In a trumped-up legal process, artfully called "reunions," the king instructed his lawyers to advance arguments in front of tribunals composed of crown-appointed jurists. The king's brief was that once France acquired territory, any of the dependencies of the newly obtained region would thenceforth devolve to France. Any subsidiary dependencies of annexed territory were, in turn, promptly arrogated, and registered.

For several years, those who had contending claims to those advanced by Louis—the Swedes, the Austrian Emperor, and the Spanish—were either too weak or too preoccupied by the Turks; for in 1683, Kara Mustafa, "The Turkish Wallenstein,"[32] stood before the gates of Vienna with 200,000 troops, including sappers and engineers lent by the French army. The seige lasted 59 days and only a Polish-German force led by Sobieski and Charles V, the Duke of Lorraine, effected Vienna's rescue. Once the Ottomans had been driven to their last Balkan redoubts some six years later, and William of Orange assumed the English throne (1688), a new coalition against Louis, backed by William of Orange, congealed. But the beginning of the Grand Alliance, the League of Augsberg, served only to stymie Louis from gaining more. At the Treaty of Ryswick in 1697, Louis XIV deigned to recognize William III as King of England; but in turn, Louis obtained acceptance of nearly all the "reunions" of the 1680s. Moreover, Parliament voted only 7,000 soldiers for William's army and reduced the navy. The Tories then forced William to send his guards away. "In fact," wrote Winston Churchill,

William reckoned he could guarantee European security . . . [instead] . . . [o]fficers and men were cast upon the street or drifted into outlawry in the countryside. . . . [I]n the name of peace, economy, and isolation, they [the Tories] had prepared the ground for a far more terrible renewal of war.[33]

The development of effective countervailing power to a greatly enhanced France, a development sometimes chronicled as inevitable as the seasons, was in fact by no means certain. It was 50 years into Louis' reign, at a point when Louis claimed the right to place a zealously Catholic king on

England's throne while attempting the unification of Spain and France under the crest of the Bourbons, that William's stratagem of perpetual coalition war would have a chance in England's Parliament. By then Spain had leagued with France—bringing along the Indies, South America, and a great part of Italy. Belgium, Luxembourg, and Savoy also rested with France. By the reckoning of military historians, it was only the leadership of Marlborough and Eugene,[34] added to the miraculous sums raised by the English Parliament, that drove Louis back to frontiers defined at Westphalia in 1648.

CAVEATS TO A "MODERATE AGE"

As noted by Chicago University's great economic historian John U. Nef, who wrote 40 years ago, war had "declined in seriousness" in the age of Louis XIV. By the end of the seventeenth century, Nef wrote, war had become more controlled and cerebral and, thus, "congenial to the thought of an optimistic and rational age." "The older conception of military campaigns persisted," as Nef put it, "only in the east of Europe."[35] Indeed, in the United States, the established canon of contemporary "liberal-realist" scholarship still holds that the management of late-seventeenth- and eighteenth-century power thorough coalition diplomacy was the period in which the forces of moderation in international society had their greatest victory.[36]

Part of the evidence that warfare in the age of Louis heralded a new moderation in international society is Daniel Defoe's observation that it had become, in his time, "frequent to have armies of fifty thousand . . . within view of each other, and spend a whole campaign in dodging or, as it is gently called, observing one another and then march off into winter quarters."[37] A half-century later Clausewitz echoed this view when he observed, "The size of the French monarch was so disproportionate to the limited nature of the war. . . . The limited intensity of the war gave rise to the opinion that for France war was a secondary matter, and in turn this point of view influenced the charter of the war."[38]

Some battles were, indeed, more formalized and less bloody than before, but war's object nonetheless almost always included destroying enemy forces. As Raimondo Montecuccoli, lieutenant general and field marshal of the army of the Austrian Hapsburgs, put it: War is the "activity in which adversaries try to inflict damage on each other by all possible means." Using a formulation later taken up by Frederick (and the German General Staff), Montecuccoli argued that armies fought until "whosoever at the end disposes of more forces intact." "Philosophers may debate," Montecuccoli wrote, "whether a permanent state of war exists in nature, but statesmen cannot doubt that there can be no real peace between powerful competing states; one must suppress or be suppressed, one must either kill or perish."

Even battlefield victory was not sufficient for Montecuccoli; those who fled had to be "hunted and annihilated"[39] lest they regroup to fight again. In sum, for most commanders of the late seventeenth and early eighteenth centuries, real combat, once begun in earnest, knew few limits and allowed little quarter.[40]

As a result, carnage, even when it could be localized, grew immense. Battlefield losses—when battle was given at places where commanders felt they either had an edge or had no choice—reached the tens of thousands. Indeed, the death tolls from late-seventeenth- and early-eighteenth-century battles—at Blenheim, Ladnen, Malpequet, Ramilles, and Oudenarde—were not regularly exceeded until the Battle of Bordino and the American Civil War. In each late-seventeenth- and early-eighteenth-century test at arms, the better-sighted guns and longer-ranged, faster-firing cannon of the day caused far higher casualties than had been the usual case at the start of the seventeenth century.

The new technology of war manufacturers was matched by a new administrative science: The lethality of combat increased as a function of the state's ability to organize a soldier's pay, vitalization, and housing, and to field a constant supply of munitions. Firepower also expanded in proportion to the spread of the new science of discipline. If cudgeled sufficiently, and marched insensate, as the disagreeable Col. M. de Martinet discovered, troops could be quick-marched in formation for a month or two while on campaign, then formed along dense, staggered lines. On command, they would produce a great continuous rain of fire while receiving in kind from their adversaries.[41]

THE IRONY OF LOUIS' FOREIGN POLICY: THE BALANCE OF POWER—AND ITS LIMITS

Any new security at the end of the seventeenth century was apparent only when measured by the ghoulish yardstick of the Thirty Years War. It was a rare year in Europe during the latter part of the seventeenth century—perhaps but four in all—that was without war. War had become nearly universal in frequency and scope, extending from the Straits of Malacca to Mexico. As Voltaire remarked in an examination of Louis' time: "It is one of the results of the ingenuity and fury of men that the ravages of our wars are not confined to Europe. We drain ourselves of manpower and money so as to go to the far reaches of Africa and America."[42]

As a result of incessant war, the period of Europe's emerging balance of power proved as deadly as the latter part of the fourteenth century. Peasants were no longer tortured for their savings; priests were no longer tied to wagon wheels to run with dogs. But ordinary citizens were hardly given much more safety than they had during the Thirty Years War. Pillage emerged as a matter of state policy, rather than being the reward of combatants, as had been the rule 50 years earlier; and a frank policy of "preventive terror" was employed by the armies of Louis—along with those of Marlborough, Leopold, and Charles XI.

Piqued at Genoa's aid to his Spanish enemies, for instance, Louis had the city blown apart; he then ordered the resultant rubble—two-thirds of every building that had once stood in the city—thrown into the sea.[43] In his campaign against Holland in the 1670s, Louis' forces savaged the potential staging areas of his enemies with such a "barbarous" ferocity that an "astonished" Voltaire found that Dutch children still read "books which recount the deed and thus inspire hatred of the French in future generations."[44]

In the last 20 years of the seventeenth century, whole provinces on the French frontier were reduced to ash and ruin to leave no forage for the enemy; to teach an enemy a lesson; to inspire fear; to exact revenge. Louis called it his "policy of frightfulness." When more than a few of his generals balked at Louis' orders, the king himself threatened their recall and disgrace. "Not a stone, not a stone," the mighty Louis intoned, as Heidelberg, Mannheim, Trier, Speyer, Oppenheim, Worms, and a host of smaller cities were given over to torch and terror.[45]

In undertaking an avalanche of war, Louis mobilized the largest forces Europe was to see until Napoleon. Taxes to support the immense armies of the day far exceeded the level that had been reached in the Thirty Years War. By the end of the century every state in Europe, save England, teetered on bankruptcy. Depleted by the ever-increasing cost of war, even the relatively well-heeled governments of the day were forced to let soldiers and sailors go during rare times of truce or peace. Former soldiers turned into brigands and highwaymen while the continent shivered under the press of a radical change in climate. Crops failed. Plague worked its way back through Europe. By 1694, Fenelon, the king's one-time religious savant, wrote: "Your people are dying of hunger. . . . All France is nothing more than a great desolate hospital without supplies."[46] But Louis had hardened beyond moral deafness. Even when the king's own brother petitioned Louis to lighten the people's burden, Louis dismissed the dead and dying as "canaille . . . not much of use on this earth . . . I pray you not to meddle in what does not concern you."

Can a nation be safe without strength?

Charles Davenant, 1696

What can be done against force, without force?

Cicero

Half Hapsburg, married to a Hapsburg, reigning over the most powerful states in Europe, Louis' undertakings could have had a manifest legitimacy by definition. As the quintessential sovereign of his day, Louis XIV could have provided a different standard for organizing international relations had he been only somewhat more temperate. But by his ceaseless claims on his Hapsburg cousins everywhere their interests touched his, Louis contested almost every element of the emerging but still fragile international order adumbrated at Westphalia. No diplomatic credential could be presented without risk that a Bourbon envoy might contest his place in a processional. No border Rhineland prince could be safe from annexation. And nearly every state in Europe was certain to know of French excesses from the 200,000 that fled in the terror of the 1680s into the Huguenot Diaspora.

Whatever territorial and administrative inhibitions he might have privately acknowledged, none were made clear by his actions. As in the case of the great dictators in this century, one can speculate that Louis may have had limits to his schemes. But Louis seemed living proof that power defines its own interests. His unremitting activity after 1668 had no real plan or design. Early on, he seemed animated by a mix of commerce, revenge, and pique. Later, his design was said to "round off French frontiers." The apogee of Louis' ambition came in his attempt to unite the Spanish and French patrimony while supporting Catholic James II's return to the English throne. But always Louis' actions seemed to illustrate that, with power, the appetite tends to grow with the feeding.

France, by becoming the leviathan state grown overstrong and predatory, posed a profound danger to any emergent European "system" comprised of autonomous states. International "society" was still inchoate when Louis assumed power. Only in the process of defending themselves did Europeans forge a new commonweal predicated on independent, sovereign power.[47] The objective of a balance of power as a desirable European condition had been a matter of prescriptive comment for some time in Louis' youth. But explicit mention of the balance of power finally made an appearance in Europe's public law at the Treaty of Utrecht in 1713. In the wake of Louis' final defeat, the signatories to Europe's peace pledged to take "care [that] suspicions . . . be removed from the mind of men and [that] . . . Peace and Tranquillity of the Christian World . . . be ordered and stabilized in a just Balance of power [which] is the best and most solid foundation of mutual friendship and lasting concord."[48]

By the time Louis had found it "easy" to leave life, he had perversely helped foster the balance of power as a general principle of European society. Louis' inadvertent legacy was a European solidity that was to moderate the first half of the eighteenth century. It hardly seems coincidental that the first proposals in modern times for new forms of international organization, based on the management—by professional diplomatists—of power with equivalent power, appeared in the wake of Europe's collective experience with Louis' incessant wars. In a work published in 1716, Callières, one of Louis' diplomatic servants, spoke of an emerging "freemasonry of diplomats" who reported through increasingly well-developed and autonomous ministries, separate from the Department of War.[49] Not long before Louis died, the (albeit short-lived) *Acadèmie politique* for training young professional diplomatists heralded the fact of a separate and increasingly professionalized diplomatic service, charged with the management of state relations in time of peace, and arranging for coalitions in case of war.[50] In the years following Louis' death, diplomatic conversations still employed the grammar of interests, but a new logic developed.

Like the liberal realists of our own time, a school of thought arose a century or so following Louis' death which held, as a major premise, that war had become an ironic but nonetheless empirical condition of international order. "[T]hough some may laugh and call them utopian dreams," Clausewitz wrote, the tendency was to "equilibrium defined by the balance of power, revealing itself only when in danger of being upended."[51] Clausewitz's argument was that once war had become bureaucratized (by the end of the seventeenth century) it inevitably ceased to function as an instrument of dynasts, and had to become an extension of rational government policy. Larger, more competent states had developed what Clausewitz called a "sensitive nexus."[52] War was intrinsically dreadful and rightly feared; European commanders and kings certainly preferred victory to defeat. But closely balanced forces, the ritualized construction of fortresses, and mannerly maneuvers and sieges allowed war, as Clausewitz argued without irony, to become but a "stronger form of diplomacy, a more forceful of negotiation . . . to be exploited at the peace conference."[53] A better peace had become the object of war. In the process of serving an improved peace, force had formed an ironic, Siamese connection with Europe's emerging public law, prosperity, and order.[54]

For awhile the expectation of equilibrium, predicated on a balance of power, did sustain the independence of states and preserve a modicum of stability. On reflection, however, it was merely an Indian summer of tranquillity that had bussed Europe at the time of Louis' passing. Three generations on, the leader of the best-organized military machine in Europe, Frederick of Prussia, a parvenu like Louis, found fame, military reputation, and the urge to expand frontiers irresistible. Notwithstanding the promise of a balance of power to preserve the independence of significant states, Poland—the savior of Europe a hundred years before—disappeared. Then, in France, all the furies capped at Westphalia erupted in the guise of nationalism, giving yet more and still bloodier proof to the truth that anarchy, aggression, and war are endemic to international society.

NOTES

1. Louis XIV, *Memoire for the Instruction of the Dauphin, 1668* (P. Sonnino, trans.) (New York: The Free Press, 1970). Reproduced in Evan Luard (ed.), *Basic Texts in International Relations* (New York: St. Martin's Press, 1992), p. 159.

2. John B. Wolf, *Louis XIV* (New York: W. W. Norton, 1969), p. 133.

3. William James Roosen, *The Age of Louis XIV: The Rise of Modern Diplomacy* (Cambridge, Mass.: Schenkman Publishing, 1976), p. 34.

4. Wolf, *Louis XIV*, p. 75; Louis XIV, *Memoire for the Instruction of the Dauphin*, p. 159.

5. Louis XIV, *Memoire for the Instruction of the Dauphin*, p. 159.

6. R. M. Hatton, "Louis XIV and His Fellow Monarchs," in John C. Rule (ed.), *Louis XIV and the Craft of Kingship* (Columbus: Ohio State University Press, 1969), p. 382.

7. Geoffrey Treasure, *The Making of Modern Europe* (London: Methuen, 1985), p. 197.

8. Hatton, "Louis XIV and His Fellow Monarchs," p. 383. In this sense, however, Louis was no less "advanced than Grotius who held that a sovereign is hardly bound by a secular instrument or authority if it conflicted with the interests of his state."

9. H.W.V. Temperely, "The Revoltion and the Revolutionary Settlement in Great Britan, 1687–1702," in Sir A. Ward et al., *The Cambridge Modern History* (New York: Macmillan, 1924), p. 395. William's remarks were made upon hearing that King Carlos II of Spain had finally died, leaving Spain and all Spain's possessions to the Bourbons. Louis, notwithstanding three undertakings to refrain from doing so, accepted Carlos' will.

10. William F. Church, "Louis XIV, and Reason of State," in Rule (ed.), *Louis XIV and the Craft of Kingship*, p. 370. Mazarin advised a young Louis, God "established kings to take care of the well-being, security, the repose of their subjects, and not to sacrifice those goods and that repose to their own passions, and if that unfortunate situation does occur . . . Divine Providence abandons them." John B. Wolf, "The Formation of a King," in Rule (ed.), *Louis XIV and the Craft of Kingship*, p. 123.

11. J. J. Mangan, *The King's Favour* (New York: St. Martin's Press, 1991), p. 70.

12. Church, "Louis XIV, and Reason of State," p. 381.

13. Mangan, *The King's Favour* p. 70.

14. John C. Rule, "Roi-Burecrate," in Rule (ed.), *Louis XIV and the Craft of Kingship*, p. 171.

15. Ibid., p. 172.

16. Mangan, *The King's Favour* p. 73.

17. Thomas Hobbes, *The Leviathan* (Harmondsworth: Penguin, 1968), p. 150; and Torbjorn L. Knutsen, *A History of International Relations Theory* Manchester: Manchester University Press, 1992), p. 88ff.

18. Hobbes, *The Leviathan*, p. 150; and Knutsen, *A History of International Relations Theory* p. 88ff.

19. Paul Sonnino, *Louis XIV and the Origins of Dutch War* (Cambridge: Cambridge University Press, 1988), p. 56. When war was a certainty, Colbert, first a courtier, wrote on the onset of the war: "If the king were to subjugate all the United Provinces of the Netherlands, their trade would become His Majesty's trade; there would be nothing else left to wish for."

20. Wolf, *Louis XIV*, p. 78.

21. Rule (ed.), *Louis XIV and the Craft of Kingship*, p. 56; and Paul Sonnino,

"The Sun King's Anti-Machiavel," in Rule (ed.), *Louis XIV and the Craft of Kingship*, pp. 356–357.

22. Louis XIV, *Memoire for the Instruction of the Dauphin*, p. 159.

23. Inès Murat Murat, *Colbert* (Robert F. Cook and Jeannie Van Asselt, trans.) (Charlottesville: University of Virginia Press, 1984), p. 172.

24. Colbert's huge memo (1670) is in Pierre Clement (ed.), *Lettres, Instructions et Memoires de Colbert*, Vol. VII (Paris: Imprimerie National, 1870, 1873), pp. 233–266.

25. Ibid.

26. C. R. Baxter, *The Anglo Dutch Wars of the 17th Century* (Palo Alto, Calif.: Pendragon House, 1974), p. 23.

27. H. R. Trevor-Roper, *The General Crisis of the Seventeenth Century in Europe: 1560–1660*, ed. Trevor Aston (London: Routledge and Kegan Paul, 1965), p. 148.

28. Louis XIV, *Memoire for the Instruction of the Dauphin*, p. 159.

29. John Baptist Wolf, *Toward a European Balance of Power: 1620–1715* (Chicago: Rand McNally, 1970), p. 2.

30. He died at the age of 64 of massive kidney stones and had to be buried at night, in a parish plot, lest the people be stimulated to riot. Murat, *Colbert*, p. 271.

31. John B. Wolf, *The Emergence of the Great Powers, 1685–1715* (New York: Harper & Brothers, 1951), pp. 16–17, 26; Wolf, *Toward a European Balance of Power: 1620–1715*, pp. 66–67; and Wolf, *Louis XIV*, p. 248.

32. Wolf, *Louis XIV*, p. 52.

33. Winston S. Churchill, *The Age of Revolution* (New York: Dodd, Mead, 1957), p. 22.

34. Duke Francois Eugène of Savoy was a child of the commandant of the Swiss guards and the chief lady in waiting to the queen, a woman who had to flee France because she had been accused of being a poisoner.

35. John U. Nef, *War and Human Progress* (New York: Russell and Russell, 1968), p. 156.

36. Among others, see H. Rothfels, "Clausewitz" in E. M. Earle (ed.), *Makers of Modern Strategy* (Princeton, N.J.: Princeton University Press, 1943), p. 99.

37. Daniel Defoe, "An Essay upon Projects, Earlier Works," in Henry Morley (ed.), *The Earlier Life and Chief Earlier Works of Daniel Defoe* (London: Routledge, 1989, p. 135, cited by Nef at p. 156.

38. Peter Paret and Daniel Moran (eds. and trans.), *Carl von Clausewitz: Historical and Political Writings* (Princeton, N.J.: Princeton University Press, 1992), p. 18.

39. Cited in Gunter E. Rothenberg, "Maraca of Nassau, Gustavus Adolphus, Raimondo Montecuccoli, and the 'Military Revolution' of the Seventeenth Century," in Peter Paret (ed.), *The Makers of Modern Strategy* (Princeton, N.J.: Princeton University Press, 1986), p. 62.

40. Cited in Rothenberg, "Maraca of Nassau, Gustavus Adolphus, Raimondo Montecuccoli, and the 'Military Revolution' of the Seventeenth Century," p. 62; Nef, *War and Human Progress*, p. 153.

41. Geoffrey Treasure, *The Making of Modern Europe* (London: Methuen, 1985), p. 218ff.

42. Philippe Erlanger, *Louis XIV* (Stephen Cox, trans.) (New York: Praeger, 1970), p. 255.

43. Previously, bombing cities from the sea had been directed against pirates who sought refuge in the non-Christian towns of Algiers.

44. "Bodegraven and Zwamerdam, two important market towns, rich and well-populated, very similar to French country towns of moderate size, were given over to the soldiers for pillage, as a recompense for their hardships. They set fire to both; and in the light of the flames rioted in debauch and cruelty. It is astonishing that French soldiery should be so barbarous, commanded as they are by so many officers who have justly gained reputations of being humane as they are brave. This pillaging made such a profound impression that more than 40 years later I have seen Dutch children's reading books which recount the deed and thus inspire hatred of the French in future generations." Jean Francois Marie Arouet de Voltaire, *The Age of Louis XIV* (London: J. M. Dent, 1951), pp. 104–105.

45. Wolf, *Louis XIV*, pp. 452–453.

46. In a letter said to be for the king's eyes only: William F. Church, "Louis XIV, and Reason of State," p. 397.

47. Herbert Butterfield, "The Balance of Power," in Herbert Butterfield and Martin Wright (eds.), *Diplomatic Investigations* (London: George Allen & Unwin, 1966), p. 140.

48. Cited in M. S. Anderson, "Eighteenth Century Theories of the Balance of Power," in R. Hatton and M. S. Anderson (eds.), *Studies in Diplomatic History: Essays in Memory of David Bayne Horn* (London: Longman, 1970), p. 192.

49. Francois de Callières, *The Practice of Diplomacy* (A. F. Whyte, trans.) (South Bend, Ind.: University of Notre Dame Press, 1963), p. 113ff.

50. Sir Herbert Butterfield, "Diplomacy" in R. Hatton and Anderson (eds.), *Studies in Diplomatic History*, p. 363.

51. Hugh Smith, "The Womb of War: Clausewitz and International Politics," *Review of International Studies* 16(1): 50ff.

52. Carl von Clausewitz, *On War* (Michael Howard and Peter Paret, eds. and trans.) (Princeton, N.J.: Princeton University Press, 1976), Book Eight, chapter 3, pp. 589–590.

53. Ibid., p. 590.

54. Smith, "The Womb of War," p. 50ff; Paret and Moran, *Writings*, "Notes on History and Politics," p. 244.

The Heyday of the Balance of Power: Frederick the Great and the Decline of the Old Regime

INTRODUCTION

By the middle of the eighteenth century, the balance of power was almost universally acclaimed as an indispensable condition of European statecraft. Yet both the moderation and consensus that accompanied the eighteenth-century international community were short-lived. Vying with the development of policies and institutions aimed at an overall European equilibrium were potent forces of disorder. Specifically, the national assertions of Prussia led to fissures of a system that relied, on the one hand, on moderation and consensus and, on the other, on opportunism and violence.

Because the balance of power failed to operate effectively, it gave way to its nemesis: unscrupulous statesmanship. Hence it can be argued—contrary to conclusions of most who refer to the eighteenth-century balance of power—that the origins of the breakdown of European order are not to be found merely in the cataclysm of the French Revolution, but instead can be traced to three additional factors: (1) an absence of central authority or even a semblance of a public monopoly of superior force in the post-Utrecht (1714) international system, (2) the incapacity of universal European values to limit the appetite of some of the more established states, and (3) the rise of ambitious parvenu states, especially Prussia and, to a lesser extent, Russia.

In our time those who almost longingly recall the old state system have seemed unmindful of the very modest success of even its best years.[1] Indeed, to many, in retrospect, the eighteenth century seemed a "golden age"[2] in the history of the nation-state system. But the period of a functioning balance of power was, in truth, more fragile and fleeting than it usually is portrayed.

INTERNATIONAL MODERATION AND CONSENSUS AND THE EIGHTEENTH-CENTURY BALANCE OF POWER

A number of social and political developments encouraged the moderation that characterized both the means and the ends of the "classic" eighteenth-century balance of power system. The great coalitions against Louis XIV had left most European states exhausted, and a bit less interested in the mere glory of nations or kings.[3] After the death of Louis XIV, France's chief government minister, Cardinal Fleury, assumed the regency for young Louis XV. Fleury was 73 years old when he took office and 90 when he died. He was not in a position (nor did he desire) to initiate great plans for the distant future. When Louis XV finally came to rule, he proved to be lazy and self-indulgent, little concerned with the glory of France. Public affairs fell increasingly into the hands of merchants and financiers disinterested in diplomatic great departures. Britain's prime minister, Sir Robert Walpole, had a personal motto that could have summarized the early eighteenth century: "Let sleeping dogs lie," he would say over and over again.[4]

Moreover, the passions of patriotism, although certainly a factor in the vast mobilizations of England, Holland, and France during the wars of Louis XIV, did not dominate international politics. For instance, it was unthinkable to ask for "unconditional surrender" or to make the kind of mass appeals as those that occurred later with the coming of nationalism, when whole peoples called for the submission of other whole peoples. National feeling existed, but the disruption of any final diplomatic settlement based on "national interests" was not permitted. In the mid-eighteenth century there was simply too much distance between those who led and those who followed. In fact, only a fraction of the population concerned itself with foreign affairs.[5] Statesmen were not yet compelled by public opinion. Bolingbroke would write to his friend, Lord Bathurst, concerning the masses.

I would rather be a dog, my lord, and bay at the moon than be obliged to roar and eternally in that note which the humor, the passion, the ignorance, and the incapacity of power sets in. The only popularity worth having is that which will sooner or later arise from the steady pursuit of national interests.[6]

Nevertheless, there was a change from the practice of the seventeenth century. As diplomatic intercourse and comity between states grew, the execution of foreign policy expanded beyond the purview of a few clerks and several ambassadors. The increase in diplomatic functions necessitated the development of foreign officers with separate departments, intelligence operations, lawyers, and a permanent staff of officers of various rank who were sent abroad to manage the affairs of their respective countries. The "interests of state" were no longer decided by the king alone (they had not been for some time in England), but by wealthy merchants, financiers, holders of title and inherited wealth, and the royal family. This devolution of foreign policy to bureaucrats and numerous groups helped to make policy both more predictable and more conservative.

International moderation was also supported by the expanded use of trade as a foreign policy instrument. As Professor Nef once pointed out, "Fighting with new weapons," in the eighteenth century, such as improved cannons and bayonets, "was not heading toward very satisfactory results" if they were calculated either in territory or trade gained. So statesmen turned increasingly to another kind of weapon, to duties, prohibitions against imports, and to preferential treatment of colonial trade."[7] David Hume had brilliantly demolished the theory of exclusive commercial exploitation, arguing that trade created mutual advantages,[8] but British mercantilist statesmen were not convinced. To them, commercial policy was "high" policy.[9] States fought for "favorable" balances of trade just as they fought for "favorable" balances of power, and this common search for expanded commercial and military power resulted in an equilibrium of power—a fact that statesmen took to be as immutable as geography.

Perhaps the most important elements of moderation in the conduct of eighteenth-century interstate relations occurred on the battlefield. The development of standing armies, the necessity of giving troops regular clothing, food, and shelter, and the improvement in discipline reduced both the incentive and the opportunity for looting and lawlessness. As the acquisition and maintenance of soldiers (and the saltpeter necessary for the manufacture of gunpowder) grew more costly, commanders hesitated to expend their resources frivolously.[10]

On the home front it became commonplace for soldiers to be stationed in garrisons, while a goodly number of others were sent to far-off colonies or to sea. Naval battles were inherently less costly in human life, and the stationing of soldiers abroad reduced the opportunities for, and the intensity of, combat in Europe. Losing armies were not annihilated on the battlefield with any great frequency. There was, in fact, an expectation that they would get away. The sight of blood revolted this rather humane epoch. And soldiers were no less sensitive to the sight of their own fluids than were gentler minds of the day. In fact, the rationale for giving troops red uniforms was to diminish soldiers' fright upon witnessing the blood of their comrades. Likewise, the decks of fighting ships were painted red so that sailors would not take undue notice of the carnage.

Soldiers' zeal for pursuit was further dampened by the invention of bayonets, which first appeared in the 1680s and gradually replaced the pike, a cumbersome weapon measuring up to 18 feet in length. By the early eighteenth century the bayonet-equipped musketeer, armed with the safer, faster-firing flintlock, could face cavalry alone, if properly drilled. Rigorous training of infantry, indeed large armies, was a consequence of the invention of an accurate rapid-fire, steel-tipped rifle.[11] Yet the prospect of using bayonets—of stabbing or being stabbed by a cold blade and then having the weapon dislodged by a bullet—was horrifying. Consequently, armies, no matter how well drilled, operated without much sanguinary passion and tended to avoid each other.[12] Moreover, almost bereft of earthly possessions, soldiers were often burgeoned into battle by brutal drill and discipline. Frequently, armies reluctantly dragooned from streets or prisons found themselves fighting on loan for some contracting principality in Europe. Such men as these rarely made for enthusiastic land encounters.

Declining enthusiasm for combat helped precipitate the eighteenth-century effort to limit and regulate battlefield engagements. International law was therefore able to moderate the conduct of hostilities by demanding that war be declared formally and ended formally. It was also increasingly acknowledged that war should be waged with due concern for noncombatants and prisoners of war. Even in time of war, Europeans traveled and traded with each other with few official impediments. It was the time of the "Enlightenment,"[13] when religious passions had finally ebbed and when the *philosophes* would speak of the reason that all men could, and eventually would, attain.

PRUSSIA: THE MILITARIZATION OF A MODERATE INTERNATIONAL ORDER

By and large, the war that broke out by the mid-eighteenth century had two loci. One was between Britain and France for commerce and colonies. The other was the competition for territory and power in east central Europe. The latter struggle was marked by Prussia's rise from a highly militarized provincial German state to a great power, rivaling Austria in power and pretense. The English–French rivalry and the contest that centered in Germany became intertwined. But, in terms of the old European order, they can be thought of separately. The Anglo-French wars were waged mainly overseas about issues that, although considered important, were hardly critical to the structure of European society. When Canada changed hands as a result of the Seven Years War, Voltaire's reaction was typical of the European attitude: He considered that part of North America to be but "a few miserable acres of snow."[14] The struggle in central and eastern Europe, however, was seen to be of more lasting importance, and it had near-fatal consequences for the norms of moderation on which the balance of power was constructed and maintained.

Frederick the Great's father, Frederick William, inherited an area that had no independent status at all until the Treaty of Westphalia (1648). Prussian nobles were known for their ferocity and skill in raising, maintaining, and directing soldiers. In all, however, Frederick William had more than an ordinary Prussian's enthusiasm for military prowess. By giving troops an iron ramrod to pound down the powder charges in muskets (instead of wooden ones, which fit poorly and splintered), and by paying extraordinary attention to close-order drill,[15] Frederick William greatly augmented that considerable army's capacity for rapid fire and maneuver. Then, too, his stringently prudent economic policies encouraged the increased conscription of his own people, rather than relying on more expensive and less dependable mercenaries, as was the mode in Europe. Proportionate to the population (1:25 as compared to 1:150 in France),[16] it was the largest army in Europe. And although not preeminent in absolute numbers (perhaps 80,000), it was a force to reckon with.

Frederick William's twin legacy was this impressive army, a centralized administrative system more autocratic than any other in Europe, and his son, Frederick II. Frederick's father had readily terrorized both the Prussian populace and his son. When the people of Berlin hid from Frederick William as he passed through the streets, he chased after them brandishing his walking stick, exhorting them not to run but rather, as he put it, to "love me, scum." Frederick William suspected his son of being in league with his enemies, the English. Because of young Frederick's interest in arts and letters, his father believed him to be not really a man.[17] Frederick often suffered his father's blows and regularly was denied food so that relatives and servants had to feed him on the sly. At one point he tried to run away to England with his single boyhood friend, but his plan was compromised. Frederick's father had his son imprisoned. Just before the adolescent Frederick fainted, he saw his only close friend beheaded on order of his father.[18]

After Frederick William's death, Prussia found itself directed by a man steeped in the Enlightenment. The young prince wrote and spoke well only in French. Many of his policies (particularly his domestic reform)—some of which began under Frederick William—produced a moderate criminal system and efficient graduated taxes, encouraged religious toleration, and made him the darling of the French *philosophes*, especially Voltaire. In external politics, however, Frederick's only limits were those established by Prussian power and a disposition in his later life toward prudence. In a sense, Frederick's foreign policy was the greatest force for disruption in the eighteenth century, exclusive of the French Revolution.

Frederick succeeded to the throne in 1740. Within the year he had seized Silesia from Austria. It was a daring campaign lasting only seven weeks. In one stroke Frederick claimed territory half again the size of Prussia under Frederick William. Silesia had been the richest province in the Austrian Empire. In contrast to the poorly endowed estates of Brandenburg and Prussia, it was a bountiful agricultural land, possessing large tracts of forest and immense quantities of coal and iron. But Frederick's claim to the people and the area was of dubious legality. The taking of Silesia by launching a war without warning was considered outrageous by most statesmen in Europe. As Frederick himself later gloated, Europe was unpleasantly "amazed" by his audacity.[19] Frederick confessed that the general view of Europe was that only a man who did not believe in God would commit such a rapacious act.[20] "That man is mad," Louis XV concluded.[21]

The seizure of Silesia overturned one of the operating principles of the balance of power as it had come to be understood by the mid-eighteenth century. The balance of power had been seen as a reliable guarantor of national independence. Previously, there had been a

general recognition that the destruction of an independent sovereignty was an exceptional and normally an unjustifiable act which ultimately protected many of the small states of Europe, some no larger than a single city, from absorption by the greater powers. Even in the eighteenth century, when the power of the larger states was increasing rapidly, contemporary opinion, influenced by the classical city-state ideal, held up the smaller states for admiration and believed in their independence.[22]

Frederick's annexation was thus "illegitimate" in both a legal sense and in terms of the reigning consensus underlying the fragile and rather recent stability of Europe. The annexation of Silesia proved to be the beginning of the final breakdown of inhibitions against large-scale changes in the status quo, implying that a case for expansion was not necessary beyond simple military ambition and the subsequent interest that any unfounded claim might require.

Frederick's action, as Karl Marx observed a century later regarding the Wars of Bismark, implied a dynamic of perpetual war:

If [territorial] limits are to be fixed by military interests, there will be no end to claims because every military line is necessarily faulty and may be improved by annexing some outlying territory; and moreover, they can be fixed finally and fully because they always must be imposed by the conquer or upon the conquered and consequently carry with them the seeds of fresh wars.[23]

To the statesmen of the day, the essential purpose of the eighteenth-century balance of power was the perpetuation of the European status quo. This balance did not require peace; quite the contrary. The balance of power relied on an assumption that any state might align itself with any other—if, by making such an arrangement, the overall European political equilibrium and individual interests of states might be enhanced. Alliances shifted and numerous wars were fought, usually with the result of restoring the *status quo ante bellum*. Still, the novelty of this short-lived balance of power system was less in its mechanisms than in its self-conscious articulation and celebration.[24] One mid-eighteenth-century essayist, Charles D'Avenant, was typical:

As the Earth is now divided into several Kingdomes, Principalities and States, between 'em Wars will happen, but the Weaker fortifie themselves by Alliances with the Stronger; so that (unless some Great Oppressor rises up to disturb the World with his Ambition) we have many more years of peace than of War; whereas in Universal Empires every day had its different Calamities.[25]

By and large, territorial compensation for victory and loss in combat or diplomacy before Frederick's seizure of Silesia had been carved out from the vast overseas possessions of the European powers. In this way states usually retained their frontiers and their dignity. For although the colonies were a source of wealth and pride, they were not yet considered integral or essential to any state's legal, political, or moral existence.

Frederick's motives in literally stealing Silesia could have been frivolously simple. Most probably he acted out of simple opportunism. He explained himself to an English admirer: "I was young, had plenty of money, a big army, and wanted to see my name in the newspapers."[26] He may have wished, in some ultimate sense, to feel himself worthy of approval and esteem from his irascible dead father.[27] Later, however, Frederick gave a more elegant, *realpolitik* justification:

The acquisition of Silesia increased Prussian revenues by 36,000 thalers. The greater part of that sum was used to increase the army. We shall presently have the use Frederick made of these troops . . . Silesia was united to Prussia. . . . The principal cause of the successful conquest was the army which had been formed in the course of twenty-two years by admirable discipline and was superior to all other troops in Europe.[28]

The "operational code" of Frederick's statecraft violated the nascent sense of European community. Good relations between diplomats were possible when the ruling houses of Europe shared the same traditions of culture and civility toward one another. One of the most eminent students of this period has written that the aristocracy and ruling houses "were forged together by family ties . . . common cultural values and . . . common moral convictions about what a gentleman was, and . . . Indeed, the gentility of the eighteenth century promoted that attention to group interests on which the system rested."[29]

But Frederick felt disdain for any contemporary code or values of interstate comity. As he revealed in a marginal note to himself in his volume of Tacitus: "No ministers at home but clerks. No ambassadors abroad but spies. Formal alliances only to sow animosities. Kindle and prolong wars between neighbors. Always promise help and never send it."[30]

Some of Frederick's contemporaries may have contemplated unscrupulous depredations like those of Frederick. For instance, one of Louis XV's advisors, the Count of Broglie, counseled, "A great power with a grand design first carries it out in spite of general indignation, then makes the reckoning with its neighbors; and the balance of the account is always favorable."[31] All in all, however, most statesmen were inhibited by more moderate norms of the time.

Yet, in Frederick's views, foreign policy was a scientific study of how to gain advantage. To Frederick, since all other states were similarly selfish, any balance of power could only be maintained, in effect, by arms races, preemptive wars, and the coupling of ends with means virtually unlimited by considerations of laws or ethics.[32] In a more or less modern international environment this was a revolutionary notion of political conduct. Few others in Europe would publicly or even privately make any such assertion as Frederick's to the effect that "European politics are so fallacious that even sages become dupes, if they are not on the alert."[33] When one of Frederick's ministers drafted a convoluted juridical explanation for the Prussian to claim Silesia, Frederick wrote on the back of the document a cynical but evidently sincere compliment: "Brave: the work of an excellent charlatan."[34]

Two principles in international law had been evolving, but were in tension with each other. One was *practa sunt servanda* (treaties must be served). This maxim held that treaties were like private contracts. To fail to live up to them just because of temporary disadvantage would be wrong. The other principle was *rebus sic stantibus* (treaties are valid only as long as conditions remain unchanged). To this latter principle, Frederick's writing and action subscribed. When a war broke out nearby, counseled Frederick, a wise prince did not stay neutral, even when obligated by formal agreements. For "by remaining neutral he risked everything and would expect to gain nothing."[35] To Frederick, treaties were but the most transient of arrangements. In the preface of his "History of My Own Times" he wrote:

The interest of the state ought to serve as the rule of the monarch. Princes are slaves to their means, the interests of states prescribe laws to them, and that law is inviolable. . . . Examples of treaties . . . broken are frequent. It is not our intention to justify them all . . . [It] appears evident that a private person ought to be scrupulously tenacious of his promise. . . . If he does an injustice [others] can have recourse to the protection of the laws. . . . [A]n individual alone suffers . . . while a sovereign may draw calamities upon nations.[36]

To Frederick, even the most fundamental elements of international law, such as sovereign immunity, could succumb to "reasons of state." Thus, in 1756, suspecting wrongly that a plot was being hatched against him and that the proof could be found in the diplomatic archives of Dresden, Frederick invaded the city without warning. The archives of state, guarded personally by the Queen of Saxony—mother of the Queen of Spain, heir apparent of France and cousin of Maria Theresa—were seized. The Saxon queen was pushed aside so that the incriminating (but nonexistent) diplomatic correspondence, which all Europeans considered privileged, might be discovered and published.

Although he was as well-bred as any Enlightenment prince, Frederick scorned civility. He insulted Empress Maria Theresa of Austria with puns and lewd jokes, and offered enormous bribes to the King of France's mistress for a favorable end to the Seven Years War, but he never "allowed himself to forget for one moment that she was descended from butlers and fish vendors and that both of her parents were procurers."[37] The Czarina Elizabeth was also the object of Frederick's obscenities. Her love of vodka and men was legendary. But his notice of it was unkind at best.

Once while Frederick was entertaining a French gentleman . . . a sprightly hussar entered the room. Pointing to him, Frederick remarked, unsmilingly, "That fellow has the handsomest penis in my dominions. I am going to send him as ambassador to Russia." The story was relayed via the Austrian and Saxon ambassadors to . . . the Russian Imperial Chancellor, who was also Elizabeth's lover. Needless to say, both were apoplectic.[38]

Frederick's misanthropy was not without purpose. He understood that in a world of gentility and at least a pretense of respect among royal houses, despicably ill-mannered words could yield an advantage. As Frederick told his longtime associate, De Catt:

As long as I breathe, my dear sir, I shall poke fun at these people who are so implacable against me. If it cannot hurt them, at least I will shock them and exasperate them as much as I can. . . . It is not difficult my friend, to point defects . . . I make it my business . . . I will in turn, employ . . . my pen and ink to hurl bolts at them which will anger them and drive them to despair. Thus, like Hercules, I will lay low this Hydra of enemies.[39]

In the eighteenth century, diplomacy moved away from the Renaissance idea that envoys were sent abroad to deceive and spy. The expanded use of diplomats with elaborate protocol and rules tempered, slowed, and regulated interstate activity. To Francois de Callieres and those schooled in the French diplomatic method (and most of the great houses of Europe would be included), a dishonest diplomat was like a shady banker or businessman: One who has a reputation for being shifty soon loses his customers, credit, and credibility. As de Callieres, in his great work *On the Manner of Negotiating with Princes*, wrote:

The good negotiator will never rely . . . on . . . bad faith. . . . [A] lie always leaves a drop of poison behind and even the most dazzling success gained by dishonesty stands on an insecure foundation, for it awakens in the defeated party a sense of aggravation, a desire for vengeance, and a hatred which must remain a foe.[40]

In commerce or relations between states, deception has rarely been good business and was never good for the business environment. By about the mid-eighteenth century many Europeans began to feel that the real purpose of diplomacy was "to harmonize the real interest of the parties concerned." The craft of an envoy was negotiation, that is, the making of agreements. Therefore, de Callieres concluded, the ambassador should be "a man of peace . . . who works by persuasion. . . . [T]he great secret of negotiating is to bring out prominently the common advantage of both parties of a proposal and so link these advantages that they may appear equally balanced to both parties."[41]

In the early and mid-eighteenth century, diplomacy was the usual means of gaining advantage. But Frederick nearly dispensed with the "new" diplomacy of the eighteenth century. Unlike other sovereigns of his day, Frederick did not use diplomats or believe it to be a diplomatic function to negotiate on behalf of sovereigns. Negotiation, to him, was merely a calculation of military potential, not the attenuation of conflicting interests. It was not that he was unwilling to negotiate; he was—but only to gain what he knew were respites in his quest for advantage.

Frederick preferred lower-rank "envoys" to ambassadors, inasmuch as such individuals, it was considered, needed less talent. Besides, to Frederick, they were essentially "letter carriers."[42] Therefore, his negotiators were neither significant individuals nor the honest ones that de Callieres advised. Frederick counseled Valoir, the French envoy to Berlin:

You are a witty man and a man of superior understanding. But in the post of ambassador you are yet a novice. I will therefore give you a piece of advice: If you have anything to negotiate, apply directly to me. My people will deceive you—that is what I pay them for.[43]

In the eighteenth century, there evolved the budding of a kind of parallel relationship between force and diplomacy. Force was a "last resort," but it could be used without undue fear because violence was not as awful as it had been or was to become. Thus force stood at the side of diplomacy, neither overshadowing it nor hindering its use. Frederick used both his army and his statecraft to his obvious advantage, with little thought to European tradition. By discounting those elements of inhibition, consensus, and civility in international society, Frederick augmented Prussian power but decreased the stability of the balance of power. This was a design of his statesmanship. In time, its effects were to take their toll on events in

Europe and the moderation and consensus that characterized the eighteenth-century international community.

THE PERILS OF AN EXPANDED EUROPE

By participating in the dismemberment of a European state, Poland—which had been a part of European society for 600 years and was closer in culture and character to Western Europe than Prussia itself—Frederick demonstrated the fragile order the balance of power gave to interstate relations. Prussia, even with the addition of Silesia, had seemed on the frontier of Europe. Indeed, Voltaire had called Frederick "King of the Border Zones."[44] By mid-eighteenth century, though, the edge of Europe was almost 100 miles to the east. The partition of Poland in 1772 was undertaken to join the geographically divided domain of east and west Prussia. Catherine the Great, who had been engaged for some time with a Polish insurgency, was willing to cooperate, as was, reluctantly, Maria Theresa, Frederick's Austrian opponent.

Maria Theresa knew her act was a violation of European norms, but the temptation of a vast new polyglot realm proved irresistible. Frederick's sardonic comment on her hesitation was, "She weeps, but she takes." Maria Theresa was not, however, unaware of the kind of effect the Polish partition was liable to have on the public order of Europe. "Long after I am dead," she despaired, "it will be known to what this violation of all that was hitherto held sacred will give rise."[45] Edmund Burke wrote: "Pray, dear sir, what is next? . . . Poland was breakfast, and there are not many Polands to be found. Where will they dine? After all our love of tranquility and all expedients to preserve it, alas poor peace."[46]

The partition of Poland, writes Oxford historian Robert B. Mowat, was a "brutal crime in the face of the known and acknowledged law of nation." Previously, annexations had been

indemnities at the end of wars, or as the result of exchanges, or of hereditary succession. . . . The annexations made by Austria, Russia and Prussia could not be defended on the grounds of costs or warfare, of exchange and of compensation. . . . They were pure brigandage, the robbing of a neighbor carried out in time of peace by those powers against a helpless neighbor.[47]

The balance of power had been held by Europeans as a guarantor of the sovereignty of the weak. But after the partition of Poland, as Albert Sorel wrote, "The weak states noted with terror the development of a practice which threatened them all. It . . . became a part of European custom and the flexible doctrine of equilibrium."[48] Indeed, the Polish example was followed by the partial division of the Ottoman Empire undertaken by Russia and Austria in 1782, followed by further partitions of Poland in 1792 and

1795. On the frontier of Europe a malign principle arose and thrived; it finally engulfed Europe.[49]

Frederick's ambition for more German land and his almost obsessive husbanding of state power forced Austria to cease opposing Russian advances to the west, which had begun with Peter the Great in the late seventeenth century. By forcing Austria to seek Russia as an ally and then by co-opting Russia into the partition of Poland in 1772, Frederick added another previously all-but-irrelevant member to international society. Russia, slowly drawn into new calculations regarding the European balance of power, was still a semi-barbarous state. In diplomacy, Russia shared few of the cultural hesitations or familial inhibitions with the rest of Europe. In warfare, Russian soldiers were known for their excesses. In 1759, for example, during the Seven Years War, warfare in central Europe returned to some of the savagery that had been the norm in the Thirty Years War. "The Russians," writes British historian Nancy Mitford, "committed every atrocity under the sun and raped everybody, including the Burgomaster of Beuthen, whose wife said she really thought they might stick to women."[50] "Nothing like it had been seen since the invasion of the Huns," read one account. "Inhabitants were hanged after their noses and ears were cut off, their limbs were torn away, their entrails and hearts opened."[51]

The addition of a still backward Russia to the European system of the balance of power and the division of most of Germany into two great states—Austria and Prussia—brought further difficulties to European equilibrium. The addition of diverse, nontraditional "actors" in the emerging eighteenth-century international system increased the potential for conflicts of interest within that system. By augmenting the number of states engaged in an arms competition, the possibility of regulating such competition diminished.[52] And by enlarging the number of potential allies, policy-making became more uncertain as misapprehension about motives increased. The addition of new "great powers" to the international system of the eighteenth century made the system inherently more unpredictable and, to that extent, more unstable. War might now occur not only because of willful strategies but also as the result of the inability to calculate and accommodate the intentions of others. This was especially the case as new "actors" refused to play by, or even give lip service to, many of the old rules that had moderated diplomatic behavior.

Disorder was exacerbated by "legitimizing" the notion that a European equilibrium could be produced by the mutual search for a competitive edge through arms races[53] and preemptive attacks. The practice of this dogma propagated by Frederick soon swept Europe. As Montesquieu despaired:

A new disease has spread through Europe. . . . It has attacked our princes and makes them maintain a disproportionate number of troops. . . . As soon as one state increases the number called into service, the others immediately do the same, with the result that nothing is gained thereby but the common ruin. Each monarch keeps in readiness as many armies as he would need if his people were in danger, and this condition of rivalry of all against all is called peace.[54]

CONCLUSION

The fragile and short-lived success of the eighteenth-century balance of power rested on moderation and consensus. Frederick's war, in tactics and aims and volume of violence, was destructive of that consensus. Richard Rosecrance, a political scientist, summarizes most recent scholarship regarding the salad days of the balance of power when he writes: "A balance of power mechanism could hardly have functioned in a context in which . . . protagonists were bent on advancing their separate interest against general European concerns. . . . A minimum homogeneity of outlook . . . [a] unit of sentiment and ideas . . . among the great powers was a necessity of such a system."[55]

The aim of the new "French system" of diplomacy had been to secure at the conference table, by adjustment of contending interests, a moderate international order wherein states could not be termed either satiated or *revanchist*. Classic diplomacy was largely predicated on reason and comity between states. Respect for sovereign immunity and other injunctions of law and protocol facilitated negotiations. As Richelieu contended, the observance of treaties is always the wisest course, for the "greatest strength of sovereigns comes from doing this."[56] His advice, however, served but two generations of European statesmen.

For a short time, war, although an instrument of diplomacy, was used mainly when diplomacy and accommodation had failed. The classic diplomatic mold was shattered when Frederick and his rival, Catherine the Great of Russia, found that diplomatic courtesy was no substitute for gains dramatically nailed to a foundation of force. In his memoirs Frederick wrote an aphorism more understandable to the revolutionary age of Mao Tse-tung than to any "golden age" of the balance of power: "(R)oyal crowns are won only by means of big guns."[57] To Frederick, war, instead of a deplorable *ultima ratio* of diplomacy, was almost a lyrical imperative. "The ox must plow the furrow, the nightingale must sing, the dolphin must swim, and I—I must make war," he explained.[58]

The Prussian system of internal governance was geared almost exclusively to external policy. Internal reforms were undertaken to facilitate the management of statecraft. The middle and lower classes were systematically denied any opportunity for much more than a rudimentary political education. Frederick's leadership, and the myth he created, made Prussia the most absolute system in European history. Prussia was, perhaps, the only real precursor of twentieth-century totalitarianism and, in fact, contributed to many of the myths that buttressed the Third Reich.[59] As one historian, Koppel Pinson, commented:

By his cult of military force and by his own example of military success, he implanted in Prussia, and through Prussia in Germany, their inordinate reliance on military strength which both the Germany of Bismarck and Hitler were to follow. He became the supreme example of the amoral national hero who hovered over and above the everyday concepts of good and evil.[60]

Prussia and Russia, as the parvenu states of Europe, faced few inhibitions about the limits of *raison d'état*. To them, security was what social scientists would today call a "zero sum" game. If you did not maintain and nourish security interests, others would see that course of action as weakness and would make you their prey. As Catherine the Great explained, aggrandizement, not negotiation or mutual undertaking, is the object of statecraft. "He who gains nothing, loses," she concluded.[61]

In the seventeenth century the balance of power after the Treaty of Westphalia was maintained by the German–Spanish connection. When that connection was broken, the Austrian House of Hapsburg and most of the houses of Germany were strong enough to maintain on the frontier of Europe a bulwark against Ottoman and Russian invasions. Even in their weakened state, the royal houses of Austria and Germany were, in the minds of many observers, the linchpin of European order. As the Abbe de Saint Pierre wrote:

The real strength of the existing order is . . . to be found partly in the play of conflicting policies which . . . keep each other mutually in check. But there is another bulwark more formidable yet. This is the Germanic Body, which lies almost in the centre of Europe and holds all other parts in their place, serving . . . for the protection of its neighbours. Its component peoples . . . make it the rock on which all schemes of conquest are doomed infallibly to break. . . . So long as that constitution endures, the balance of Europe will never be broken . . . and the Treaty of Westphalia will perhaps forever remain the foundation of our international system.[62]

After Frederick, the fundamental territorial alignments and moral assumptions of the Westphalia system were subjected to strains from which the old order would never really recover. The "golden age" of the balance of power was a fleeting moment, partially realized. Memory seems to exaggerate the durability of the most temperate features of the balance of power. Nonetheless, many students of international affairs seem to harbor a subconscious urge to locate empirically an idyllium. Perhaps there is reassurance in the thought that an international system predicated on power can, after all, find a tolerable order.

NOTES

1. The portrayal of a European balance of power distinguished by its brevity and tentativeness is a minority position, to be generous. Still, there are even harsher judgments. For a flawed but powerful statement that European politics before the French Revolution was a mere extension of the dictums of *raison d'état* and *sauve qui peut*, see Albert Sorel, *Europe and the French Revolution: The Political Traditions of the Old Regime* (Alfred Cobban and J. W. Hunt, eds. and trans.) (Garden City, N.Y.: Anchor Books, 1971).

2. The common understanding of the eighteenth-century international system as a "golden age" is reflected in the following volumes: Walter L. Dorn, *Competition for Empire: 1740–1763* (New York: Harper & Brothers, 1940); Edward Vose Gulick, *Europe's Classical Balance of Power* (New York: Norton, 1955), pp. 36–40, passim; Kyung-Won Kim, *Revolution and the International System* (New York: New York University Press, 1970), especially chapter 1; Hans J. Morgenthau, *Politics among Nations*, 5th ed. (New York: Knopf, 1973), p. 189; Robert B. Mowat, *The European State System* (London: Oxford University Press, 1929); Richard N. Rosecrance, *Action and Reaction in World Politics: International Systems in Perspective* (Boston: Little, Brown, 1963), especially chapter 1.

3. See Sorel, *Europe and the French Revolution*, pp. 33–35; and Penfield Roberts, *The Quest for Security: 1715–1740* (New York: Harper, 1947) pp. 2–3 and 37, passim.

4. Robert R. Palmer, *A History of the Modern World*, 2nd rev. ed. (New York: Knopf, 1960). p. 243.

5. Roberts, *The Quest for Security*, p. 4.

6. H. T. Dickenson, *Bolingbroke* (London: Constable, 1970), p. 254.

7. John U. Nef, *War and Human Progress* (Cambridge, Mass.: Harvard University Press, 1950, pp. 165 and 254, passim.

8. David Hume, "Of the Jealousy of Trade," *Essays Moral, Political and Literary*, Vol. 2 (London and New York: Longman's, Green, 1898), p. 348.

9. As Walter Dorn puts it: "What appears absurd as an economic measure maybe sound common sense from the point of view of military strategy. Great Britain and France fought each other with navigation acts and the 'Exclusif' with navies and privateers, by keeping their respective trade routes open and closing those of their rival, but they fought also with normal peacetime commerce and shipping, with trade monopolies and the economic self-sufficiency of the respective colonial empires. This, power and politics and economic policy became interchangeable terms." Dorn, *Competition for Empire*, p. 9.

10. John B. Wolf, *The Emergence of the Great Powers, 1685–1715* (New York: Harper & Row, 1951) p. 174, passim.

11. Richard A. Preston and Sydney F. Wise, *Men in Arms: A History of Warfare and Its Interrelationships with Western Society*, 2nd rev. ed. (New York: Praeger, 1970), p. 140.

12. See Frederick's own comments in Frederick the Great, "History of My Own Times," *Posthumous Works*, Vol. 1 (London: C.G.J. and J. Robinson, 1789), pp. 71–72. (Hereafter, Frederick's *Posthumous Works* are cited by title and volume number.)

13. The military doctrine of the day was beholden to the Enlightenment. Hence, strategists stressed the importance of maneuver, reason, and cleverness in battle. Commanders often attempted to prolong campaigns merely to exhaust an opponent's treasury rather than to attempt to defeat the opposition. Some, as Michael Howard once called them, "visionaries" objected to this mode of warfare, and with the rise of national armies and nationalism, battlefield casualties rose dramatically.

14. Ludwig Dahio, *The Precarious Balance of Power* (New York: Vintage Books, 1962), p. 115.

15. Generally, every eighteenth-century European army was as brutally drilled. Martinet, after all, was a Frenchman. But even so, Prussia under Frederick William and his son Frederick had a reputation for excess. See Jay Luvas, *Frederick the Great and the Art of War* (New York: The Free Press, 1966), pp. 12–13; E.W.Q. Lloyd, *A Review of the History of Infantry* (London: Longman's, Green, 1908), pp. 154–155.

16. Geoffrey Barraclough, *The Origins of Modern Germany* (New York: Capricorn Books, 1963), p. 400.

17. Toward the latter charge, there is testimony of a Swiss physician who claimed that Frederick's adolescence was marked by a catastrophic surgical attempt to cure a "social disease" that resulted in a permanent physiological impairment. In any case, after adolescence, Frederick never showed any evidence of interest in women. See Dr. J. G. Zimmermann, *Select Views of Life, Reign, and Character of Frederick the Great, King of Prussia*, Vol. I (London: Hookham & Carpenter and F. Newberry, 1972), pp. 44–67.

18. Henri De Catt, *Frederick the Great: The Memoirs of His Reader*, Vol. 1 (Boston and New York: Houghton Mifflin, 1917), pp. 6–63.

19. Frederick the Great, "History of My Own Times," Vol. 1, p. 108.

20. See Frederick's own account of European reaction. Ibid., pp. 108 and 151.

21. Edith Simon, *The Making of Frederick the Great* (Boston: Little, Brown, 1963), p. 216; and Louis L. Synder and Ida Mae Baker, *Frederick the Great: Prussian Warrior and Statesman* (New York: Franklin Watts, 1968), p. 68.

22. Alfred Cobban, *National Self-Determination* (Chicago: University of Chicago Press, 1948), pp. 170–171.

23. "Second Address of the General Council of the International Working Men's Association on the Franco-Prussian War," in Karl Marx, *Selected Works*, Vol. 1, V. Adoratsky (ed.) (New York: International Publishers, 1936), p. 441.

24. Gulick, *Europe's Classical Balance of Power*, p. 39.

25. Charles D'Avenant, essays: *I. The Balance of Power; II. The Right of Making War and Peace, and Alliances; III. Universal Monarchy* (London: printed for James Knopton at the Crown in St. Paul's Churchyard, 1701), p. 291.

26. Frederick the Great. Letter number XXXI to Jordon, 3 March 1741, "Correspondence," Vol. IX, p. 63.

27. As Frederick told his reader, "My father would want me to be a soldier, but he never suspected that one day I should in this respect be what I am. How astonished he would be . . . he would not believe his own eyes." De Catt, *Frederick the Great*, Vol. 1, p. 131. De Catt adds that on a "thousand occasions" Frederick would return to this matter of his father's esteem; ibid., p. 132. As Frederick confided "[E]ven amid the pleasures I enjoy, the image of my father rises up before me to weaken them. . . . In spite of all . . . I have not ceased to venerated." Ibid., p.

136. Frederick said this when he was almost 50 years old, a time when his dreams were obsessed with memories of his father's beatings and anger. Ibid., p. 64.

28. Frederick the Great, "History of My Own Times," Vol. 1, p. 174.

29. J. Morgenthau, *Politics among Nations*, p. 221.

30. Nathan Ausbel, *Superman: The Life of Frederick the Great* (New York: Ives Washburn, 1931), p. 533.

31. Cited in Albert Sorel, *Europe under the Old Regime* (New York: Harper & Row, 1964), p. 19.

32. As Frederick states, "Princes should personally watch the proceedings of their neighbors. They should apply thmeselves with extreme attention to their plans, and anticipate their enterprise. They should take precautions which good alliances afford against the politics of these turbulent spirits that never cease . . . like the canker, eat into and consume whatever they touch." *Posthumous Works*, Vol. 4, p. 386.

33. Ibid., Vol. 5, p. 17. Also see Frederick's purported remarks in Henrich von Treitschke, *The Confessions of Frederick the Great and the Life of Frederick the Great* (New York: Putnam, 1915), p. 69.

34. Frederick's "Preface" to his "History of My Own Times," pp. xiv–xvi.

35. D. B. Horn, *Frederick the Great and the Rise of Prussia* (London: English University Press, 1964), p. 33.

36. Cited in J. Ellis Barker, *Foundations of Germany* (Port Washington, N.Y.: Kennikat Press, 1917, 1970), p. 69. See also Gerhard Ritter, *Frederick the Great* (Berkeley: University of California Press, 1968), p. 82.

37. Ausbel, *Superman*, pp. 608–609.

38. Ibid., p. 609.

39. De Catt, *Frederick the Great*, Vol. 1, p. 30. In another instance, Frederick wrote on a "rough draft" of the Letter of Madam Pompadour to the Queen of Hungary which demanded the reinstitution of chastity. It was "accidentally" published, Frederick told Voltaire. Ibid., p. 13.

40. Francois de Callieres, *On the Matter of Negotiating with Princes: On the Uses of Diplomacy: the choice of Ministers and Envoys; and the Personal Qualities Necessary for Success in Missions Abroad* (Boston: Houghton Mifflin, 1919), p. 48.

41. Ibid., pp. 55 and 111. To de Callieres, it was important that an ambassador be a "good Christian" with a "well-equipped service" and also be a "man of letters." Ibid., p. 62.

42. Treitschke, *The Confessions of Frederick the Great*, p. 72.

43. Ausbel, *Superman*, p. 546. As Frederick confided to De Catt: "I often hide my designs from those who are about me. I even mislead them, because suspecting what I have in my mind they might speak about it . . . I can only save myself by secrecy." De Catt, *Frederick the Great*, Vol. 1, p. 14.

44. Ritter, *Frederick the Great*, p. 93.

45. Nancy Mitford, *Frederick the Great* (New York: Harper & Row, 1970), p. 273.

46. Edmund Burke, *Correspondence of the Right Honorable Edmund; between the Year 1744 and the Period of His Decease in 1797*, Vol. 1 (London: F. and J. Ribington, 1844), p. 403.

47. Robert B. Mowat, *A History of European Diplomacy: 1451–1789* (New York: Longman's, Green, 1928), pp. 275–276.

48. Sorel, *Europe under the Old Regime*, p. 31.

49. Ibid., p. 32.

50. Mitford, *Frederick the Great*, p. 229. Even Frederick was taken aback by the behavior of Cossacks. De Catt, Vol. 11, p. 54.

51. Sorel, *Europe under the Old Regime*, p. 72.

52. Some of these issues are raised in Richard N. Rosecrance's "Bipolarity, Multipolarity and the Future," *The Journal of Conflict Resolution* 10 (1966): 314–326, in James N. Rosenau, *International Relations and Foreign Policy: A Reader in Research and Theory* (New York: The Free Press, 1969), pp. 325–336, passim. The Rosenau reader is a classic. Many of the permutations raised by Rosecrance are noted in the section entitled "Theories of Balance and Imbalance," pp. 289–345. Also see Felix Moreley, *The Society of Nations* (Washington, D.C.: Brookings Institution, 1932), for an assertion that as the number of states increases arithmetically, the possibility of conflict increases geometrically.

53. "Arms races" may be a bit of a misnomer inasmuch as the quality of weaponry remained equally accessible to almost all powers before the Industrial Revolution. But competition regarding leadership, finance, supply, and mobilization capability was intensified as a result of Frederick's brand of state buccaneering.

54. Charles Louis De Secondat, Baron de le Brede et de Montesquieu, *The Spirit of the Laws* (London: G. B. Bell and Sons, 1900), Book XIII, number 17, p. 234.

55. Richard N. Rosecrance, *Action and Reaction in World Politics: International Systems in Perspective* (Boston: Little, Brown, 1963), p. 27.

56. Sorel, *Europe under the Old Regime*, p. 21.

57. Barker, *Foundations of Germany*, pp. 97–98.

58. Ausbel, *Superman*, p. 634.

59. Sorel, *Europe under the Old Regime*, p. 11.

60. Koppel S. Penson, *Modern Germany: Its History and Civilization* (New York: Macmillan, 1954), p. 6.

61. Horn, *Frederick the Great*, p. i.

62. "Abstract of the Abee De Saint Pierre's Project for Perpetual Peace," in Murray G. Forsyth et al., *The Theory of International Relations* (New York: Atherton, 1970), pp. 139–140.

Chapter 4

The French Revolution: "A *Virus* of a New and Unknown Kind"

DECONSTRUCTION

According to Carl von Clausewitz, a military witness to the French Revolution from the age of 13, the French Revolution stemmed wholly from the "views of the philosophers."[1] It was the French *philosophes* "who wanted to base everything on the rights of man . . . as a force opposed to the absolute monarch . . . setting . . . limits on [its] power . . . [but] [o]nce the colossal breach occurred in France, it was inevitable that the rest of Europe would be affected by it"[2] (emphasis added).

The French Revolution demonstrated that states could fuse ideology with society so that, as Goethe observed, "[e]very thing" could be "firmly directed to one single purpose."[3] Once the "masses . . . counted for nothing," Clausewitz recalled. But when the demands of the dispossessed came to be accepted by the middle class, then their combined weight was "four or five *hundred* times" larger than the old ruling elites (emphasis added). Their very enormity constituted an "essential" and "irresistible" claim to power.[4]

The "elemental fury" of the newly enfranchised, "untrammeled by any conventional restraints," haunted Clausewitz, for the war the new masses waged was wholly free "from . . . ancient diplomatic and economic bonds."[5] "The . . . French had attacked the traditional ways of warfare like acid," Clausewitz recalled. "To their own surprise and everyone else's," explained Clausewitz, "the French learned that a state's natural power and a great simple cause were far stronger than the artificial structure of international relations by which other states were ruled."[6]

Even much later, as keen an observer as Alexis de Tocqueville was not able to wholly fathom the Revolution's passion. "[T]here is something unexplained in its spirit. . . . It is a *virus* of a new and unknown kind. There have been violent Revolutions in the world before; but the immoderate, violent, radical, desperate, bold, almost crazed and yet powerful and effective character of the [French] Revolutionaries has no precedents"[7] (emphasis in original).

France presented a unique and nearly fatal threat to the whole state system as it had evolved since Westphalia. Europe's classic diplomatic repertoire failed and failed again. France's novel claims and unique method of struggle could not be met by limited measures. The only effective counter to France's revolutionary challenge was, ironically, to employ the Revolution's own invention—democratic war. As Clausewitz concluded, "a war with France would [be] . . . not only a struggle against a government, but also against a people and therefore a struggle of life and death."[8]

But in a historic act of denial, most European statesmen failed to comprehend either the extent or the implications of an "old military system that [had] collapsed." Clausewitz allowed that it could not "be expected that the great change" would be "immediately understood."[9] But even in his most generous reflections, Clausewitz chastised the old order for not grasping the sweep of change brought about by the new power available to revolutionary France. In fact, as we shall see, general apprehension of the threat revolutionary France posed was not fully translated in political-military reality until mid-1813.

PROPHECY

In England, Edmund Burke, unique in so many ways, was singular in understanding almost at once that France's Revolution presaged "inexplicable war" with Europe's established order.[10] To Burke, even in the early months of 1790, the French Revolution was, *perforce*, for export since the revolutionaries aimed not at "national interests" or a bit of disputed territory, but rather the "Rights of Man"—a formula which could know no limits save those the framers of those rights might independently adduce from their understanding of "nature."[11] Burke saw clearly, well before war broke out between France and its German neighbors, that a society of virtual outlaws had launched an "inexplicable war" not just against the ruling order of France, but against the whole of international society.[12]

Burke was especially struck by the use of a language that evoked murderous incivility while calling itself "virtue." Burke allowed that if "the revolutionaries were to mind their own affairs" intervention would not be allowable. But France's neighbors faced, at a minimum, endless "conspiracies and sedition which," if not the result of outright conquest, in themselves were certainly aggressive war in their "resemblance." The mere example of revolutionary France was pernicious and destabilizing. "The influence of . . . a France," Burke argued, "is equal to a war." In fact, the French "example" was "more wasting than a hostile eruption."[13]

In the long run, Burke was convinced, from the start of the 1790s, before war had erupted, that revolutionary France would never allow real reconciliation within itself or with its neighbors.[14] Anything like a reconciliation between France and its neighbors was necessarily temporary and fraudulent. French diplomacy after the Revolution could not offer anything but the dissimulations of a "cabal." Unsurveilled and left to their devices, French diplomats would subvert "all normal rendering of rules and etiquette."[15] France's newly "powdered," "perfumed," and "plumed" envoys might have traded in their "rags" for "fine clothes." But these "Ambassadors for the Rights of Man" were as unlike Richelieu and Mazarin as silk is from earth.[16]

With "this republik" [*sic*], Burke thundered, nothing "independent can co-exist": "The very idea of negotiation . . . implies some confidence in their faith. . . . [W]hat hope can we have of . . . [them], as the[ir] very basis of the negotiation, assume[s] ill-faith and treachery?"[17]

Burke's insight, prefiguring Clausewitz's, was that if war is to mean anything it needs to be linked intimately to its purpose. Burke understood, therefore, that the end of a war against France was not mere "victory" over the Revolutionaries; it was also to bring France back into the European political system. Hence, Burke insisted at the onset that at the conclusion of what he knew would be a great struggle, France would have to be restored, not vivisected like Poland or extirpated from Europe's political life like Silesia. Even after extensive French gains, Burke did not see any necessity to roll back French frontiers to where they were in 1789. Instead, he only hoped to "see France circumscribed within moderate bounds."[18] After the Revolutionaries' defeat, Burke suggested, France would have to be "nursed" to normalcy instead of being irremediably "exhausted" by a punitive peace.[19] Indeed, even the revolutionary ringleaders, Burke suggested, should be shown leniency.[20] Burke's forecasts and prescription were an accurate prologue to events.

WITHOUT KINGS, "UNIVERSAL LIBERTY" KNOWS NO BOUNDS

Soon enough, Burke's predictions were confirmed by the course of the Revolutionaries. The Revolution's endemic bellicosity surfaced on the Rhine. Since 1648, Alsace had been jointly ruled by Austrian princes and the King of France. But in August of 1790, the Assembly announced that the "Alsatian people" were now "united to the French people." The warrant for this union was the French people's "will alone, [and] not the Treaty of Munster."[21] Along the entire Rhine, Rhenish princes were declared "illegitimate."[22] From now on, proclaimed the Revolutionaries, the "will of the people" would determine political authority.

In June 1791, Louis and his family were arrested after an attempt to flee to Austria. The royal entourage was escorted back to Paris under armed guard and handed over for the keep of the Assembly. The escape attempt seemed to confirm that, inevitably, Austria would side with Louis and his Austrian-born wife. For some time, exiled French aristocrats and royals had mustered troops on the Austrian side of France's northern border, in Belgium.

With Louis' arrest, ominous broadsides advertised ineluctable war. *Les Révolutions de Paris*, a sheet addressed to the National Assembly, argued:

> We shall have war.
> We shall have it if Louis once more defiles the throne.
> We shall have it if he is dethroned.
> We shall have it if the law caries out vengeance on him.
> We shall have it if we conserve the monarchy.
> We shall have it if we establish a regency council.
> We shall have it if we constitute ourselves a republic.

As a republic, argued *Révolutions de Paris*, France could be "free, clear of all fetters"; hence able to "strike a great blow" against the reign of kings everywhere. Regicide, terror, and the people's holy war, as Burke had warned, were now postulates of inextricable necessity:

Let the head of Louis fall . . . [M]ake way for a . . . republic; let . . . the first campaign . . . of our new republicans . . . exterminate all despots, to plant the standard of liberty even in the very heart of Germany. We . . . anticipate the war . . . others are anxious to carry into our territory . . . and France will have the glory . . . of having conquered, not Europe for France, but the universe for liberty, purging it of kings, emperors, and tyrants of all descriptions.[23]

In January 1792, one of the Revolution's great orators, Maximilien Robespierre (the leader of the governing twelve-man Committee of Public Safety), cautioned against expanding the Revolution by dint of arms. The real beneficiaries of war, he said, would be officers in the armies, conspirators, and speculators.[24] It was simply "extravagant," said Robespierre, "to suppose that one people has only to enter another's territory with arms in its hands to make the latter adopt its Constitution."[25] "No one," he predicted, would love "armed missionaries."[26]

The new logic, Robespierre feared, knew no limits. If the Revolutionaries were serious about their universal message, then perhaps no nation, even China, was immune from being the target of armed French ministrations. By 1792, France's revolutionary dynamic had, in fact, arrived at the point where peace meant counterrevolution; and revolution could mean only war.[27] Burke and Robespierre were proved prophets by events.

In answer to the desperate entreaties of the imprisoned Queen Marie Antoinette, an Austrian coalition confidently assembled at the frontier.[28] One Prussian official told a group of officers: "Do not buy too many horses; the comedy will not last long. The army of lawyers will be annihilated . . . and we shall be home in autumn."[29]

Neither France's initial military leadership nor French forces inspired much respect. On April 28, 1792, a French column caught sight of Austrian forces massing at the frontier and fled without a shot directed at the enemy. The French commander, General Comte Thèobald Dillon, was shot by his panicking troops and his body tossed in a campfire.[30] Another poorly equipped French force sent to attack Mons also fled. Some 250,000 soldiers were expected to report—but a third less showed up. Only 83 of some 169 battalions were able to form, due to an absence of officers.[31] Burke's prediction that untrained French volunteers were incapable of acting like soldiers appeared to have been validated.[32]

TERROR BEHIND THE LINES

On July 25, 1792, the Duke of Brunswick, commander of an Austro-Prussian army, declared that Paris should "submit at once. . . . [I]nhabitants . . . who may dare to defend themselves . . . shall be punished. . . . If the least violence [were] offered to . . . the . . . Royal family [it would beget] ever memorable vengeance. . . ."[33]

But Brunswick's chilling message had totally unintended effects.[34] Napoleon, an eye witness, recalled seeing the congregation of the most frightening rabble ["canaille."] in Paris.[35] Municipal authorities responsible for safeguarding the king fled as the crowd surged forward. But 900 Swiss guards remained to defend the king at the Tuileries. Most were killed in the advancing stampede, but the Swiss had given the royal family time to escape with their lives to a refuge on the grounds of the Tuileries. The few pathetic, living Swiss guardsmen were left stripped of their uniforms by the enraged mob. Most were castrated and beheaded. The monarchy had been effectively ended, as Burke had feared, at the hands of a mob.

Dr. Paul Marat, another member of the Committee on Public Safety, wrote, in "L'Ami du Peuple," that only when Paris was secure from traitors behind the lines would the men of the city be able to leave for the front in order to meet the advancing Austrians. The next day, a Sunday, a carriage full of priests who had refused to swear allegiance to the Revolution was stoppped short of its prison destination and attacked. Soon, a crowd had entered the prison and forced the incarcerated through a savage gauntlet. Most were killed. In one case, a General Lalue had his heart torn from a wound.[36]

On September 5, 1792, the Convention authorities proclaimed terror "the order of the day."[37] Instead of making efforts to quell vigilantes, the mob had received a patina of legal sanction from the Revolutionaries and their well-cowed legislative supporters.

VALMY

Two weeks later, on September 20, 1792, some of Europe's finest soldiers, sick with dysentery, met the rag-tag but numerically superior French force at Valmy, a three-day quick march from Paris. French cannons fired first.[38] The Austrian commander, Commander Brunswick, surveyed his forces and announced: "We do not fight here." With that, Europe's counterthrust into France was finished.[39] The British ambassador in Vienna, the Seventh Earl of Elgin, reported in honest shock: "The finest army that ever was collected . . . commanded by the most famous general in Europe" was routed by "an undisciplined horde of volunteers without officers."[40] The poet Goethe, with the Austrian field staff, said the troops had seen a "new era in world history and you can all say that you were present at its birth."[41]

For the Revolutionaries, Valmy marked the dawn of the universal dominion of the "Rights of Man." Barré, a member of the Committee on Public Safety, thundered,

In ordinary wars after such success one would have sought . . . peace. . . . But in the war of liberty, [successes] are only a means . . . of exterminating despots. . . . Monarchies need peace; the Republic needs martial energy. Slaves need peace; republicans need the ferment of liberty. Governments need peace; the French Republic needs revolutionary activity.[42]

SERENDIPITY SOURS

At first, the collapse of the traditional martial class and the chaos that gripped France seemed to Britain's policy-elite but another link in the great chain of English serendipities. Most of England's leading politicians viewed the onset of war with France's neighbors with self-satisfied equanimity. While the Austrians advanced on Paris, Lord Grenville, Britain's leading diplomat, announced that British interests were preserved only by observing the "most scrupulous neutrality."[43] The British Prime Minister, William Pitt, assured the House of Commons that Britain could remain aloof from war. Indeed, England, said Pitt, could anticipate at least 15 more years of peace.[44]

Valmy had not brought England to consider war, but it had gained English attention to the issue of the conjunction between power and sedition. A wave of domestic unrest was unsettling. Civic disorder seemed to be linked to the startling proliferation of English "clubs." The proliferation of these "associations" appeared to the English "establishment" much like the Jacobin Clubs of Paris. The English response was to investigate, legislate, and repress. On May 21, 1792, a Royal Proclamation against seditious publications was issued.[45] The printer of the publicist of the American Revolution was jailed. Thomas Paine himself was charged and forced to flee to Paris.

Soon, the Duke of Portland, the Whig opposition leader, aligned himself with Burke, saying he now did "not believe there is [any] other means of preventing the dissemination of those French doctrines but by force."[46] Soon there was a consensus reflected in a parliamentary committee that stated that France's stunning success at Valmy in September put "the safety of the country . . . [and] constitution" into question.[47]

BRITAIN'S INTERESTS

French revolutionary forces, on the exuberant rebound, captured first Brussels, then Antwerp.[48] The new French position in the Low Countries threatened England. As Napoleon later told his generals in 1801, Antwerp was "a pistol aimed at the heart of England,"[49] for it was the jumping-off place for any cross-channel invasion. From Antwerp it was not hard to assemble a flotilla of landing craft that could be shielded from English men-of-war in the Scheldt Estuary. In the late fall or early spring, a cross-channel invasion could be mounted at night. If a disciplined infantry were landed along the Thames, in Essex, or East Anglia, the whole south of England could be split all the way to the London docks.

Holland was even more strategic than Antwerp for England. The Dutch Republic had been central to England since the days of William and Mary. On March 29, 1790, three years before France's attack began, Burke spoke of England's long commitment to Holland, which "might be considered as necessary a part of this country as Kent."[50] If access to Holland and Belgium were sealed, the British could be blocked from the continent's most lucrative trade. French statesmen could not be oblivious to England's interest in the Lowlands. When France's Revolutionaries threatened to "hoist the Cap of liberty on the Tower of London" if Britain dared defend Holland,[51] even the most adamantine Englishman agreed that a Dutch request for assistance in case of attack had to be honored.[52]

"WAR, FREED FROM ALL CONVENTIONAL RESTRICTIONS"

Holland aside, France's revolutionary leadership believed it would have war with England when Louis XVI was executed in January 1792.[53] When the news reached Lord Grenville, he alerted Auckland, his most trusted diplomat, that war was inevitable: "The business [of the execution] has now brought us to crisis and I imagine that the next dispatch to you . . . will announce the commencement of hostilities."[54]

Expecting England to join an Austro-Prussian counterattack, the French began to mobilize more and more resources. On April 6, 1792, the Committee of Public Safety was given the power to requisition men and munitions. By August 23, 1793, the Committee decreed a *levée en masse*, placing all the resources of the country at the disposal of the war effort:

All Frenchmen are in permanent requisition. . . . The young men will go to combat; married men will forge weapons and transport food; women will make tents and uniforms and serve in the hospitals. Children will make bandages from old linen, old men will present themselves at public places to excite the courage of warriors, to preach hatred of kings and the unity of the Republic.[55]

Twenty-five years earlier Rousseau had written of the strength of an army imbued with *l'amour de patrie*,[56] yet the notion, no less than the reality, of the masses in arms had seemed for most statesmen at once far-fetched (both organization and discipline seemed insurmountable obstacles) and dangerous to civil authority. But the French state had already gained the ability to muster all matter of property and talent. The intellectual distance to the summons of persons for war was not all that great. It was, in fact, a matter of simple logic.[57] But as Clausewitz observed, the *levée en masse* changed everything:

In 1793 such a force as no one ever had conceived made its appearance. War had . . . become an affair of the people, and that of a people numbering thirty millions, every one of whom regards himself as citizen of the State. . . . By this participation of the people in the war . . . the means available . . . had no longer any definite limits. . . . [T]he element of War, freed from all conventional restrictions, broke loose.[58]

In the summer of 1793, France's enemies had resumed the offensive. Mainz was taken by the Prussians; Valenciennes fell; and Toulon lay under siege by the British. Royalist and Roman Catholic insurgents controlled much of the Vendé and Brittany. Lyons, Marseille, Bordeaux, and other important localities were in the hands of the breakaway "moderate" Revolutionaries, the "Girondists." But by early winter of 1793, France surpassed its rivals in equipment, men called into arms, and, most of all, zeal. France's new army of citizens proved more effective and better motivated than that of any of its adversaries. Fluid French formations and ad hoc harassment of retreating forces broke the drill-book rule of using "squares" of pikemen. The legacy of France's ancient drill master, Martinet, gave way to new self-discipline and, most important, a new community between the army and the population.

Carnot, whom Napoleon reverentially called the military "architect" of the Revolution, wrote—in the classic revolutionary idiom of dichotomous antinomies—that war has but two locations. It can be waged in the territories of one's enemies, or one can wait until the enemy presses in on the homeland. Obviously, it was better at a distance—"*a l'outrance*"—and with the fullest effort. He who exacts the highest price in the shortest time, in Carnot's logic, "won." Carnot exhorted: "We must exterminate to the bitter end."[59] It was the prescriptive injunction of total war.[60]

Eventually, the *levée en masse* dried up unemployment. The gardens of the Tuileries were blanketed with arms manufacturers. Scientists, chemists, and engineers were pressed into service. Capital was conscripted. The army, as the phrase born in 1793 put it, had become the "school of the nation."[61] At year's end, 645,000 men were mobilized; the next year, at 750,000, the French army was larger than any Europe had ever seen.[62] In the winter of 1796, though "bark had to be scraped from the trees for soup" and Parisians, dressed in rags, sighted wolves on Paris' outskirts.[63] France's forces were 1,169,000 men strong. France had become irresistible.

REVOLUTIONARY ARMIES AND PROFIT

More than ideology kept France's armies in the field. From the onset, the Revolutionaries were frank about the requirement of France for war. As one minister put it: "Peace is out of the question. We have three hundred thousand men in arms. We must make them march as far as their legs will carry them, or they will return and cut our throats."[64]

The Revolution's army never provided itself with adequate supplies. From the start, the army lived more in the manner of Wallenstein in the Thirty Years War than in the fashion of the old regime.[65] France's new breed of military contractors, in service of the state and working on commission, extracted 10 million francs in gold in 1793 from the Palatinate alone.[66] In the first occupation of Belgium, Carnot declared that "all that is found in Belgium must be sent back to France. . . . It is necessary to despoil the country and make it impossible to furnish the enemy the means to return."[67] Of course, if the enemy—in this case, the Austrians—did not return, it was not clear how the people of Belgium would survive.

By the start of August 1794, the Revolution in its most radical sense was over, but the Revolution's wars tramped on.[68] The Rhineland was reoccupied in October 1794 with a new government "based on the sacred principles of justice." But the bills incurred by France's army in the area were exacted from the new beneficiaries of liberty themselves. In 1795, one of the Revolution's "Directors" exclaimed: "Make peace! And what will you do with the Generals? Would they cultivate greens?"[69]

Expansion and extortion on a grand scale soon became a kind of Ponzi scheme. Each expansion paid only part of the last, and in turn required yet another. As Napoleon wrote later: "The Directory . . . needed a state of war as other governments need a state of peace."[70] French ambition was a stranger to limits. In March 1798, the French occupied Bern and seized a store of some six million livres in gold coin. The conquest of Switzerland financed Napoleon's expedition to Egypt; and Egypt, it was hoped in turn, would be but a stepping stone to India, where treasures of immense value were said to await liberation.[71]

By the time Napoleon assumed dictatorial powers at the end of 1799, the compulsion to expand seemed almost a species of imperial satyricism. As Bonaparte confided to one of his confederates: "The French state needs brilliant deeds, and, in consequence, war. It must be the first of all states or perish. In our situation I regard any conclusion of peace as a short truce and feel myself . . . destined to fight almost without interruption."[72]

COMPREHENDING THE THREAT

Europe's classic wartime methodologies proved perpetually insufficient.[73] The message, armies, and administrative method of the French Revolution jeopardized everything and threatened the very existence of Austria, Prussia, Russia, and even England as autonomous states. The old forms of coalition warfare calculated interests in terms of property, souls, and commerce. But always, at the peace that followed, the "great powers"—no matter how they were diminished or fatigued—remained. France's war aims were different. France's wars were far more than wars of expansion and exploitation. As Karl Marx understood it, France offered a species of international class war: "Napoleon was the last stand of *revolutionary terror* against *bourgeoisie society*. . . . *He carried the Terror* to its conclusion by *replacing the permanent revolution with permanent war*[74] (emphasis in original).

France's immense new energy and the threat that energy posed to European order was not, however, at first, well understood. Perhaps it was because the dimensions of the threat were so novel; or perhaps it was because of some kind of combination of intellectual ossification and unwarranted self-satisfaction. But whatever the reason, the fact was that each of France's opponents at one time or another sought independent arrangements with France—as if *they* were immune from what was befalling others.

With the exception of most English statesmen after 1794, there was little understanding in Europe about the scope of France's revolutionary threat. Goethe was an exception.[75] A few days after Valmy, he foresaw that Prussia too would "plunge into the destruction of the crowd," and that Europe might require "a thirty years' war to appreciate what would have been sensible in 1792."[76] In fact, Goethe was seven years off.

Europe's powers generally treated France as if it were but passing through a phase, like adolescence; and that its political priapism would, in time, diminish. Time and again, policies were developed to meet French appetites, as if they could be satiated through accommodation.[77] Finally, the British, after a few years of indecisive war and diplomacy, turned to generally consistent analysis of the French threat. As William Pitt informed the House of Commons on February 3, 1800, France's very existence and system, no matter what its current policy, was "in itself a declaration of war against all nations."[78]

Even when Napoleon became attached to much of the paraphernalia of the old regime—primogeniture, gilded robes, and the crown of an emperor—most leading British politicians realized that France threatened not just England's classic attachment to the balance of power, but England's own internal order as well.[79]

In 1797, English troops at outposts as distant as Capetown and as close as the North Sea mutinied. One parliamentary report claimed that disloyalty among the English forces had been promoted and financed by French agents. In 1798, Ireland rebelled. Some 140,000 English troops, twice as many as had ever served in Europe before Waterloo, were sent to repress the uprising and fend off invading French.[80] Among Irish sympathizers to France the threat of French stabilization was, as one Irish street ballad went:

> Oh! may the wind of Freedom
> Soon send young Boney o'er
> And we'll plant the Tree of Liberty
> Upon our Irish Shore![81]

ANOMALOUS PEACE

The one interruption for Britain's long struggle with the Revolution, the Peace of Amiens, was signed March 27, 1801 (it lasted through the next year). By the end of 1802, as Talleyrand allowed, France had "everything" it might reasonably want.[82] But Napoleon understood it was but a lull; for, in his words, "[b]etween the old monarchies and a young Republic the spirit of hostility must always exist."[83]

The peace was more an armistice. A French-style constitution was forced on Holland after an unwanted plebiscite was held in which 400,000 "absentee ballots" were thrown into the hopper. Along the Rhine, 45 out of 51 free cities were incorporated into France. This action so reduced the number of Catholic votes in the Holy Roman Empire that no Hapsburg could ever gain the emperor's throne in the traditional Diet. At the same time, Spain was reduced to vassalage. Even the ancient Swiss Republic was humbled, and required to provide 16,000 soldiers like so many bushels of Baltic grain.

PERPETUAL WAR

England took up arms again in 1803.[84] Russia and Austria joined with England. France parried by constructing a fleet of warships and assault craft. But Nelson caught France's invasion fleet on October 21, 1805. Off the southwest coast of Spain in the straits of Trafalgar, in an unheard-of maneuver, Admiral Horatio Nelson divided his fleet into two columns and drove them perpendicularly through France's horizontal line of ships at two points. French ships, thus separated from one another's supporting fire, were annihilated. It was the greatest English victory at sea since 1588. On land, however, the coalition found much less success. A Russian-Austrian army met the French at Austerlitz on December 2, 1805, and was destroyed.[85] With hardly the means to secure their own frontiers, Austria and Russia withdrew, leaving Britain to war on alone.

England was isolated by the peace that Napoleon had constructed on the continent. Prince Klemens Wenzel Nepomuk Lothar von Metternich, the Austrian statesman, described Britain as "outside this world like the moon."[86] Never had Britain been more in danger.

Prussia, whose neutrality had done nothing but aid Napoleon against the failed British-led coalition, was reduced to the status of lowly satrap. Forty-nine percent of Prussia's population was removed from Prussian control. Prussia's Frederick William was required to pay an "indemnity" for the crime of standing aside in war. Since the amount exceeded Prussia's annual revenue, France's administrators exacted claims in kind—from the forfeiture of mortgages, forts, custom houses, and trade concessions. A labor force was impressed by French overseers to make roads to connect French strongholds. The once proud Prussian army was broken down to the level of a bare constabulary force of 42,000—of whom 16,000 were promised to France in war. A protest to Laforest, the French representative at Berlin, bespoke the betrayal of class and privilege: "I thought," complained the Prussian Foreign Minister, that "you were a gentleman."[87]

France's former adveraries sued for peace. Tsar Alexander I met Napoleon on a raft in the river Niemen at Tilst on the border between Russia and a wholly colonized Prussia in early 1807. Bedazzled by Napoleon's conjury of new Russian positions from Turkey to India, the Tsar was only too pleased to agree to France's "free hand" in the West. It was the only winning hand Napoleon would ever play.

By the fall of 1809, Austria had also become an abject dependent of Napoleon's, symbolized by the marriage of Maria Louisa, the Hapsburg Emperor's daughter, to the hitherto heirless Napoleon. The irony was substantial. From the start, the luckless Marie Antoinette's purported crime was that she was too Austrian.[88] Now, as Caesar did to Gaul, Napoleon married into Austria and then divided it into three parts: Bohemia, Hungary, and Austria. Some of the remaining lesser states were cobbled together and handed over to Napoleon's brother Jerome. Another brother, Louis, was made King of Holland. Most of Italy, including the papal states of Lombardy and Venice, was delivered to Napoleon's stepson. Napoleon's uncle in Corsica received a cardinal's cap. Lettia, Napoleon's mother, walked the halls of her son's Imperial Court, muttering to herself, "If only it lasts!"[89]

THE SPANISH "ULCER"

In 1808, French troops arrived in Iberia. The Spanish Bourbon king abdicated, and Napoleon's brother Joseph assumed the throne. But soon the remains of Spain's old order—the titled, clergy, and the people of Madrid—rose in revolt. The first explosion of popular fury occurred on the evening of May 2, 1808. As memorialized in Goya's mesmerizing series, "Horrors of War," French troops responded with astonishing brutality.[90] Suppression only fueled more rebellion. Especially in the countryside, France's imposition of an anti-clerical regime provoked a storm of xenophobic rage.

The British saw Spanish resistance as a great opportunity. Integrating defecting Spanish regulars and with irregular Spanish and Portuguese forces, Arthur Wellesley, the Viscount Wellington, marched from Lisbon to meet the French. Napoleon rushed huge forces across the Pyrenees and threw Wellington back. But victory in large battles yielded nothing in the way of French control. Anti-French guerrilla forces never let up, and almost as soon as they were armed by the French, Spanish troops defected to the guerrillas.

Napoleon's communication with his forces became extremely difficult. Two hundred men were required to see to it that just one dispatch from Paris got through.[91] The arid Spanish countryside proved unable to support French forces. French supply convoys moving south were regularly plundered. Some 90,000 French forces were tied up just to hold one supply road. Stragglers were picked off in rear areas. French deaths in the Peninsula averaged a hundred a day.[92] Soon 370,000 of France's best forces were called in—with no change in fortune.[93] Over a five-year period, some 180,000 French were killed trying to hold the Peninsula. Guerrilla losses were but 25,000.[94]

Fighting "without a front," complained Napoleon, the guerrillas had become a nightmare, a "hideous leopard."[95] In the end, as Clausewitz concluded, Spain was Napoleon's "greatest error."[96] Bonaparte's "enormous effort," wrote Clausewitz, "crippled him in one arm."[97] As David Chandler, one of England's distinguished historians, noted, "[T]he simple fact" is that Britain

stumbled upon a secret that made a permanent French occupation of Spain as impossible as . . . [the] United States' . . . in South Vietnam. . . . [A] small, but well-trained regular army operating in association with . . . widespread guerrilla forces . . . is bound to make a permanent occupation by [an] army not enjoying the full support of the local population impossible.[98]

Maxims of guerrilla war were not articulated until later, but the rules that, for instance, Mao Tse-tung adduced were perhaps discovered first, in practice, by the Spanish. As Mao wrote, famously:

> The enemy advances,
> We retreat;
> the enemy camps,
> we harass;
> the enemy tires,
> we attack;
> the enemy retreats,
> we pursue.[99]

Antoine Henri Jomini, a Swiss officer and military theorist who served in Napoleon's forces, remembered a night in Spain when no Spanish troops had been reported within 50 miles, yet an entire French corps was wiped out—by priest-led peasants. "Any soldier," wrote Jomini, would have preferred the older warfare, for all its blood, to the "organized assassination" of the new wars of the nation.[100] But the new warfare—a thing of France's own invention—would, Clausewitz recalled, "bring the French to utter ruin."[101]

The irony of Napoleon's defeat in Spain, and coming defeats elsewhere, was that the Revolution's successful export of popular war had made Europe ungovernable by force.[102] For as the second decade of the nineteenth century began, it was clear that the "secret" of a "people in arms" was no longer a French monopoly. Napoleon's enemies—in Spain, Prussia, Italy, and Russia—all, in time, turned to popular war.

NOTES

1. Cited by Peter Paret and Daniel Moran (eds. and trans.), *Carl von Clausewitz: Historical and Political Writings* (Princeton, N.J.: Princeton University Press, 1992), p. 341, a fragment translated as a "Agitation," probably written in the early 1820s, pp. 341 and 350ff.

2. Paret and Moran, *Writings*, "Agitation," p. 346; and Carl von Clausewitz, *On War* (Michael Howard and Peter Paret, eds. and trans.), with introductory

essays by Peter Paret, Michael Howard, and Bernard Brodie, and a commentary by Bernard Brodie (Princeton, N.J.: Princeton University Press, 1984), see pp. 591–593.

3. Friedrich Meinecke, *The Age of German Liberation, 1795–1815* [*Zeitalter der deutschen Erhebung*] (edited with an introduction by Peter Paret; Peter Paret and Helmuth Fischer, trans.) (Berkeley: University of California Press, 1977), p. 413.

4. Paret and Moran, *Writings*, "Agitation," p. 346.

5. Paret and Moran, *Writings*, "On Sharnhorst," p. 102; and in Clausewitz, *On War*, p. 593.

6. Paret and Moran, *Writings*, "Observations on Prussia," p. 76.

7. Tocqueville, cited by François Furet, *Interpreting the French Revolution* (Elborg Forster, trans.), *L'Ancien Regime*, Book 3, chapter 1 (Cambridge: Cambridge University Press, 1978), p. 163.

8. Referring to Prussia, specifically in 1806. Carl von Clausewitz, *Nachichtren uber Pruessen in seiner grossen Katastropje, Kreigesgeschichliche Einzelschriften*, Vol. 10 (Berlin, 1888), p. 469, cited by Peter Paret, *Understanding War: Essays on Clausewitz and the History of Military Power* (Princeton, N.J.: Princeton University Press, 1992), p. 78; Paret and Moran, *Writings*, "Observations on Prussia," p. 76.

9. Paret and Moran, *Writings*, "On Sharnhorst," p. 102.

10. Thomas Copeland et al., *The Correspondence of Edmund Burke*, Vol. 6 (Chicago: University of Chicago Press, 1958–1978), pp. 42, 36.

11. Letter on the Regicide Peace 11, "On the Genius and Character of the French Revolution as in Regards Other Nations," in Henry Bohn (ed.), *The Works of the Rt. Hon. Edmund Burke*, Vol. 18 (London: Bohn's British Classics, 1854–1889), p. 217.

12. Thomas Copeland et al., *The Correspondence of Edmund Burke*, Vol. 7, p. 60.

13. Second Letter, in Paul Langford (ed.), *Writings and Speeches of Edmund Burke*, Vol. 9 (Oxford: Clarendon Press, 1981–1991), p. 289.

14. Speeches in the Debate on the Army Estimates, 9 February, 1790, *Works of Edmund Burke*, Vol. 5, p. 187; Letters on the Regicide Peace, 1 August 1792, "On the Overture of Peace," *Works of Edmund Burke*, Vol. 8, p. 185; Letter to Grenville, 18 August 1792, cited in Alfred Cobban, *Edmund Burke and the Revolt against the Eighteenth Century* (London: Allen and Unwin, 1929), pp. 120–121.

15. Fourth Letter, in Langford et al. (eds.), *Writings and Speeches of Edmund Burke*, Vol. 9, pp. 72–78ff.; Jennifer M. Welsh, *Edmund Burke and International Relations* (New York: St. Martin's Press, 1995), p. 143.

16. Stanley Ayling, *Edmund Burke: His Life and Opinions* (London: John Murray, 1988), pp. 249–250; Georges Lefebvre, *The French Revolution from 1793 to 1799*, Vol. 2 (John Hall Stewart and James Friguglietti, trans.) (New York: Columbia University Press, 1964), p. 12.

17. First Letter, in Langford et al., *Writings and Speeches of Edmund Burke*, Vol. 9, p. 257.

18. Letter to Earl Fitzwilliam, February 8, 1790, cited by Welsh, *Edmund Burke and International Relations*, p. 10.

19. Remarks, in Langford (ed.), *Writings and Speeches*, Vol. 8, p. 491.

20. Welsh, *Edmund Burke and International Relations*, p. 164.

21. A. Armstrong, *Revolution and World Order: The Revolutionary State in International Society* (Oxford: Clarendon Press, 1993), p. 90.

22. J. Mavidal and E. Laurent et al. (eds.), *Archives parlementaires, recueil complet des débats législatifs et politiques, des Chambres francaises de 1789 à 1860,* Ser. 1 (Paris, 1868–1870), Vol. VIII, p. 397; Crane Brinton, *A Decade of Revolution, 1789–1799* New York: Harper & Brothers, 1934), p. 95.

23. Helen Maria Williams, *Eye-witness Account of the French Revolution: Letters Containing a Sketch of the Politics of France* (Jack Fruchtman Jr., ed.) (New York: Peter Lang, 1997), p. 45.

24. Simon Schama, *Citizens: A Chronicle of the French Revolution* (New York: Knopf, 1989), pp. 591–597.

25. The emperor attempted to propitiate the French still. Schama, *Citizens*, p. 595; Stephan Walt, *Revolution and War* (Ithaca, N.Y.: Cornell University Press, 1996), p. 70; J. M. Thompson, *Robespierre* (Oxford: Basil Blackwell, 1988), pp. 202–209.

26. R. R. Palmer, *The Age of the Democratic Revolution: A Political History of Europe and America, 1760–1800*, Vol. 2, *The Struggle* (Princeton, N.J. : Princeton University Press, 1969–1970), p. 13.

27. Furet, *Interpreting the French Revolution*, p. 127.

28. Peter Paret, *Clausewitz and the State*, rev. ed. (Princeton, N.J.: Princeton University Press, 1985), pp. 24–29, 64; Paul W. Schroeder, *The Transformation of European Politics, 1763–1848* (New York: Oxford University Press, 1994), p. 94.

29. Albert Sorel, "Dumouriez; Un géneral diplomate au temps de la Révolution," Vol. 64, *1884*, p. 323, cited by T.C.W. Blanning, *The French Revolutionary Wars, 1787–1802* (London and New York: Arnold, 1996), p. 116.

30. Francois Auguste Marie Alexis Mignet, *The History of the French Revolution* (London: J. M. Dent, 1926), p. 178; Heinrich von Sybel, *History of the French Revolution*, 3rd ed., Vol. 1 (W. C. Perry, ed.) (London: J. Murray, 1867–1869), p. 448.

31. Jean Favier and Thomas André et al., *The Chronicle of the French Revolution, 1789–1799* (London: Chronicle Publications Ltd., 1989), p. 266.

32. Kyung-Won Kim, *Revolution and the International System: A Study of the Breakdown of Stability* (New York: New York University Press, 1970), p. 38; Jeremy Black, *British Foreign Policy in an Age of Revolution: 1783–1793* (Cambridge: Cambridge University Press, 1994), p. 389.

33. Lefebvre, *The French Revolution*, Vol. 1, p. 216. The manifesto may well have been written by émigrés, perhaps the infamous Artois himself. See Karl A. Roeder, *Baron Thugut and Austria's Response to the French Revolution* (Princeton, N.J.: Princeton University Press, 1987), p. 99.

34. Baron John Emerich Edward Dalberg Acton, *The French Revolution* (John Neville Figgis and Reginald Vere Laurence, eds.) (London: Macmillan, 1910), p. 232.

35. Mignet, *The History of the French Revolution*, p. 196.

36. Albert Mathiez, *The French Revolution* (Catherine Alison Phillips, trans.) (New York: Russell & Russell, 1962), p. 160.

37. Lefebvre, *The French Revolution from 1793 to 1799*, Vol. 2, p. 68.

38. Prussian troops were sick from eating too many grapes, according to one tale. Mathiez, *The French Revolution*, p. 222.

39. Maj. Gen. J.F.C. Fuller, *The Conduct of War, 1789–1961* (New Brunswick, N.J.: Rutgers University Press, 1961), p. 31. Clausewitz wrote: "the Duke of Brunswick . . . left the required courage at home. A war conducted in such a timid fashion could not feed itself; the whole burden soon fell on Prussia's finances, which were soon exhausted. . . . The energy needed . . . was lacking. Prussia concluded the Peace of Basel, and left her allies in the lurch." Clausewitz, "Three Observations," in Paret and Moran, *Writings*, p. 64.

40. Black, *British Foreign Policy*, p. 404.

41. Schama, *Citizens*, p. 640.

42. Armstrong, *Revolution and World Order*, p. 88.

43. John Ehrman, *The Younger Pitt, The Reluctant Transition*, Vol. 1 (London: Constable, 1983), p. 42.

44. J. J. Holland Rose, *William Pitt and the Great War* (London: G. Bell and Sons, Ltd., 1911), p. 32.

45. Black, *British Foreign Policy*, p. 390; Maurice Philip (ed.), *The French Revolution and the British Popular Politics* (Cambridge: Cambridge University Press, 1991), p. 412ff.

46. Black, *British Foreign Policy*, p. 411.

47. Ibid., pp. 412–413.

48. The invading general was a South American named Miranda. Overall command was Dumouriez, who was fighting a flanking action at Liège.

49. David Hamilton-Williams, *Waterloo: New Perspectives: The Great Battle Reappraised* (London: Arms and Armour Press, 1993), p. 33. Just as worrying was the open-ended resolution, passed on November 19 by the Convention, that France wished to grant "brotherhood and assistance to all those peoples who want to recover their freedom."

50. William Corbett (ed.), *Parliamentary History of England*, Vol. 29, *1849*, p. 219, cited by Blanning, *The French Revolutionary Wars*, at pp. 47, 50. The point that Blanning makes is that the French Revolution's exertions abroad do not stem fully blown from ideology, but had recognizable *realpolitik* antecedents.

51. Black, *British Foreign Policy*, p. 416.

52. Burke to Grenville, November 27, 1792, in "Report on the Manuscripts of J. B. Fortescue, Esq.," edited by Great Britain Historical Manuscripts Commission (London, 1882–1927), Vol. 11, pp. 463–66; and Grenville to Auckland, December 27, 1792 and December 4, 1792, in Vol. 2, pp. 341 and 351, cited by Kyung-Won Kim, *Revolution and the International System*, p. 58.

53. T.C.W. Blanning, *The Origins of the French Revolutionary Wars 1787–1902* (New York: St. Martin's Press, 1986), p. 137.

54. Black, *British Foreign Policy*, p. 447.

55. See, on this, R. R. Palmer, *Twelve Who Ruled: The Committee of Public Safety during the French Revolution* (Princeton, N.J.: Princeton University Press, 1958).

56. See R. R. Palmer, "Frederick the Great, Guibert, Bulow: From Dynastic to National War," in Edward Meade Earle (ed.), *Makers of Modern Strategy* (Princeton, N.J.: Princeton University Press, 1943), pp. 49–74; and Bruce D. Porter, *War and the Rise of the State* (New York: The Free Press, 1994), p. 131ff.

57. Lefebvre, *The French Revolution*, Vol. 2, *1793 to 1799*, p. 66.

58. Clausewitz, *On War*, Book Eight, chapter 3, pp. 591–592.

59. Michael Howard, *War in European History* (London: Oxford University Press, 1976), pp. 80–81.

60. Charles Townsend, "Militarism and Modern Society," *Wilson Quarterly* (Winter 1993): 75.

61. Cited by Townsend, "Militarism and Modern Society," p. 77.

62. Bruce D. Porter, *War and the Rise of the State*, pp. 131–132ff.

63. Simon Schama, *Patriots and Liberators* (New York: Knopf, 1977), p. 11.

64. Cited by Winston S. Churchill, *The Age of Revolution: A History of the English Speaking People*, Vol. 3 (New York: Dodd, Mead, 1957), p. 285.

65. David E. Kaiser, *Politics and War: European Conflict from Philip II to Hitler* (Cambridge, Mass.: Harvard University Press, 1990), p. 229, especially n. 47.

66. Ibid., p. 218. Not unimportant was the motivation of the Directory in seeing Napoleon as far from France as possible. Schroeder, *The Transformation*, pp. 94, 177.

67. David Silverman, "Informal Diplomacy: The Foreign Policy of Robespierrist Committee on Public Safety" (Ph.D. dissertation, University of Washington, 1974), pp. 228–230, cited by Walt, *Revolution and War*, p. 95 n.135.

68. William H. McNeil, *The Pursuit of Power* (Chicago: University of Chicago Press, 1982), p. 193; and Lefebvre, *The French Revolution from 1793 to 1799*, p. 145.

69. Sydney Biro, *The German Policy of Revolutionary France: A Study in French Diplomacy during the War of the First Coalition, 1792–1797*, Vol. 1 (Cambridge, Mass.: Harvard University Press, 1957), p. 375; and Walt, *Revolution and War*, p. 103.

70. Denis Woronoff, *The Thermidoran Regime and the Directory, 1794–1799* (Julian Jackson, trans.) (New York: Cambridge University Press, 1984), p. 167, cited by T.C.W. Blanning, *The French Revolutionary Wars*, p. 196.

71. Schama, *Citizens*, p. 709. The Napoleonic expedition to Egypt effectively began the modern era in Middle Eastern history.

72. Cited by Kaiser, *Politics and War*, p. 257; and Martin Phillipson, "La paix d'Amiens et la politicque géneéral de Napoléon I?" *Revue Historique* 76 (1901): 76.

73. Blanning, *The French Revolutionary Wars*, p. 196.

74. Cited by Furet in *Interpreting the French Revolution*, p. 129.

75. Derek McCay and H. M. Scott, *Rise of the Great Powers, 1648–1815* (New York: Longman, 1983), p. 273; Alfred Cobban (ed.), *Debates on the French Revolution* (London: Crosby, Lockwood and Son, 1918), pp. 460–462; Walt, *Revolution and War*, p. 98.

76. Cited by Gordon Craig, *The Politics of the Unpolitical; German Writers and the Problem of German Power, 1770–1871* (New York: Oxford University Press, 1995), p. 14.

77. Kaiser, *Politics and War*, p. 250.

78. Cited by Armstrong, *Revolution and World Order*, p. 104.

79. Except for a curious intermission in 1802, England fought France continuously for 23 years. Hamilton-Williams, *Waterloo: New Perspectives*, p. 304.

80. R. R. Palmer, *The Age of the Democratic Revolution*, pp. 491, 498.

81. Ibid., p. 336.

82. Schroeder, *The Transformation*, p. 233. Napoleon could not abide stasis. During the year of "peace," some 30,000 troops were sent to retrieve Haiti from what proved to be one of history's few successful slave revolts. French frigates blockaded American shipping in New Orleans, a source of supplies for Haiti's rebels. The action provoked an undeclared war with the United States.

83. Cited by David Chandler, *On the Napoleonic Wars* (London: Greenhill Press, 1994), p. 5.

84. Schroeder, *The Transformation*, pp. 94, 231.

85. At this point Napoleon contemplated a French Empire that would include Russia and Austria and ally itself with Russia against Britain.

86. Cited by Schroeder, *The Transformation*, p. 351.

87. Ibid., p. 285.

88. Antonia Fraser, *Marie Antoinette: The Journey* (New York: Doubleday, 2001), passim.

89. Palmer, *A History of the Modern World*, p. 400.

90. Gunther E. Rothenberg, *The Art of Warfare in the Age of Napoleon* (Bloomington: Indiana University Press, 1978), p. 49.

91. Chandler, *On the Napoleonic Wars*, p. 174.

92. Ibid., p. 160; and Rothenberg, *The Art of Warfare*, p. 156.

93. Chandler, *On the Napoleonic Wars*, p. 173, citing King Joseph's military aide.

94. General Bigaree, cited by Chandler, *On the Napoleonic Wars*, p. 173.

95. Ibid., pp. 179–180.

96. Paret and Moran, *Writings*, "The Campaign of 1812 in Russia," p. 201.

97. Ibid.

98. Chandler, *On the Napoleonic Wars*, pp. 159–160.

99. John Shy and Thomas W. Collier, "Revolutionary War," in Peter Paret (ed.), *The Makers of Modern Strategy* (Princeton, N.J.: Princeton University Press, 1986), p. 840.

100. See John Shy's essay on Jomini in Paret (ed.), *The Makers of Modern Strategy*, p. 170.

101. Clausewitz, *On War*, Book Eight, chapter 8, p. 615.

102. Henry A. Kissinger, *A World Restored* (New York: Grosset and Dunlap, 1964), p. 316.

Chapter 5

War and Order: The "Juggernaut of War" Meets a "Legitimate" Peace

Napoleon had grown fat and removed from the contemporary calculus of power. He refused to countenance a real understanding with Europe, even on the basis of French conquests the year following Louis XVI's judicial dispatch.[1] Perhaps, given what he deemed the essence of his position, he could not concede there was an alternative. To Napoleon—more a fifteenth-century condottiere[2] than a nineteenth-century Revolutionary— his power, and indeed that of France, required victories.[3] Perhaps Napoleon's position was now that of the Revolution's ineluctable dynamic. As Clausewitz concluded, France had become a "juggernaut of war," "pulverizing through Europe"; for France, every "breath" was "an act of force" in which "moderation would be just as irrational for her as slackness would be for anybody else."[4]

The only valid—that is, the only competent—response to the challenge of total war would be its mirrored counterpart.[5] Yet it was not until 1813 that France would be met by coalitions universally informed of war's changed nature; and it was not so much a discovery as an organic reaction to France's method. For wherever Napoleon's forces traveled, the message of popular politics traveled with them. Clausewitz observed the etiology of Europe's counterstroke to the protracted challenge presented by the French Revolution. First, an "interest in politics grew more and more widespread among the upper classes."[6] In time, "the reaction set in."[7] With sufficient experience at war, and with the masses both introduced to and used in war, their numbers became in aggregate an explosive force equal to the French. Then, and only "[j]ust in time,"[8] as Clausewitz writes, were whole peoples gathered up against France. Their *"mobilization"* had proved to be the defining "spark that would touch off the mine"[9] (emphasis in original).

THE RUSSIAN BREACH

Napoleon counted on Russian neutrality in his final campaign against Austria and England. Hence, he was incomprehensibly shocked to discover the Tsar possessed the temerity to issue a "ukase" or decree on December 31, 1810, that announced a break with Napoleon's "Continental System" (a design that deprived Russia's huge landowners of their right to export grain—a trade that was their sole source of wealth). To Napoleon, it was insult enough that the Tsar would pretend he was dealing with an equal. A formal declaration of autonomy, however, was intolerable.[10]

"HERE YOU WILL FIND ONLY ASHES": THE ROAD TO MOSCOW

As had every French general since 1792, Napoleon decided that the best solution to political differences was a mass attack. By mid-1812, Napoleon's *Grande Armée* was some 700,000 strong. This incredible mass of men—the largest ever collected for war—was assembled from every corner of the French Empire. Spain, as Clausewitz noted, had depleted most seasoned French troops. Still, some 200,000 committed French nationals were available for the Russian campaign.[11]

Napoleon's onslaught began in June of 1812. Marching east, France's vast army carried supplies sufficient for a few weeks. Faced with his awesome numbers, a Russian army of semi-savage peasants led by the inexperienced or the febrile would, Napoleon figured, cut and run.

Three long months later, on September 7, 1812, in an open space near the village of Borodino some 60 miles west of Moscow, a French force depleted to 130,000 advanced on a Russian position.[12] Although his army was strung out along an 800-mile-long supply line,[13] Napoleon still managed to bring up some 200 cannon. Wheel-to-wheel, for 10 hours, firing two 12-pound balls a minute, French artillery pounded down on 50,000 of Russia's best troops.[14] It was the largest battle the world had yet to know.

Clausewitz, a witness then serving as an advisor to the Tsar's general staff, wrote that in the face of the superior French guns, Russians backed away "no more than 2,000 paces. . . . Thus Russians maintained their cohesion throughout these ten hours."[15] With the day's battle done, Clausewitz saw "no trace of the disorganization" that an army in defeat might show. On the contrary,

[t]he number of Russian prisoners may have reached a few thousand, the number of guns lost between twenty and thirty. . . . French trophies were . . . insignificant. . . . The author scarcely remembers a single light cavalry regiment unsaddled during the retreat. . . . [T]he Russian army remained physically in very good shape. Its numbers were reduced only by casualties . . . and it lost few men from sickness or straggling.[16]

Although he lost 30,000 men, to Napoleon, Borodino seemed a victory. The way to Moscow was open. The only oddity was the absence of Russian prisoners taken at battle's end, a curiosity he ascribed to the savage discipline Russian officers inflicted on their troops.[17] As with the people of Spain, Napoleon seemed incapable of understanding that others could field successful national armies. In any case, Napoleon was convinced that the Tsar would soon negotiate.[18] But upon capturing Moscow on September 12, 1812, Napoleon could not find a single party with whom he might hold a discussion, no less a surrender.[19]

Caulaincourt, Napoleon's closest aide in Russia, remembered that, far "from having found any of the civic authorities" they had hoped would negotiate,

they discovered . . . not . . . so much as a single prominent inhabitant. All had fled. Moscow was a deserted city. . . . As was the case in most of the private palaces, nothing had been disturbed in the Kremlin; even the clocks were still going. . . . No one remained but a few [French tutors], a few foreign shopkeepers, the servants in some of the hotels, and . . . people of the lowest classes of society.[20]

Although most of the Russian estates were merely abandoned, one, owned by a man named Rostopchin, had been put to the torch. Rostopchin left a notice on a sign pointing to his estate. It read:

For eight years I have improved this land, and lived happily here in the bosom of my family. . . . [O]ne thousand seven hundred and twenty dwellers [who lived] on my estate are leaving it at your approach . . . I am setting fire to my mansion rather than let it be sullied by your presence.

Frenchmen!—in Moscow I have abandoned to you my two residences with furniture worth over a half a million rubles. Here you will find only ashes.[21]

On the first evening of Napoleon's occupation of Moscow, flames broke out in the suburbs. By morning, a huge vault of fire consumed the city's wooden houses. One of the most beautiful cities Napoleon said he had ever seen nearly disappeared. At first, the emperor disparaged the fire as symptomatic of a people so backward that they would "burn their houses to prevent our sleeping in them for a night."[22] But if Moscow's fire wasn't a deliberate Russian tactic, it obviously worked against the French. For, as Clausewitz reported, it "became a way of enraging the Russian people further." And it consigned the "possibility of peace negotiations" to even "more remote" regions of "the Czar's mind."[23]

Napoleon had hoped for peace before winter. But the Tsar would not so much as entertain a conversation. To compound Napoleon's vexations, winter settled in early, with temperatures below 34 degrees Fahrenheit in the first days of October.

Clausewitz recalled that the French army now numbered only some

90,000 of exhausted men and horses, at the point of a narrow wedge driven 550 miles into Russia; to its right was an enemy army of 110,000; on all sides a population in arms forced to face the enemy in all directions, without depots, without adequate supplies . . . that does not add up to a situation that one could tolerate through winter.[24]

Napoleon occupied Moscow for 35 days. With the Russian capitol and countryside laid waste, there was no choice but to retreat. But the Russians, as Clausewitz wrote, "burned villages" along the way back from Moscow as they had burned Moscow itself. The great chain of fires across the steppes, Clausewitz adduced, seemed to have become at "first" an act of "thoughtlessness and carelessness" but, "gradually [it] became policy." Across the steppes, Napoleon found "the inhabitants were already gone . . . the food . . . used up . . . [B]ridges were also torn down, and the numerals were hacked out of the mileposts. . . . [T]he French must have often found it difficult to know where they where on the highway."[25]

"Never," Clausewitz wrote, had there been "such thirst; the filthiest puddles were emptied to quench the fever; and washing was out of the question."[26] Starved men and horses froze where they fell. Russian regulars and Cossack raiders harassed and sniped stragglers—the latter forces, Napoleon had to concede, were "the best light infantrymen in the world." Partisans—priests, villagers, housewives with bread knives—attacked French stragglers by night. Bridging equipment was lost. Ice-jammed rivers had to be forded on improvised pontoons; frost-bitten soldiers staggered up onto the banks only to be greeted by more blasts from "General Winter." In a trek of over 900 miles, a mere 100 Guardsmen were able to enter Paris in formation. Some 270,000 wolf-ravaged corpses, 200,000 horses, and 1,000 cannons littered the ice and mud between Moscow and Westphalia.[27]

The touchstone of Napoleon's downfall was that which had brought him to the apex of world power—the armies of peoples. The Russians had stumbled "unintentionally," Clausewitz observed, upon Europe's counter-stroke.[28]

AUSTRIA PIVOTS

As Napoleon left Moscow, the outlines and preconditions of yet another coalition started to surface. By February 1813, a national rising in Prussia—like that which gripped Spain, anti-foreign and religiously inspired—allowed Prussia to defect from France's abasing grip. In June 1813, Britain offered a huge subsidy, an astounding 32 million pounds,[29] to Austria if it were to follow Prussia and take up arms in a "grand coalition."[30] Austria's policy makers considered the offer, but were pleased to hear from Napoleon as well. Hence, when Metternich received an invitation from Napoleon at the end of June (a summons from "my evil star")[31] Metternich was gratified that Austria now had options.

In the nine hours of discussions, Metternich told Naopoleon he was facing an end to his absolute domination of Europe. If Austria were to join a coalition against France, then Napoleon's ultimate defeat was now possible.[32] On the other hand, Metternich suggested, Napoleon could come to terms for the sake of Europe and his own security as emperor. If France were to retreat, it could have expanded borders, and retain its ideals and Napoleon.

But, Napoleon replied, if he were to renounce claims and positions, neither he nor France would survive the resulting turmoil within France. None of the coalition members—save Russia, and perhaps Poland—acquitted themselves on the battlefield so that they might "deserve" any gain at French expense.[33] How then could he explain or justify a withdrawal?

Metternich—according to his own recollection—held the position that Napoleon would now have to know some limits. The justification was requirement for a stable European order and a restoration of the balance of power. Up to the present, "[b]etween Europe and the aims you have hitherto pursued," Metternich scolded, "there is an absolute contradiction. . . . Today you can still conclude peace; tomorrow it may be too late!"[34]

Provoked, Napoleon flung his hat and shouted, "You are not a soldier, you know nothing. . . . I grew up on the field of battle, and a man such as I am cares little for the life of a million men." Then, with more calm, he added a disturbing prospect, "I may lose my throne, but I shall bury the whole world in its ruins."[35]

As Austria, Britian, Prussia, and Russia mustered huge forces, Caulaincourt, the emperor's plenipotentiary, appealed to Napoleon to "dissolve the hostile Coalition by peace."[36] But, as Caulaincourt despaired, Napoleon clung "to ideas which flatter his preconceptions. He seems convinced now that Austria will never take up arms against him, as he was in Moscow that Alexander would negotiate."[37]

So sure was Caulaincourt that disaster loomed in Napoleon's limitless hubris, that he secretly urged Austria on. "Conduct us back to France either by war or armistice," Caulaincourt urged, "and thirty million Frenchmen will thank you."[38]

A NEW KIND OF BALANCE

The "French," Clausewitz noted, seemed wholly "contemptuous of the political calculus with which other governments anxiously weighed enemies and alliances."[39] But a successful coalition never "revealed" itself to Europe's statesmen before. It was only at the point where, as Clausewitz put it, the "balance of power *system*" (emphasis in original) was exposed to its maximum "danger of being lost," when all Europe seemed to be subsumed, that statesmen realized Napoleon could not be halted by diplomacy.[40] At long last, it came to be understood throughout European chancelleries that France presented a wholly novel problem, and that lasting victory would only be possible when there was an appreciation of "the danger that France posed to everyone."[41]

France, it was finally apprehended, could not be contained or propitiated. It would have to be remade, and the unique means for doing so would have to be the Revolution's own method: a war of a people in arms. What would patriotism do to multinational Austria or Russia? For other states, such as England and Prussia, oligarchs were unsure if self-consciously national armies would remaim cohesive. And could states dependent on mass armies stay together, not just in battle, but later? It was an open question until almost the last battle, for in established national states like Prussia and England, national armies undercut the old verities of class and privilege. In the cobbled, patchwork continental empires—Austria and Russia—the problem of national armies was fraught with even more abundant dangers.

The goal of victory over Napoleon alone had proven insufficient, and victory itself was likely to remain insufficient. For total war requires a total military *and* political response. This was the point at which Clausewitz made his central observation about the inextricable relationship between war and policy. The relationship betwen war and policy "outcome" is clearer as the exertion in war increases. As Clausewitz mused to a friend, "War is not an independent phenomenon, but the continuation of politics by different means. Consequently, the main lines of every major plan are *largely political in nature*, and their political character increases the more the plan encompasses the entire war and the entire state"[42] (emphasis in original).

The huge effort required for "simple" victory made the requirement of war incommensurate with each separate coalition partner's national interest. European states arrayed against Napoleon would have to come up with an agreement on political ends, as well as means. Without a collective vision of the postwar order, individual state interests would carry a more powerful purchase on each state's political leadership and public. Separate peaces, after all, are the bane of coalitions. The great paradox is that if coalitions cannot stand a separate peace, they usually find it all but impossible to define a vision of collective peace that can carry them through to victory and beyond. Only when all the larger states of Europe could sustain a vision of concerted action that implied an alternative world order—an order that excluded coming to terms with Napoleon—was success both in battle and in peace possible for the Allies. But this was not an understanding easily apprehended. Indeed, the requirement of vanquishing Napoleon and reconstructing Europe's political order only materialized when Napoleon himself rejected moderate terms as incompatible with his own honor and the requirements of France. And only then were Napoleon and the Revolution he had captured overcome.

Clausewitz had observed firsthand that when the coalition placed victory prior to—and over—a common peace, the results were intrinsically problematic. And Clausewitz came to realize that once peace awaits military developments, instead of being in the forefront of strategy, the eventual peace itself is distorted by—and in fact a slave to—the tide of battle.[43]

The French nation-in-arms produced the counterforce necessary, but not sufficient to bring about Napoleon's defeat. Large national armies would be necessary to bring about Napoleon's end. But would there be an incentive for the armies to stay together so that France was vanquished? Then what? France, even in defeat, was a great state. To break it would invite Russia and Germany into a power contest as far west as Calais. Britain would never countenance it. To reconstruct France, while keeping millions who had loved the tricolor in political chains, would require an enormous occupation—perhaps in perpetuity. Who would provide the troops? France would seethe, and eventually leadership would arise among the most self-consciously nationalist peoples who would, over time, succeed in overthrowing their oppression or wholly draining their repressors.[44]

The realization as to what peace required had to dawn on all of France's enemies. France would have to consider the peace "legitimate." As early as 1799 to Burke first, and then in Britain generally, it was clear that it was not really a choice to try to lop off great chunks of France, as had been Poland's lot until it was finally all but extinguished. As England's Secretary for War William Windham warned Pitt, if France were to be crippled, Austria and Russia acting together would be needed to "cover" vast French-speaking areas with permanent garrisons. Russian power would then be in a position to perpetually jeopardize England's access to the continent. Sea lanes from Bologne to Istanbul would find themselves near a Russian thumb. Jailing France would fail in any case, Windham believed, since no matter how energetic the occupation, some Jacobin "poison" would leak out and "corrode and infect all of Europe." The coalition, Windham wrote, would never be able to effect France's restoration by itself. France would have to be a willing patient. It would be about as easy "to establish a good government in France, without the aid of the . . . inhabitants of that country," Windham suggested, as it would be "to get a child single-handed and without the concurrence of a female."[45]

The outline of France's reconstruction—and, indeed, the construction of European order—would be, as Metternich put it, the "moral" requisite for Europe's defeat of Revolutionary France.[46] The Allies, after trying more simple underpinnings of sustaining their coalition, were reluctantly obliged to agree on both the means and the ends of the conflict. Only when the coalition could see its collective interest in not just defeating France but reordering it—and to collectively sustain the peace that would follow— was any meaningful "success" possible. The apprehension of consensus regarding the character of the peace was as critical.

One reason that meaningful peace was so long in coming was because of a puzzling truth: A large element of French cooperation, which was essential, seemed as difficult as it seemed unlikely. But the determined and sustained involvement with France in Europe's postwar world, in common with the Allies who defeated France's armies, was the only war in which Europe might hope to find security from the threat of Revolution unleashed in the early 1790s.[47]

Once total means like those of the French were adopted by France's adversaries, and married to a vision of the ultimate postwar order (and what that order would require), then the "moral" conditions were in place for the fifth and final coalition to organize. This coalition would take France beyond a conquest to a peace that "made sense." The collective realization of what the coalition had to do to be successful occurred in mid-1813—when Metternich guided Austria's vast weight to the side of Russia, Britain, and Prussia for the last time.

A TWENTY-YEAR COMPACT

In October 1813, two huge multinational forces assembled near Leipzig, in Saxony. The French gathered some 190,000 troops; the coalition perhaps twice as many. Austria offered 150,000 soldiers, most of them drawn from Austria itself—an amount equal to the army of Russia and twice that of Prussia. The battle at Leipzig dwarfed that of Borodino, and it came to be called, for its immense size and national armies, the "Battle of Nations." The results in three days were some 40,000 dead and the decisive breaking of Napoleon's main force.[48]

Napoleon raised yet another army, and for the first time in nearly 20 years it was all French. But as it assembled at the end of November 1813, news that the dreaded Cossacks were closing from the East panicked the French ranks. French soldiers fled their barracks and tents, losing them-selves in the woods or the cities. Napoleon's draft masters beat in vain for soldiers to reappear.

As allied troops passed French frontiers, British Foreign Secretary Lord R. Stewart Londonderry, the Second Marquess of Castlereagh, called together senior diplomats from Austria, Prussia, and Russia. Agreement was reached at the French town of Chaumont on March 1, 1814. Recalling, purposively, Westphalia, the Treaty of Chaumont would read: "The present Treaty of Alliance having for its object the maintenance of the balance of Europe, to secure the repose and independence of the Powers, and to prevent the invasions which for so many years have devastated the world." Unlike Westphalia, however, the operative phrase, "the High Contracting parties" vowed to extend whatever postwar arrangements they made in common for "twenty years from the date of the signature."[49]

Russian forces arrived in Paris first. Napoleon fled. France's remarkable Foreign Minister, C. M. de Talleyrand-Périgord, ignoring the emperor's orders, stayed in Paris and offered himself to mediate with the Tsar. The two immediately worked out an arrangement for a Bourbon restoration under a constitution.[50] But French garrisons salted around Europe still provided Napoleon considerable leverage. Hence, when Napoleon offered to abdicate in the first week of 1814, his conditions were met by the Allies. Napoleon would receive a kingdom of his own, "somewhere." The Treaty of Fontainebleau, the following week, delivered to Napoleon the Mediterranean island of Elba, an annuity. His followers could keep their personal property. The Allies also promised to evacuate France in exchange for French withdrawal from the fortresses it still held outside of France. France's 1792 borders were actually improved.[51] A number of colonies acquired since the Revolution were retained. The remaining issue of European peace was to be settled in what was hoped would be a short, formal conference, to be held in Vienna in November of 1814.

THE MANAGEMENT OF ORDER

Poland

As in the Yalta and Potsdam conferences of World War II, Poland proved to be the great stumbling block to accord. Divided among the powers under French auspices in 1797, Poland's status was, said Prince Talleyrand, a matter of international law. In reality, it was an assertion that seemed to augment France's leverage among the powers, since the argument hardly suited the Tsar. Employing a tactic to be finely honed in the Soviet era, guilt was piled on necessity: "I thought France owed me something," he complained.

The Duchy of Warsaw is mine by right of conquest from Napoleon's Empire. The entire continent of Europe had been in league against me, when I repulsed a most unjust aggression. Nevertheless, I did not hesitate to come to the aid of these same powers with an effort equal to that which had saved Russia. Now that victory has enabled the principal states of Europe to be reconstituted as they were before . . . and even enabled several of them to gain . . . , it is only fair that my subjects be indemnified for so many sacrifices and that a buffer state guard them forever from the dangers of a new invasion.[52]

If Russia acquired Poland, Metternich feared it would be either a boiling salient of repressed nationalism or a stalking horse of Russian power.[53] To Castlereagh, Poland was but a residuum of the balance of power. It could be divided and disposed of as it had been under the press of Frederick, Catherine, and Maria Theresa's cooperation 80 years before. The Tsar dispensed with the English suggestion quite plainly in his first informal meeting with Castlereagh: "I am in occupation of Poland. I possess a large army. If England or anyone else does not like it, they can come and turn me out."[54]

Castlereagh felt a Russian salient in Poland could be managed well enough by a revived Prussian counterweight. This was clear from Castlereagh's only instructions from London (on Poland or anything else). Anything the Congress of Vienna was likely to discuss would not warrant a British commitment to arms. "HRH cannot contemplate . . . without entertaining the most serious apprehension . . . the renewal of war. . . . It is unnecessary for me to point out to you the impossibility of HRH consenting to involve this country in hostilities at this time for any of the objects . . . hitherto under discussion at Vienna."[55]

In the end, as at Yalta at the close of World War II, without a willingness of the leader of the alliance to use arms on the ground, Russia would gain a great mass of territory. Like at Yalta, Poland was reduced to dependence on Russia, Germany was reconfigured by a Conference of the Powers. Prussia was "compensated" in the West at Vienna for territories "lost" in the East.[56]

The Congress of Vienna was not unique in moving peoples around as if their nationality and history were residual to state necessity. Nor would it be the last time Europeans attempted to rejigger geography in consequence of conflicting demands. But from the Congress of Vienna on, each fix derived from the movement or exchange of peoples carried unexpected and eventually insupportable baggage. When weighed by the animus and eventual counterclaims and "rectifications" they provoked, it was no wonder that Europeans decided in the mid-1970s to declare the borders of Europe all but frozen. But in the early 1990s, just when Europeans were celebrating the triumph of liberal values, the old politics of the Balkans, like the forgotten vagrant uncle who appears at a wedding, resurfaced.

THE MANAGEMENT OF ORDER

Germany

As the Scottish philosopher David Hume observed, after traveling widely through Germany at the middle part of the nineteenth century: "Germany is undoubtedly a very fine Country, full of industrious, honest People, and were it united it would be the greatest power that ever was in the world."[57]

German nationalist stirrings, especially in Protestant Germany, presented a serious obstacle to the "conservative" order imagined at Vienna in 1815. Austro-German troops had proved indispensable to victory. But a weak German center of the Westphalian design had proved essential for Europe's order since Westphalia.

If any German state or "states" in combination were too strong, all their neighbors could be overwhelmed. But if Germany were especially weak, France might be tempted. Or the Austrians, or Prussians themselves might be arroused to "undo" the balance. If the threat of Austria's power was too large, then there was the issue of what Russia might do. Before 1812, Russian power had been hypothetical. But as the congregants and their entourages at Vienna dined, danced, and deliberated over long months, even more Russian troops passed through Germany to beef up their patrols of Parisian streets. All the Western powers hoped Russia would retreat. But a condition of Russian "containment" proved to be a stronger Germany than had ever before been considered.

In the end, the Vienna settlement came down somewhere in the middle of the polar possibilities of a weak Germany, as was the Westphalia design, on the one hand; and, on the other, a Germany more closely knit together, with huge reserves of potential and actual power. Austria reemerged as a Great State, as did Prussia. Indeed, in some ways, they had never been greater. Hence, Prussia was assigned a virtual hegemony in North Germany, while Austria was given a leading position in the rest of Germany. The remaining aggregation of German-speaking satrapies, bishoprics, and free cities of the now defunct Holy Roman Empire were situated in a jury-rigged political farrago governed by a "Diet" in Frankfurt under Metternich's watchful eye. The Diet was the formal responsibility of both Austria and Prussia. To be sure, Germany was still divided, but this time the whole of Germany was the providence of two powerful *German* rivals.[58]

Of the two, Prussia and Austria, Prussia was potentially the more powerful. It had, under press of Napoleon's humiliating defeats, well reformed its military and finances. By mid-century, Prussia's finances and military were in good order and modernized, while Austria's finances and military were a shambles. In an era of rising nationalism, Prussia was more Germanic, while Austria retained a tenuous hold on the peoples of Northern

Italy, Central Europe, and the ever-troubled Balkans. Meanwhile, throughout German territory, Francophobia smoldered, heated by the Napoleonic
occupation and misuse of mostly Prussian manpower (almost all of the
200,000 Prussians impressed into Napoleon's 1812 Grand Army had died
on the way to Moscow or in the miserable retreat). Indeed, the blossoming
German arts were obsessed with a regnant France. Beethoven's "Eroica"
Symphony, for instance, celebrated England's Wellington's victory over
French forces in 1813; and the German painter Caspar David Freierich
evoked in oils a faceless French soldier overwhelmed by an archetypical
Teutonic forest while watched portentously by a raven of doom.

THE CONGRESS "SYSTEM"

The territorial rearrangements of the Congress of Vienna were grounds
for continuing discord. But interstate contention could be successfully suf-
fused as long as the major governments of Europe shared similar outlooks.
And while the states of Europe shared the same views of nationality and
legitimacy, it was possible to construct a new bedrock of a future *institutional order.*

Most of European trade was carried along inland waterways. The provision for international control of the Rhine, Neckar, Moselle, Main
Meuse, and Schedlt was therefore a significant step economically and politically, and an important datum in explaining the great expansion of trade
that ensued as the century unfolded.

The Congress also took to regulating diplomatic rules. A whole series of
accords regarding embassies and envoys were approved. The Congress of
Vienna also made a start toward the outlawry of the slave trade. Issues of
precedence were addressed at Vienna for the first time since the Pope had
issued an edict in 1504.[59]

THE REPUBLICAN CAULDRON: ELBA TO ST. HELENA

At the apogee of a tide of European cooperation, Napoleon attempted
to retrieve his position from his Elba redoubt. Napolean's last stand, in
itself, it turned out, was a significant epilogue to the Congress of Vienna.
For although Napoleon's grand gesture underscored the troubling reality
that the *idea* of a great revolutionary nation in arms had not been extinguished, Wellington's ability to rally the coalition and defeat the French at
Waterloo validated that the Congress system was already working.

Napoleon's attempted comeback began in February of 1815. French
army units sent to arrest him joined his ranks instead. By March 13, 1815,
the Congress declared Napoleon an international criminal. The response of
the conference at Vienna presaged both Versailles (in its unfortunate proclamation that the Kaiser was a "war criminal") and Nuremberg in 1945;

and of course, in mid-June, Wellington's multinational force defeated the last of Napoleon's armies at Waterloo.

In a sense, Napoleon's effort was something of a near thing. A huge number of veterans had rallied to his side. But Napoleon had no army and had to gather what veterans and volunteers he could on the move while avoiding all the strong points in France occupied by forces belonging to the Congress. Many supporters who otherwise might have rallied to Napoleon's side were driven underground by the early Bourbon- and Congress-backed campaign of repression.[60] And even if Napoleon had gained the upper hand at Waterloo—and it was a very close call—the 1.2 million–man allied occupation force that arrived in France by the summer of 1815 would have probably proved dispositive against further efforts to revive France's Revolution bellicosity.[61]

So confident were the Allies of their upper hand that the Congress was able to wrap up its work before Waterloo (June 18, 1815). Their confidence war rewarded with the result that Napoleon was soon shipped out to St. Helena. In the fall, France's borders were somewhat diminished from those agreed to earlier, yet it had a net gain from its pre-Revolutionary position since the agreed frontiers were pushed to those of 1790 (instead of 1729, as had been agreed before Napoleon's return from Elba). Louis XVIII inherited a police apparatus as thorough as any in Europe. A stiff five-year indemnity was imposed.

The Republican cauldron boiled in the hearts of veterans, intellectuals, and middle-class countrymen who bore the return of privilege in hushed bitterness. Indeed, republicanism and nationalism, deep and sullen, daily impeached authority and government across the face of Europe. For Prussia, German nationalism was less of a threat, perhaps, than were Republican institutions. For the English, the ideological challenges of republicanism and nationalism were co-opted by reforming ministries. For Russia and Austria, repression was immediate, unabashed, ruthless, and lasting; but never wholly successful. In short, while French power would never recover from the wounds of the Revolution, its legacy remained.

TOO SOON FOR NATION-STATES AND TOO LATE FOR THE BALANCE OF POWER

Europe, after the French Revolution, faced three logical alternatives for achieving public order, given public sentiments, on the one hand, and the restored position of the old elites on the other: (1) a system of nation-states, (2) a system of equilibrated power, (3) a system of managed, "concerted" power.[62]

The first option, so clear a century later, was all but inconceivable to the diplomats gathered at Vienna. To the diplomatists of the day, states were a function of basic power, interests, and perhaps even dynastic right. But "nations" (that is, the masses who might believe themselves French, English, etc.) had no real standing; certainly not in the international law, neither then nor in the next half-century, at least in the Chancelleries of the day. National self-awareness was rising, however. In Hapsburg lands and further east, as Metternich well understood, the much vaunted *Volk* had begun to seek their own political autonomy. Intellectuals in Poland, Hungary, Bavaria, and Italy began to reject a uniformity imposed by "others." Yet to the ruling classes these were the notions of "professors," as Clausewitz acidly relegated his radical nationalist contemporaries.[63] The masses might count in their sanguinary wartime service, but that was it, at least for the next several decades.

A BALANCE OF POWER?

A reconstructed balance of power system was embraced in theory by all the major powers at Vienna, with the important exception of Russia. The Tsar's conception of the postwar "system" was a mystical combination of a return to religion by peoples and the worldwide elevation of patriarchal Christian authority. The founding document of the Holy Alliance read, at Russian insistence: "The Sovereigns have become convinced that . . . the relations of powers . . . must be replaced by an order founded on the the exalted truths of eternal religion."[64]

In the end, however, even the Tsar accepted the analysis of Frederick von Gentz, a Prussian diplomat charged with drafting the language of the Congress of Vienna's final convention, that war arises in the first instance from "the excessive overweight" of states.[65]

The "golden age" of the balance of power was the ideal to which Clausewitz, for one, hoped states would return to after the settlement of 1815. For Clausewitz, a rational international order had occurred when states would be "safe from total ruin, [and] aware of their own limitations, they would . . . restrict their own aims."[66]

Before Napoleon, Clausewitz remembered, there were times when states were content with the flags, profit, and honor of war. Indeed, in ages when feudal values still held some sway, simple "victory" could be its own reward. Clausewitz's Elysian yearnings were for a return of the time when "every campaign . . . ended with the winning side attempting to reach a state of balance. . . . At that point, the progress of victory stopped."[67]

Napolean was a fearful "God of War" who had joined "vast resources" with "vast goals," and exacted a commensurate price.[68] The toll of Europe-wide wars resulting from the French Revolution easily exceeded five million battlefield deaths.[69] Like those who live in the tropics, who need to have boards, nails, and sandbags on hand in case of typhoons and hurricanes, Clausewitz hoped that mindfulness of the threat of total war would obviate its damage. For Clausewitz, like all German philosophers of his day, the *ideal* war was a moderate one; and the policy that war furthered would be moderate as well.

Clausewitz understood that the spreading appeal of patriotism had made things different. But Clausewitz—anticipating Bismarck's social policies, perhaps—hoped the state would offer enough to patriots so that they would have reason not to feel "compelled to have recourse to the final desperate remedy of national revolt."[70] If the people could be satisfied, Clausewitz hoped that reason and proportion would prevail, and war would again function as a reliable regulatory instrument of order.[71]

Clausewitz knew, however, that even if war were to be regulative and purposeful, states would have to prepare, from then on, for war "in the extreme . . . in which every element calls for policy to be eclipsed by violence."[72] The conferees at Vienna faced a conundrum that Clausewitz and his successors were to struggle with ever more frequently: Limited goals are hard to square with vast efforts undertaken at great costs.

In our present time, we can look to the American experience with managing war for stakes that were held to be less than "total victory" in Korea and Vietnam. Clausewitz sensed and despaired that the reality of the French Revolution may have signaled an end to moderate war. This was the root of his dark injunction: "Woe to the government, which, relying on half-hearted politics and a shackled military policy, meets a foe, who, like the untamed elements, knows no law other than his own power."[73] "[S]ooner or later," Clausewitz memorably cautions, "someone will come along with a very sharp sword and hack off our arms."[74]

SUPERSEDING THE BALANCE: COLLECTIVE SECURITY

The specter of force untrammeled haunted all of Vienna's serious participants and vitiated whatever urge they might have had to restore the old equilibrium of power as best they could and then stop there. For the truth was that war, at least war in its extreme form, made the balance of power all but impossible. As Henry Kissinger once noted, only in eras when people are "convinced that irretrievable disasters are impossible" can statesmen conduct delicate kinds of "diplomacy with . . . shifting alliances," compromises, and palliating conclusions. In moderate times, there are few "unbridgeable schisms." Then diplomacy, with its "seeming cynicisms," can work. For in an era of limited differences, "risks are limited." And wars are "limited" as well. When diplomacy fails to produce peace, the resulting reduced war "reveal[s] that differences [were] peripheral."[75]

Hence, diplomats at Vienna, and later in the nineteenth century and for much of this century as well, did not reject the balance of power as much as they attempted to supersede it as an autonomous imperative of order. For the prime movers of statecraft, Metternich and Castlereagh especially, the time of the balance of power had passed. Castlereagh knew he could not dismiss the balance of power. But it was "only one element . . . what he really desired was to create some permanent institutional device which would enable the United Nations [*sic* . . . meaning the coalition powers, plus France] to cooperate indefinitely in preventing the threat of war wherever it might arise."[76]

Castlereagh was unclear in his own mind if the Congress system or his own government would ever wholly dispense with England's classic position as a "pivot"—a part of Europe yet apart from it, except *in extremis*. But it was Castlereagh's clear hope that the Congress "system"—the formula of great powers meeting together to hammer out collective decisions— might prove to be, in his words, something of a "new discovery in European government, at once extinguishing the cobwebs with which diplomacy obscures the horizon . . . and giving the councils of the Great Powers the efficiency and the simplicity of a single state."[77]

Prince Metternich remarked in 1820 that the "Concert system"—a system of constant meeting and consultation—had, in fact, met with success. For five years the underlying premise of collective action, that no individual state would seek specific claims in "question of general interests," had been met.[78] For decades, in fact, the norms of cooperation and collective interests becalmed international disputes. The territorial arrangements of the conferences at Vienna lasted well into the mid-1800s (no mean achievement by the measure of the past). But the Congress "system" endured until the end of the century and even beyond, and has been at least partially resuscitated thereafter.[79]

By and large, the mechanics of succeeding Congresses involved heads of governments or Foreign Ministers, while conferences were largely attended by ambassadors and hosted by a Foreign Minister. Regardless of who attended, the protocol of the day required elaborate preparation of the venue. Perhaps since the meetings were largely ad hoc, the time exacted in making the baroque arrangements (and the weeks required to travel from capital to capital with a large retinue) allowed passions to cool.[80]

In any case, extensive prior consultations and, most importantly, the common diplomatic culture that evolved from irregular but extensive and frequent meetings, put a premium on success. Many of the disputes that occupied European diplomats, moreover, were less than critical. In fact, most of the serious disagreements Europe entertained in the years leading up to World War I, with the exception of the Franco-Prussian War, pertained to the politics of Europe's periphery—largely colonial questions and those relating to the disintegration of the Turkish Empire. Since the issues were not deemed, in present-day argot, "vital" interests to the Great Powers, they became, in effect, defined as much technical issues as matters of prestige, commerce, or security.

Even the Crimean War was in a sense a technical accident, the result of a breakdown in the process of transmitting a formula that had been agreed to in a timely fashion. As the doyen of American international relations experts, Hans Morgenthau, once wrote, the Crimean War was the result of one of several "accidents. Had any one of these accidents failed to materialize, war would have been avoided."[81]

One twentieth-century diplomat and Oxford-based academic wrote that "in almost every case after the . . . 1820s, unanimous agreement was reached among the powers. In this sense, the Conference [i.e., Congress] system, as Henry Kissinger put it, constituted a "government of Europe."[82] Generally, the decisions taken were effectively implemented, and in a number of cases joint action was taken, including the use of armed force in cases of the collective repression of nationalist revolts. Coordinated polices against revolutions were referenced in a series of conferences that followed Vienna, in 1818, 1819, 1821, and 1822. All of these meetings resulted in collective action, which in today's argot might be called prototypical exercises in "peace-enforcement."[83]

Post–Congress of Vienna, "peace-making" enterprises advanced as fast as the capacity of states to organize more violence. The legal neutralization of Switzerland at the conference of Vienna was confirmed at the London Conference of 1839. Belgium was given status as independent-neutral in the London Conference convened in 1830, its neutrality guaranteed by a pledge of the Great Powers. The same conference confirmed Greek independence. In 1865, Luxembourg's neutrality was guaranteed by most of Europe.[84]

To Europeans of the time, membership in the Congress system meant much the same thing as the entry into any exclusive London "gentleman's club." It implied good behavior in international society. As Professor Hedley Bull once wrote, the Congress system elaborated "a standard of civilization laid down by Europeans—the test which Turkey was the first to pass when under Article VIII of the Treaty of Paris of 1856 she was admitted to 'the public law and concert of Europe.' "[85]

The order produced by the Congress system was different.[86] Rules, procedures, institutions, and the kernel of what are currently tagged by political scientists as "regimes" advanced from the important work of the Congress of Vienna.[87] The Congress of Paris in 1856 regulated maritime law. An 1884 Congress of Berlin offered some guidelines for establishing colonial claims in Africa. Rules managing postal and telegraphic communications appeared in 1868. In 1874, international health agreements were derived and a permanent office appeared to supervise their implementation. Offices to standardize international weights and measures were established in 1875. In 1899, the Hague Conference revised and formalized laws of war.[88]

EVERYTHING SETTLED?

Almost all Europe's outstanding issues were settled in the years immediately following the Vienna settlement. The Congress of Vienna had left no major disputes; it had humiliated no existing government. A punitive peace, contemplated by the smaller powers, was rejected. Colonial questions were largely fended off and a kind netherworld was adduced and marked off. Areas of competition in Africa, the Middle East, and Asia were distant enough in nature and emotion that major states could make claims without involving or eliciting any wholly fateful contentions.[89] In consequence, for 70 years, most colonial interests seemed more a prestigious "diversion" than a substantive prize of great consequence. The "Great Game" shifted some of the energy away from the more disruptive claims within Europe, which in turn allowed the post–Congress of Vienna "system" to be largely sustained.

Only Napoleon was singled out, and even he was not treated especially harshly. Writing from St. Helena, Napoleon could not comprehend Castlereagh's moderation: "One cannot understand how a sensible nation can be governed by such a lunatic." "After twenty years of war," Napoleon wrote,

after all the wealth she has expended . . . after a triumph beyond all expectation—what sort of peace is it that England has signed? Castlereagh had the continent at his disposal. What great advantage, what just compensations, has he acquired for his country? The peace he has made is the sort of peace he would have made if he had been beaten. . . . Thousands of years will pass before England is given a second opportunity equal to this opportunity.[90]

HARBINGERS

After Napoleon's banishment, as Elizabeth Barrett Browning put it, kings and lords were able "to creep out to feel the sun again." But for all the goodwill among Allies, their future was uncertain; for where France did not extirpate and outlaw the old order, feudal vestiges provided the best evidence of their own obsolescence. The most repressive empires of the East fixed on the specter of revolution. Even enlightened constitutional monarchies seemed unable to command thoroughgoing legitimacy. Asa Mon says, in Goethe's *The Natural Daughter* (Die Natürliche Tochter):

> So crumbles into formless rubble
> The outward show of pomp and circumstance.

Nationalism was the ghost in the great machine Metternich, above all, hoped to keep going after the Congress of Vienna. As Clausewitz observed of simmering social unrest throughout German-speaking lands: For Germany's youth, "it was easy," to think "Germany could suddenly achieve national unity . . ." after the Congress of Vienna, After all, the

idea of establishing a German empire that would improve on the Holy Roman Empire of old captivated the academic community. The Vienna Congress . . . created not a German empire, but only a German Federation, [which produced] a longing for national unity. . . . [T]he people's efforts in the war with France were extolled; the conduct of their princes was condemned; and so, compounded of truth and falsehood, reasonable ideas and absurd ones, some to the point, others pointless, a fermentation began.[91]

Castlereagh privately approved of the collective action of eastern monarchs and Bourbons against revolutionary change and rising nationalism: "We are always pleased to see evil germs destroyed, [but we are] without the power to give our approval openly."[92] English intervention or assistance to Austrian or Russian armed intervention in Germany, Spain, or Greece would have broken any British government. And no British government could welcome a huge Russian gendarmerie in the heart of Europe.

When an international conference at Troppau in early 1821 resulted in some 90,000 Russian troops joined to 80,000 Austrians in repressing uprisings across Northern Italy, Castlereagh found himself the object of parliamentary and public obloquy. The rest of the British cabinet repudiated what was taken as Castlreagh's assent for a "general European police" force engaged in acts of repression that were wholly offensive in their extremity.

In the summer of 1822, Castlereagh's cabinet's hostility intensified. Depressed by his colleagues' rejection of his arguments,[93] troubled by blackmailers who had attempted to falsely link him to a homosexual scandal,[94] overwhelmed by work, Castlereagh, the great prime mover of the Congress system, opened his throat with a shaving razor.[95]

The cleft between nationalism and legitimacy was never bridged.[96] Nationalism and republicanism, first in France but later throughout Europe, augured pandemic war. Moreover, it was war against the ruling class. Madame de Staël's ditty, written in 1799, captured what was to become a widespread fear of Europe's ruling classes:

Shorten giants by the neck
Raise the small up—what the heck!
Everyone at the same height
That's true happiness and light.[97]

By mid-century, it was plain that "national" considerations would vie with "reason of state." Vast increases in firepower, and militant notions regarding nation, class, property, power, and justice seemed poised to combine. With this new social macramé, the permanent problem of international anarchy was made far less tractable. For the statesmen who inherited the Congress system, a new international sociology enervated collective governance, and made each effort—of necessity—conditional and problematic.

NOTES

1. R. R. Palmer, *Twelve Who Ruled: The Committee of Public Safety during the French Revolution* (Princeton, N.J.: Princeton University Press, 1958), p. 384; Felix Markham, *Napoleon* (New York: Mentor Books, 1963), p. 108.

2. Condottiere were the mercenary soldiers during Italy's incessant wars of the fourteenth and fifteenth centuries. They fought for the highest bidder and on occassion even ascended to rule themselves.

3. Paul W. Schroeder, *The Transformation of European Politics 1763–1848* (Oxford: Clarendon Press, 1994), p. 471; Paul Schroeder, "Napoleon's Foreign Policy: A Criminal Enterprise," *Journal of Military History* 54(2) (1990): 147–161.

4. Cited by Peter Paret and Daniel Moran (eds. and trans.), *Carl von Clausewitz, Historical Political Writings* (Princeton, N.J.: Princeton University Press, 1992), "Political Declaration," p. 295; and Carl von Clausewitz, *On War* (Michael Howard and Peter Paret, eds. and trans.), with introductory essays by Peter Paret, Michael Howard, and Bernard Brodie, and a commentary by Bernard Brodie (Princeton, N.J.: Princeton University Press, 1984), Book Eight, chapter 3, p. 592.

5. This is Clausewitz's suggestion. See *On War*, Book Eight, chapter 3, p. 593.

6. Paret and Moran, *Writings*, "Political Declaration," pp. 74–76.

7. Clausewitz, *On War*, Book Eight, chapter 3, p. 592.

8. Ibid.

9. Paret and Moran, *Writings*, "Political Declaration," pp. 74–76.

10. De Caulaincourt, Vol. 1, p. 540, cited by Schroeder, *The Transformation*, p. 337.

11. Paret and Moran, *Writings*, "The Campaign of 1812 in Russia," p. 201.

12. The author, in his own words, was the "senior quartermaster general of the First Cavalry Corps under General Uvarov." Paret and Moran, *Writings*, "The Campaign of 1812 in Russia," pp. 151–152.

13. David H. Chandler, *The Campaigns of Napoleon* (New York: Macmillan, 1966), p. 858.

14. Viscount Montgomery of Alemain, *A History of Warfare* (London: Collins, 1970), p. 348.

15. Paret and Moran, *Writings*, "The Campaign of 1812 in Russia," pp. 146–147.

16. Ibid., pp. 159 and 161.

17. General De Caulaincourt, *With Napoleon in Russia* (edited and abridged by Jean Hanoteau) (New York: Grosset and Dunlap Universal Library 1935), pp. 102–103.

18. "That happened in 1807, after the battle of Friedland, and it had also worked in 1805 and 1809 with the Emperor Francis after the battles of Austerlitz and Wagram. . . . Should we then ignore the actual results of the campaigns of

1805, 1807, and 1809, and, by the test of 1812 alone, proclaim . . . their success to be a breach of natural law? . . . That would be a very forced conclusion." Clausewitz, *On War*, Book Two, chapter 5, pp. 166–167.

19. "Napoleon," in Peter Paret (ed., with the assistance of Gordon A. Craig and Felix Gilbert), *Makers of Modern Strategy* (Princeton, N.J.: Princeton University Press, 1986), pp. 131 and 136.

20. De Caulaincourt, *With Napoleon in Russia*, pp. 111–112.

21. Ibid., p. 127.

22. De Caulaincourt, *With Napoleon in Russia*, p. 85.

23. Paret and Moran, *Writings*, "The Campaign of 1812 in Russia," p. 169.

24. Ibid.

25. Ibid., p. 163.

26. Ibid., pp. 162–163.

27. Clausewitz, *On War*, Book Eight, chapter 9, p. 629; David Chandler, *On the Napoleonic Wars* (London: Greenhill Press, 1994), pp. 206ff, 213; Paul Kennedy, *The Rise and Fall of the Great Powers* (New York: Vintage Books, 1989), p. 136.

28. Clausewitz, *On War*, Chapter Eight, book 8, p. 615.

29. R. R. Palmer, *A History of the Modern World*, 6th ed. (New York: Knopf, 1984), p. 416.

30. For Britain, Castlereagh's ministry, replacing Spencer Perceval's, was as important as Churchill's replacing Chamberlain's. Castlereagh accepted the unconditional nature of the war Napoleon had offered and, like Churchill, combined it with a firm idea of the kind of peace he had in mind: France and the balance of power restored—with the Netherlands and Italy set up as barriers against France while retaining maritime supremacy and rights.

31. Henry A. Kissinger, *A World Restored* (New York: Grosset and Dunlap, 1964), p. 77.

32. Palmer, *A History of the Modern World*, p. 416.

33. Markham, *Napoleon*, p. 205.

34. Ibid.

35. Most of this Dresden conversation is taken from the memoirs of Metternich. Cited by David Hamilton-Williams, *Waterloo: New Perspectives: The Great Battle Reappraised* (London: Arms and Armour Press, 1993), p. 34ff. There is available Napoleon's version as well. But his rendition is no more reliable. See, however, Napoleon Bonaparte, *Corespondance de Napoléon 1er: publiée par ordre del'Emperereaur Napoléon 1111*, ed. A. du Case. Paris, Volume 25, p. 20175ff.

36. Kissinger, *A World Restored*, p. 81.

37. Ibid.

38. Ibid.

39. Paret and Moran, *Writings*, "Observations on Prussia," p. 76.

40. Paret and Moran, *Writings*, "Notes on History and Politics," p. 244.

41. Clausewitz, *On War*, Book Eight, chapter 3, p. 593.

42. Clausewitz, "Two Letters on Strategy" [1827], in Peter Paret, *Understanding War: Essays on Clausewitz and the History of Military Power* (Princeton, N.J.: Princeton University Press, 1992), p. 126.

43. As Professor Paul Schroeder notes, a goal of simple "victory" tends to "de-

cide political issues by default." See his "Collapse of the Second Coalition," *Journal of Modern History* 39 (June 1987): 287 n.97, 288.

44. Henry Kissinger, *Diplomacy* (New York: Simon and Schuster, 1994), p. 81.

45. Windham to Pitt, May 22, 1799, in Harvey Mitchell, *The Underground War against Revolutionary France: The Missions of William Wickham, 1794–1800* (Oxford: Clarendon Press, 1965), p. 233.

46. This is perhaps Henry Kissinger's most important insight. But Kissinger also separates war and peace in a way that might make Clausewitz uncomfortable: "The logic of war is power, and power has no inherent limitations. The success of war is victory; the success of peace is stability. The conditions of victory are commitment, the condition of stability is self-restraint. The motivation of peace is intrinsic . . . a peace built on the myth of an enemy is an armistice. It is the temptation of war to punish; it is the task of policy to construct. Power can sit in judgment, but statesmanship must look to the future." Kissinger, *A World Restored*, p. 139.

47. Schroeder, *The Transformation*, p. 470ff.

48. Friederick Meinecke, *The Age of German Liberation, 1795–1815* (Berkeley: University of California Press, 1977), pp. 12–21.

49. Gordon A. Craig and Alexander L. George, *Force and Statecraft* (New York: Oxford University Press, 1983), pp. 26–27.

50. Louis, when he did come to Paris at the end of the month, refused a constitution that the senate had drawn up—on the basis of divine right—but agreed to accept one on his own volition on the basis agreed with the senate.

51. Talleyrand resigned on this point, and subsequently the differences between the positions of 1790 and 1972 were reconciled in favor of more defensible French frontiers.

52. K. Lutostanski, *Le Partage de la Pologne et la lutte pour l'independance* (Lausanne: Payot & Cie., 1918), p. 345, cited by Guglielmo Ferrero (Theodore R. Jaeckel, trans.), *The Reconstruction of Europe: Talleyrand and the Congress of Vienna 1814–1815* (New York: G. P. Putnam & Sons, 1941), pp. 147–148.

53. Paul W. Schroeder, "Did the Vienna Settlement Rest on a Balance of Power?" *The American Historical Review* (June 1992): 703.

54. Hamilton-Williams, *Waterloo*, pp. 147–148.

55. Ibid., p. 224.

56. At the Yalta conference, Poland was moved west. Part of historic Polish lands were taken by Russia. Part of historic Prussian lands were taken by Poland. The German speakers, some 3 million, were forced to move to what was, for nearly 50 years, the two German states that were constituted from the ashes of the Reich.

57. Cited by Tim Blanning, "Napoleon and German Identity," *History Today* 48(4) (April 1998): 38.

58. Austria's police soon became the dominant agent of order throughout the empire. Foreign study was banned. The press was strictly censored. Universities were subject to the political guidance. Austria became a classic "police state," a "prison-house of nations." The Emperor Francis II possessed exceedingly reactionary notions. As he told the president of a student group: "New ideas are being advanced. . . . Hold them in suspicion. . . . I have no need of learned men. I want faithful subjects." These were sentiments that Metternich, as Austria's first diplomat and jailer-in-chief, applied throughout Austria's German, Italian, Polish, and Slavic

dominions for the next three decades. Paul Louis Leger (based on the work of Paul Louis Leger) [William E. Lingelbach, trans.), *L' Histoire de l'Autriche-Hongrie* [Austria-Hungary] (New York: Arno Press, 1971 [1906]), p. 320.

59. Diplomatic precedence was a serious business, though not without with some elements of farce. Shoving matches and duels were not that uncommon. At a court ball in 1764, a French envoy found that his place had been commandeered by the Tsar's representative. When the Frenchman tried to squeeze his way into what he considered his rightful place, a melée ensued which, in turn, produced a duel. Harold Nicholson, *The Congress of Vienna* (London: University Paperbacks, 1946), p. 218.

60. William Lloyd McElwee, *The Art of War: Waterloo to Mons* (Bloomington: Indiana University Press, 1975), p. 5ff.

61. Schroeder, *The Transformation*, pp. 532–535ff.

62. A.J.P. Taylor, *From Lenin to Napoleon* (New York: Harper & Row, 1966), p. 12.

63. Paret and Moran, *Writings*, "Agitation," p. 350.

64. Kissinger, *A World Restored*, p. 189.

65. Paul R. Sweet, *Freiderich von Gentz: Defender of the Old Order* (Madison: University of Wisconsin Press, 1951), p. 55.

66. Clausewitz, *On War*, Book Eight, chapter 3, p. 590.

67. Ibid., Book Seven, chapter 22, p. 570.

68. Paret and Moran, *Writings*, p. 295.

69. See, on this point, "Napoleon and the Expansion of War," in Paret, *Makers of Modern Strategy*, p. 128.

70. Michael Howard, "The Military Philosopher," reviewing Raymond Aron, *Clausewitz: Penser la guerre*, Vols. 1 and 2, *L'age euroéen* and *L'age planétaire*; and Peter Paret, *Clausewitz and the State*, in *The Times Literary Supplement*, London, 25 June 1976, p. 754. There is also a letter to Gneisenau in 1818 cited by Aron to the same effect. See Aron, "Clausewitz's Conceptual System," *Armed Forces and Society* 1(1) (November 1974): 59 n.8. There is something of this kind of rumination as well in Clausewitz, *On War*, Book Eight, chapter 3, p. 593, but it is more despairing: "once barriers—which in a sense consist only in man's ignorance of what is possible—are torn down, they are not easily set up again."

71. See the memorandum written in 1812; Clausewitz wrote that future wars might not require either the arming of the masses or the overthrow of the enemy state. See Raymond Aron, *Clausewitz: Penser la guerre*, Vol. 2, *L'age planétaire* (Paris: Gallimard, 1976), p. 137.

72. Clausewitz, *On War*, Book One, chapter 1, section 26, pp. 87–90; and Bernard Brodie's concluding essay, "A Guide to Reading *On War*," p. 645.

73. Clausewitz, *On War*, Book Three, chapter 16, p. 218.

74. Ibid., Book Four, chapter 11, p. 260.

75. Kissinger, *A World Restored*, p. 214.

76. Nicholson, *The Congress of Vienna*, p. 244.

77. Castlereagh, letter to Liverpool, 20 October 1818, cited by Evan Luard, *Types of International Society* (New York: The Free Press, 1976), p. 330.

78. Cited by Richard B. Elrod, "The Concert of Europe: A Fresh Look at an International System," *World Politics* 28 (January 1976): 164.

79. "Chaque nation a ses driot particliers; mais l' Europe aussi a son driot C'est

l'orde social qui le lui a donné," cited by F. H. Hinsely, *Power and the Pursuit of Peace* (Cambridge: Cambridge University Press, 1963), pp. 224–225.

80. Elrod, "The Concert of Europe," p. 168.

81. Hans J. Morgenthau, *Politics among Nations* (New York: Alfred Knopf, 1948), p. 368. See Hinsely, *Power*, p. 213n. Between 1815 and 1885 there were 7 congresses and 17 conferences, according to Hinsely, excluding very technical meetings such as the tolls on the river Scheldt or meetings at the ambassadorial level. Elrod, "The Concert of Europe," p. 172.

82. Kirby C. Nichols Jr., *The European Pentarchy and the Congress of Verona, 1822* (The Hague: Martinus Nijhoff, 1971), p. 325; Elrod, "The Concert of Europe," pp. 159–174; and Henry Kissinger, *Diplomacy*, p. 82.

83. Evan Luard, *Types of International Society* (New York: The Free Press, 1976), p. 330.

84. As Evan Luard noted, new states created in Europe in the nineteenth century were formed not as a function of "private dealings between the leaders of an emerging people and the previously sovereign power, [rather it] was a question to be jointly determined by the concert of powers managing the affairs of the continent as a whole." Luard, *Types of International Society*, p. 331.

85. See Hedley Bull, *The Anarchical Society* (New York: Columbia University Press, 1977), p. 34. Hedley Bull was an Australian-born legally trained scholar of immense influence. He taught for years at the London School of Economics and Oxford. This author benefited greatly from his lectures and work.

86. Gordon A. Craig, "The System of Alliances and the Balance of Power," in *The New Cambridge Modern History*, Vol. 10 (Cambridge: Cambridge University Press, 1960), p. 267.

87. The literature is vast. The reader might consult for a review and bibliography in the work edited by Volker Rittberger and Peter Mayer, *Regime Theory and International Relations* (Oxford and New York: Clarendon Press and Oxford University Press, 1995).

88. Luard, *Types of International Society*, pp. 330–335. See also the fine essay by Adam Roberts, in Michael Howard, George J. Andropolous, and Mark R. Shulman, *The Laws of War* (New Haven, Conn.: Yale University Press, 1994), pp. 116–140. Mark Shulman's comments on this chapter were very helpful. Dr. Shulman, of course, bears no onus for anything save his kind help.

89. Stanley Hoffman, *The State of War: Essays in the Theory and Practice of International Politics* (New York: The Free Press, 1965), p. 95.

90. Nicholson, *The Congress of Vienna*, pp. 236–237.

91. Paret and Moran, *Writings*, "Agitation," p. 350.

92. Nicholson, *The Congress of Vienna*, p. 269.

93. See on this Kissinger, *A World Restored*, p. 229.

94. Alan Palmer, *The Chancelleries of Europe* (London: George Allen & Unwin, 1983), p. 36.

95. David Hamilton-Williams also claims that Castlereagh was depressed by the squalid court case involving homosexuality, in *Waterloo: New Perspectives: The Great Battle Reappraised*, p. 291. The charge of scandal is heatedly dismissed by Charles K. Webster, *The Foreign Policy of Castlereagh: 1815–1822*, 2nd ed. (London: Bell and Sons, Ltd., 1958), p. 486.

96. Morgenthau, *Politics among Nations*, p. 368.

97. Baronee de Staël, "Des Circonstances actuales qui peuvent terminer la ré-veolution et des principes qui doivent fonder la république France (1799, ed. John Vinénot, Paris, 1906), p. 82, cited by Eugene Weber, "The Nineteenth Century Fallout," in Geoffrey Best (ed.), *The Permanent Revolution* (Chicago: University of Chicago Press, 1989), p. 175.

Chapter 6

On Appeasement and Parvenus:
Managing the Challenge of New Power

INTRODUCTION

When British policy makers assembled in a cabinet meeting on the January 11, 1896, they faced two unexpected challenges. The first was an impending confrontation with the United States in South America. The second was young Kaiser Wilhelm's uninvited interference in South Africa. Both crises were contained and eventually petered out; and both had lasting but opposite effects. The course of Anglo-German relations after January 1896 swelled in ever-amplified waves of irritation while, in contrast, the Anglo-American spat over Venezuela proved to be a catalyst for a lasting Anglo-American rapprochement.

Britain's example, on the one hand, of a successful accommodation of one great power, the United States; and Britain's failure to either co-opt or tame the rising aspirations, on the other, is instructive. America, in no small way, is now in Britain's stead. Like Britain, the United States is a leading power. And today, as old challenges slip away, again, on the periphery—in China, India, and perhaps, elsewhere—new aspirants challenge American hegemony as both Germany and America once contested British primacy at the close of a previous century.

Essentially, there are only two possible reactions of a preeminent power to novel claims for status, position, influence, and wealth: confrontation or appeasement. In the abstract, either strategy could be employed, depending on the circumstances and interests at risk. At the moment, for instance, when faced by a rising Chinese challenge, the United States finds itself painfully pursuing, at the same time, seemingly divergent paths: on the one side, trying to "engage" China and "enlarge" Chinese markets and freedoms; and, on the other, attempting in Asia an artful policy of containment.[1] No matter how resistant statesmen are to placing a decisive bet on one policy line or another, a single direction eventually becomes clear, perforce.

THE RISE OF AMERICAN POWER

A hundred years ago, Europe was the center of international politics. Japan was still a power in the making. China was in the grips of rapacious colonialism and endemic civil war. American power, by Europe's standards, should have counted for more. But in Europe's cosmology, as English historian A.J.P. Taylor once noted, "[t]he United States seemed . . . not merely on another continent, but on another planet."[2]

Europe's estimation of America was confounded by a tendency to overvalue classic mercantile badges of international standing: gold, trade, and naval power. Only in the classic raw calculus of souls available for battle did the United States seem imposing. The American population growth, its "multiplication table," had been an essential source of American self-confidence since colonial times.[3] While European birthrates had been in decline for years, Europe's export of people increased. About half of the nearly 40 million who had left Europe in the last part of the nineteenth century made their way to the United States.[4] Yet even America's vast numbers failed to impress many European military planners at century's end. As Admiral Jackie Fisher, a leading naval officer of the day,[5] wrote dismissively: "Only ¼ of the population of the United States are what you might call natives; the rest are Germans, Irish, Italians and the scum of the earth!"[6]

While the American navy could barely limp from one coastal port to another until the latter part of the 1890s, Britain successfully held to a standard of retaining twice the naval power of her nearest rivals until well into the twentieth century.[7] British combat arms were vastly superior. At the close of the nineteenth century, even the venerable Dupont Company still produced munitions in a primitive fashion. Observers from England reported, in evident shock, that the Delaware workmen had kneaded nitroglycerine by simply jumping on a concoction of dynamite and blasting gelatin with their hobnailed boots.[8]

Yet, had Europeans engaged in the sort of statistical reckoning now commonplace, American power might have been apprehended more certainly. By aggregate measures, Britain's growth seemed to have slackened in its "maturity," averaging well less than 3 percent growth per year at the end of the 1880s. Germany expanded at a more robust rate of 4.5 percent. But the American rate of growth was faster, at around 5.2 percent per year.[9] By the end of the 1890s, the United States held a plurality of all global manufacturing, some 23.5 percent (virtually today's level, as well). In comparison, Britain's share of world manufacturing stood at 18.5 percent; while Germany's share of world manufactured production stood in third place, at 13.2 percent.[10] In terms of the character of finished goods and in terms of the sophistication in the way they were produced—except in the manufacture of heavy arms—the U.S. lead was substantial and accelerating. If wealth and power were measured by industrial innovation, or by ability to raise huge amounts of investment capital, or if it were calculated in terms of management sophistication, or even if it were judged by the standard of industrial worker education, then the American lead was not just significant, but accelerating.[11]

MARITIME ZESTS

Brooks Adams, the unusually well-born social commentator of the late 1880s, was certain that America would soon turn outward and, in consequence, develop political interests akin to those of the Old World. But American attention to the outside world was hardly an axiomatic function of rising American power. In December 1883, President Chester Arthur announced that he wanted "no part of" any naval policy that might bring the United States into collision with the "great powers of the world."[12] Five years later, in 1889, Senator Henry Cabot Lodge would lament that America's "relations with foreign nations" excited "only languid interests."[13]

But change was imminent. In 1890, Alfred Thayer Mahan, the stern 50-year-old president of the fledgling Naval War College, took his case for a "blue water" navy to the public. Mahan's *The Influence of Sea Power upon History* proved a sensation. Mahan's readership knew they stood at the cusp of technological marvels. Naval ships were the summary of the glamour and hope of a new, technically sophisticated liberal age. There were new ways of fashioning metal hulls to withstand ice and storms. The same metal-forming processes allowed fruits to be kept in tins.

For the first time, ships were beginning to operate with electric illumination. A generation earlier, the only source of fresh meat for crews on long voyages was the huge South American sea turtles that were stacked high in hulls (where they could live for months until they were consumed). But with electric generation, meat could be frozen. The notorious plagues of the sea—scurvy and rickets–disappeared from the fleets of the world's leading navies.

Naval competition was not for the financially embarrassed. Iron-hulled, steam-driven vessels in the 1880s were six times more expensive than the wind-powered ships they replaced.[14] Innovation in navigation and munitions made battleships even more exorbitant at the same time their useful life contracted. But Mahan promised that great ships in great numbers delivered abundant recompense. If America would only emulate England, America would reap rewards such as those England had gleaned when "there was none to dispute the sea to her. Where she would, she went. . . . Ruler of the seas . . . used the sea in peace to earn its wealth.[15]

But notwithstanding Mahan's popularity, progress to a blue water naval presence was halting until President Grover Cleveland began his second term in 1893 with a substantial naval initiative. Some five battleships were purchased, at a cost of some $2.5 million each, and an "armored cruiser" at over $4 million was proposed as well.[16] But Cleveland's naval program was less a response to the arguments of Mahan and more a means of workmen's relief in the face of a severe economic downturn.[17]

Cleveland's naval program faced few hurdles. Democrats were eager to support their party standard bearer. Republicans, the majority in Congress, were increasingly inspired by national revivalists. Spread-eagle, drum-thumping rhetoric, never absent from nineteenth-century politics, ascended new heights. Jingoism—a term derived from a doggerel about a fishing dispute between Canada and the United States—became as common as firecrackers on the fourth of July. "We do not want to fight," the well-known verse sounded,

> But, by jingo, if we do.
> We'll scoop in the fishing grounds
> And the whole Dominion too.[18]

The leading Republican worthies of the late nineteenth century put the lie to the canard that democracies are somehow, by their very nature, less bellicose. The usually constrained Captain Mahan, for instance, excitedly described the virtues of a people "aroused to effective action . . . by the sense of wrong done, or right to be vindicated."[19] A prominent New York politician echoed this sentiment when he spoke at the Naval War College. "No triumph of peace," Theodore Roosevelt announced, "is quite so great as the supreme triumphs of war."[20]

TARGETS OF OPPORTUNITY

Cleveland's Republican opponents attacked him as much on foreign as on economic issues. Lodge was especially agitated by Cleveland's indifference to Britain's demands on an impoverished and irresponsible Nicaraguan government. When, a few months later, Britain took to landing troops in Nicaragua, Lodge's hometown *Boston Journal* joined the senator in charging that Cleveland let the Monroe Doctrine depreciate to a point where it was "not worth the paper it is written on."[21]

The rising American interest in Latin America was, for William Lindsay Scruggs, a chance at redemption. At his last post as U.S. Minister to Caracas, Scruggs had conveyed an American business bribe to the Venezuelan government. Scruggs was cashiered.[22] A Republican with no future in the

Democratic administration of Grover Cleveland, Scruggs approached the Venezuelan mission in Washington for employment.

Scruggs understood wherein lay the bankrupt Venezuelan government's salvation. The Orinoco River basin, an area one-third the size of Venezuela itself, once had yielded the largest gold nugget, some 509 ounces, ever discovered. But the Orinoco basin had long been claimed by the British. Scruggs, a former newspaperman, penned a pamphlet, "British Aggressions in Venezuela, or the Monroe Doctrine on Trial in the fall of 1894 that described a fallow El Dorado." "[O]nly five days sail from New York"[23] America's hitherto unknown failure to contest Britain's unjust claims had signaled not just the abandonment of markets but the surrender of the Monroe Doctrine, along with America's "international prestige and influence." "The people," Scruggs forecast, would "never ratify such an act of pusillanimity."[24]

DOCTRINE AND DICTA

Scruggs' pamphlet proved as successful as any American propaganda since Thomas Paine's "Common Sense."[25] The resulting agitation from Scruggs' "British Aggressions in Venezuela, or the Monroe Doctrine on Trial," forced President Cleveland to announce, in his annual address to Congress on December 4, 1894, that it was America's "established policy . . . to remove from this hemisphere all causes of differences with powers beyond the sea."[26] But as the winter of 1895 neared an end, Scruggs grew impatient with the Fabian pace of American policy and got his hometown congressman to take up the cause on the House floor. By March 1895, a resolution condemning Britain's position in Venezuela had passed both Houses of Congress by unanimous votes.

Privately, President Cleveland complained that the clamor for action on behalf of Venezeula seemed to be "incessantly ringing in our ears,"[27] but he remained upbeat about diplomacy's prospects in the Venezuelan matter well into the spring of 1895. The Venezuelan boundary question had not, however, found any resolution when, in early May, Cleveland's Secretary of State, Walter Quintinn Gresham, was laid low by a spring cold. By the end of May, Gresham was dead.

THE EAGLE SCREAMS

Richard Olney, the new secretary of state, had gained a reputation for ruthlessness by his command of the suppression of striking Pullman car railroad workers the year before. When President Cleveland asked Olney to take Gresham's place in the first week of June 1895, the president understood he was gaining a foreign policy officer who had no instinct to retire from events. Olney redrafted Gresham's note to England and hand-delivered the missive to the president at his New York home over the July 4 holiday: "I read your deliverance on Venezuelan affairs the day you left it with me," Cleveland wrote back to Olney on July 7, 1895. "It's the best thing of the kind I have ever read and it leads to a conclusion that one cannot escape if he tries."[28]

But Olney's draft had transformed Gresham's oblique expression of concern into a ringing indictment. The note charged Britain with unjustly depriving Venezuelans of the "hope to establish [its] claim," by refusing to arbitrate. American interest, in this matter, the note argued, was predicated both on American power and President Monroe's 1823 edict. "Today the United States is practically sovereign on this continent," read the note:

Its fiat is law . . . Why? It is not because of the pure friendship or good will felt for it . . . It is because, in addition to all other grounds, its infinite resources combined with its isolated position render it *master* of the situation and practically *invulnerable* as *against any or all other powers.*[29] (emphasis added)

So serious, Olney warned, were British actions in Venezuela, that the president was prepared to bring the matter to Congress for a declaration of war: "While the measures necessary or proper for the vindication of that policy are determined by another branch of the Government, it is clearly for the Executive to leave nothing undone which tend to render such determination necessary."[30]

The real harms and injuries of a boundary quarrel some 1,200 miles from the nearest American port were nowhere as clear as Olney's threat. But like the proverbial discipline Southern farmers are said to reserve for recalcitrant cattle, Olney deemed a rhetorical two-by-four applied to John Bull's thickest parts a necessity of circumstances since, as Olney put it, "in English eyes," the United States "was then so completely a negligible quantity."[31]

A PRACTICED LANGUOR

If Olney's July message was designed to at once grab British attention, then it failed its own test. Lord Robert Arthur Talbot Gascoyne-Cecil Salisbury, a ninth Earl and Third Marquis, traced his government service to James I. Salisbury, who had been Prime Minister on three different occasions, and foreign secretary in four cabinets. Famously absent-minded and sarcastic, it was hard to know when one failing ended and the other began. On another occasion, Lord Robert Salisbury loudly asked the name of an orator several rows away in the House of Lords. Upon learning the man's name, Salisbury blurted out quite audibly, "I thought he was dead."[32] Salisbury was not to be hurried. The Prime Minister's initial take, as he told an embarrassed American ambassador, was amazement that such an elaborate statement of "principle" had been marshaled to forward "a subject so small."[33] The American note was detailed to the end of a long British foreign policy queue.

DIPLOMACY AT A DISCOUNT

Olney's note, like American diplomacy itself, said Salisbury, was the stuff of "amateurs."[34] Many Americans readily agreed. For years, American administrations plumbed murky depths to find candidates for the U.S. diplomatic service. President Grant's first secretary of state, for instance, was an army friend who was given the job for less than two weeks, sufficient to gain experience enough to enable him to move on to the position of U.S. Minister to France.[35] After the laying of another transatlantic cable, a headline in the *New York Herald* in 1892 summarized perhaps most Americans' sentiments at the time: "Abolish our Foreign Ministers! Recall our farcical diplomats!"[36]

In contrast, the British Cabinet was widely seen as the most able in England's history. Salisbury, at 65, was the visible embodiment of late-nineteenth-century diplomacy. It was already the last days of November 1895, when Salisbury received back from his legal staff a proposed draft reply to Olney's July note. Salisbury believed the date of Cleveland's annual message to be some weeks later. Had the American ambassador availed himself of transatlantic telegraph there would have been time for Cleveland to argue that the English were taking the American interest seriously—at least to the extent the English were admitting the American concern of sufficient weight to reply in time for Cleveland's annual speech, as had been requested in the July note. Instead, Salisbury's messages were placed in a diplomatic pouch for delivery by steamship. Olney, not knowing of the deliberate delay by the U.S. embassy in transmitting the British reply, took the note's delivery date—hours before the annual message was scheduled—as an "intentional contumely."[37]

AN ENGLISH ANTIPHON

As it was, the language of Salisbury's reply went no distance toward meeting American concerns. Instead, the English reply drove home an essential point: The United States had no standing in the dispute, not by treaty, nor by law, nor by dint of substantive interest. The British, therefore, would not accept American intercession, especially under duress, since it was a controversy with which the United States had "no practical concern." Given the American lack of standing in the Orinoco question, Salisbury issued a rhetorical question of a type rarely seen until the diplomatic exchanges of the Cold War. It might be "reasonably asked," wrote Salisbury, if the United States would "consent to refer to the arbitration of another

Power" if Mexico raised to that power an issue of the recovery of "large tracts of territory" acquired by the United States some 50 years before.[38]

AWAY FROM THE BRINK

The United States

Cleveland was shocked by Salisbury's didactic rebuff. Although he received the British reply too late to take it into account for his speech on December 6, he decided to deliver an immediate, independent message to Congress 11 days later. The president's rush to regain the initiative would, he hoped, reinforce the message of the validity of America's diplomatic interests—and, in the same breath, offer Britain a means of settlement that might avoid a showdown. But if Cleveland's December 17, 1895, special message to Congress on Venezuela was designed neither to "threaten nor invite war," the president's tone seemed hardly less than a loudly sounded tocsin.

The administration pledged to "resist by every means in its power" any "willful aggression" against America's "rights and interests" in South America.[39] The crucible of war, Cleveland suggested, would be no worse a "calamity" than a "submission to wrong and injustice and the consequent loss of national self-respect and honor beneath which are shielded and defended people's safety and greatness."[40]

In the summer, Olney had said that a British refusal to arbitrate would invite an imposed American decision. In Cleveland's message of December 17, however, the threat of force retreated to the end of a seven-part process, wherein Congress would appropriate funds for a commission which would eventually report to the president, who would then, in turn, transmit the report to Congress. Underneath Cleveland's jacket of bellicosity lay a benignant fabric of delay.

BACK-TRACKS

Senator Henry Cabot Lodge caught none of the tone in the *sotto voce* overture to Britian that was contained in Cleveland's message to England. Instead, Lodge took special satisfaction at no longer being "alone in the wilderness" crying "out about Venezuela." "[L]ast June," he recalled, he had been "called a Jingo for my pains." Now, there were "[j]ingoes . . . plenty enough."[41]

"Personally," Theodore Roosevelt wrote, "I rather hope the fight will come soon." He did "not care," Roosevelt added, "whether our seacoast cities are bombarded or not; we would take Canada."[42]

British officials were perplexed. Joseph Chamberlain, the Cabinet's expert on America, was asked if "President Cleveland's . . . mad thirst for war" was "merely electioneering."

Then, Chamberlain responded to his own question: "I do not think it is due entirely to electioneering. . . . I am sorry to say . . . that . . . a majority . . . of Americans would look forward without horror to a war."[43]

Although some in England argued for chastising American insolence, a surprising chorus for peace sounded from—what had become in the several decades since the Crimean War—an indefatigable peace lobby: Quakers, Unitarians, Baptists, and Presbyterian "nonconformists" rose in alarm. William Ewart Gladstone, the opposition leader, urged that "common sense" bring tempers under control.

In the United States, rumors of an impending confrontation circulated even before the message was delivered and U.S. gold reserves started to plummet. Forty-eight hours after Cleveland's message, a spectacular stock market fissure suddenly opened, and vast amounts of American investment capital hemorrhaged. American opinion leaders began to take another look at the balance between the rewards of defending an equatorial boundary and the costs of a rupture with America's most significant financial partner.[44]

The Kaiser Deflates Venezuela

England's own rather poor military condition buttressed forbearance. British military intelligence, for instance, confirmed that Canada was virtually indefensible. And the Prussian General Staff, in a study of British vulnerabilities at the time, concluded that Britain was so overextended, it had little latitude for any new initiatives in the Americas or anywhere else.[45] But more than anything else, however, the Venezuelan dispute was deflated by the appearance of an unexpected challenge to Britain from another quarter.

In South Africa, on the last weekend of 1895, Dr. Leander Jameson assembled a party of armed riders to foment an uprising among disenfranchised "Utlanders" (mostly English-speaking "outsiders.") in the Transvaal. At the first news of Jameson's raid, Kaiser Wilhelm sensed a scheme by the Duke of Wales and Jewish financiers to capture the Transvaal's gold by stealth.[46] Since the Transvaal was populated by Dutch-speaking people of a "Lower Saxon-German," Wilhelm claimed he was bound to be "sympathetic because of the racial relationship."[47]

Wilhelm informed his counselors that he had decided to wire Transvaal President Paul Kruger a public note of congratulations. One advisor cautioned that the Kaiser's telegram would be viewed as untoward and insulting in England. German State Secretary Marschall Von Bieberstein, the Kaiser's most senior minister, countered, "You have no idea of the suggestion being made in there. Everything else is even worse."[48]

Wilhelm's telegram was offensive. It indicated that had Kruger's own means not been sufficient, Germany would have taken up arms on Kruger's behalf. But above all, the Kaiser's undisguised satisfaction over what he took as a reverse for a covert policy was nothing if it was not insulting.

The telegram, said the future Edward VII, was a "most gratuitous act of unfriendliness."[49] Popular reaction was less restrained. Dock workers assaulted German sailors as they boarded ships. Shops with German names were attacked. German tourists were beaten in shops and as they boarded ships. Salisbury's colleagues realized that two crises at once were all but unmanageable. The Venezuelan imbroglio, they understood, could probably be resolved by modest concessions in form. But, as Chamberlain informed his colleagues, the German challenge required "an Act of Vigor." "[W]e ought to defy someone," Chamberlain mused of the twin German and American challenges. Given public animus, a waspish response to Germany was clearly "preferable."[50]

Conserving Enemies and Appeasement

Like a violent storm that announces a bountiful spring, the change in Anglo-American relations after the Venezuelan dispute announced a new season. On January 15, 1896, Arthur Balfour, Leader of the House of Commons (and Salisbury's nephew) told the House that the time had come when "some statesmen of authority, more fortunate even than President Monroe, will lay down the doctrine that between English-speaking peoples war is impossible."[51] And on January 26, Joseph Chamberlain—who had not that much earlier argued for firmness in the face of American pressure—seemed to experience a lasting conversion. As Chamberlain informed his Birmingham constituents, from then on, he would "look with horror upon anything in the nature of a fratricidal strife" [and he would] "look forward with pleasure to the possibility of the Stars and Stripes and the Union Jack floating together in defense of a common cause sanctioned by humanity and justice."[52]

A year later, Lord Lansdowne, secretary of state for war and future head of the foreign office, recommended against increasing British defenses in the Americas since the United States was now capable of increasing its strength in the area "indefinitely." "[I]f we included the United States [in our estimates]," wrote Lansdowne, then British strategy would simply become "a curiosity before we are much older."[53]

Entente

Britain had faced two choices: It could have accommodated America's extensive claims or it could attempt to overawe the Americans. The latter seemed expensive, potentially unnecessary, and, perhaps, out of reach. Olney and Cleveland, by dint of unmitigated brass and luck, had extracted from the world's greatest power an acquiescence to America's self-proclaimed preeminent interest, not just in a country, region, or continent, but in a whole hemisphere. After the Venezuelan crisis, British concessions reined in on each other. There was to be a capitulation on the border disputes with Canada, the relinquishing of claims on an Isthmus canal, and the yielding to the American position on fishing rights. In the Venezuelan matter's conclusion, the British acceded to arbitration as the methodology of choice in deciding virtually all-important bilateral disputes.

In contrast, the effect of Wilhelm's pressures over the Transvaal was, over time, quite different. British policy soon migrated from passive support of German external aims to an all-but-steady state of irritation.

Wilhelm was not invited to celebrate the sixtieth anniversary of Victoria's accession in 1897. Cecil Spring-Rice, at his next assignment in the Berlin embassy, applauded. The Germans, Spring-Rice wrote, "have been kicking us for years, on the assumption they were kicking a dead ass. It is a great surprise to see starting up a live lion."[54]

The difference between the reaction of Britain to the United States, on the one side, and Germany, on the other, was in the analysis of threat posed by the growth of naval power in Germany and the United States. A rising American naval competence, unlike the simultaneous assault on British naval supremacy from Germany, was reckoned by British policy makers to be benign in most instances and helpful in others.

On Appeasement and Parvenus

In his last years, Olney expressed the hope that historians would see his stewardship of the Venezuelan crisis as the first great breach with George Washington's Farewell Address. In a sense it did, for a time, and ultimately saw the United States intervene decisively on the side of Britain and France in World War I. Ironically, the purposes to which that intervention were consigned by Woodrow Wilson were undercut by the common apprehension of the Monroe Doctrine that arose at the instigation of Scruggs, Olney, and Cleveland. For opposition to Wilson's hope that the United States might retain an active praetorian of a more just and democratic world order was fatally undone, in part, by Senator Lodge's "reservation" that the Monroe Doctrine—as it had been defined in the mid-1890s—was not accounted for in the Charter of the League of Nations.[55]

But it is undeniable that the Venezuelan boundary dispute marked the point where the United States made its real debut as an actor rather than a subject in Europe's classical balance of power. Cleveland and Olney's "formidable" diplomacy was remarkable not so much in the stumblings surrounding the forwarding of a rather artificial interest, nor in the breezy disregard of Venezuela. What is astonishing, especially in contrast to the difficulties encountered by Germany, was that an American ascent to the councils of power exacted so few real costs.

For Britain, "appeasement" of the United States made sense. Appeasement's great merit is that it usually avoided war, at least in the short run. If a rising power's appetite for status, influence, or territory can be sated, then perhaps a good bit of the status quo can be salvaged. The net effect of a strategy of appeasement for a dominant power is that an existing system, which a preponderant power has largely defined and managed to its own benefit, is retained.

Appeasement would have been a limited strategy even if there had not been the experience at Munich, for democracy tends to limit its use. Leadership in states responsive to the public cannot freely pick and choose those with whom they can and cannot come to terms. Some states and some leaders are an anathema. The Cabinet diplomacy of the old regime could engage in undertakings with pariah states and statesmen. But as states have gained more representative institutions, the Wilsonian abhorrence of secret diplomacy made distasteful arrangements more problematic.

Managing Chinese Power

Like Kaiser Wilhelm II upon the involuntary retirement of Bismarck in 1890, China's Jiang Zemin's quest for national self-assertion has combined a rhetoric of victimized nationalism with rising defense budgets and an obvious aspiration to play a pivotal role in regional and international diplomacy. China has announced itself a rising power.[56] The evidence that Jiang Zemin's "major power strategy" ("daguo zhanlue")[57] is aimed at a kind of break-out similiar to that attempted by the Germans from the late 1890s is not hard to find.

First, there is the recent rash of undertakings with states from Iran and Pakistan to Yugoslavia, but especially Russia, aimed directly at countering American influence and power. Second, there is a 50-billion-dollar-a-year military modernization that is proceeding at double-digit pace.[58] Third, there is the constant public conversation about imminent war with Taiwan accompanied by an odd dismissal of America's power and standing in Asia in general, and the Taiwan Straits in particular. Finally, in Beijing, one hears and reads invective about American purposes that seems to border on the hysterical.

America, it is claimed, has resurrected the methodology of John Foster Dulles. Hence both increased American–Japanese defense cooperation and American plans to work on anti-missile technology with Australia, Japan, and perhaps Taiwan are deemed part and parcel of expanding NATO to Asia.[59] The United States, one leading academic told a conference on North East Asian security, is anxious to "red-line" China. Talk about China's human rights, a prominent academic told the gathering discussing North

Asian security, is nothing less than an attempt to "extend manifest destiny to China." A senior and well-placed expert on American foreign policy told me that the reason he and all Chinese were convinced that NATO planes bombed a Chinese embassy in Belgrade in 1999 is that many American planners simply "hate China" and want to show China that it can do nothing in the face of American power. Defense Secretary William S. Cohen, in his July 2000 visit to Beijing, was so impressed by Chinese official invective that he was moved, unusually so for an American official, to actually complain in public about another country's tendentious and abusive "Characterizations of the United States as being a hegemony, as a country determined to dominate the world and to contain and dominate China."[60]

Analysts who examine China can come up with at least five explanations for China's peculiar brand of vitriol. First, its language is not unusual either in terms of Leninist discourse, which routinely tarred one's enemies as meanly as possible. Second, there is the wounding history of humiliation at the hands of colonial powers.[61] Third, there is the real frustration of surrounding the remnant of China's civil war—Taiwan—a reminder to China's leadership that their victory was incomplete. Fourth, the fires of Chinese nationalism have been fixed to this last, unrecovered territory. America, especially, is viewed as the great impediment to China's full stature and territorial integrity. Finally, there is the widespread insecurity of China's ruling class. The leadership of China is widely loathed. China's leadership—fearful, corrupt, and incompetent—has found some success in deflecting popular anger by the manufacture of enemies.

As unsettling as Chinese rhetoric is the anachronistic way China apparently apprehends the world. Using hoary arguments vaguely like those of the quintessential American academic "realists," whom many studied in U.S. graduate schools in decades past, Chinese analysts assert that America believes "multipolarity dangerous and hence wants to perpetuate a unipolar world."[62] The American urge to dominance is likened to that of Britain or even Roman imperial practices. Hence, the NATO humanitarian intervention in Kosovo and, specifically, the American bombing of China's embassy in Belgrade in the spring of 1999 led to a passel of alarms that the United States was prepared to intervene in China in case of political disorder, ethnic disputes, regional clashes in the South China Sea, or on behalf of Taiwan.

Whose World Order?

Because Chinese Communist leadership is steeped in the Maoist-Leninist literature and advised by counselors who have been schooled in American academic Cold-War notions of realism, China's leaders are all but unable to apprehend globalization and multilateralism. And, even when these trends are given some credence, the American understanding of multilateralism and interdependence is frequently seen as mostly a disingenuous American cloak for the American will to power.

The international order that Americans study and promote is one that places a premium on transparency and economic flexibility. It is a world quite contrary to China's essentially Leninist Party's traditions and interests. Chinese dissatisfaction with an international order that it is increasingly enmeshed within, but which it did not construct, is similar to the reaction of Germany's political elite at the end of the nineteenth century. The reasoning is similar: The benefits of the extant system are dispersed asymmetrically, and most of the dividends are seen as devolving to American hegemonic power.

That is not to say that the current crop of Chinese academics and policy makers can find no objective benefit to China in the current international system. They recognize that it offers China more stability, security, and prosperity than at any other time in more than 150 years. But the current international order does not comport with what the Chinese feel is their due; and to that extent, they feel it part of continuing injustice perpetrated by a power far greater than they.

Chinese Chairman Jiang Zemin's "major power strategy" is, in fact, an attempt to break out from what American pundit Thomas Friedman calls the golden straightjacket of American-led globalization.[63] Jiang's reponse appears to be predicated on the conjury of classic routines of "balancing" major powers as an answer to American hegemony. Japan and Russia are seen as candidates for manufacturing a configuration in which American hegemonic instincts are constrained.

But to an American observer, Jiang's answer to American power appears both anachronistic and fanciful. First of all, neither Russia nor Japan is a "major power" in the nineteenth-century sense. And it is unlikely they will become so within the next few generations. Russia has no economic wherewithal. Russia's ability to help China is also attenuated by the substantial and disruptive migrations of Chinese into Russia's Far Eastern provinces.[64] Japan is even a poorer candidate than Russia for abetting Beijing. In China, there is the legacy of Chinese bitterness about Japan's behavior in the 1930s and 1940s and the absence of any public sense, in Japan, that there is anything to apologize about. More important, of course, is the fact there is no market or security incentive that China can tender to Japan that would reasonably lure Japan away from the security and trade benefits it enjoys by virtue of its intimate association with the United States.

Taiwan—What Policy? What Chance?

If China were to pose a challenge to American hegemony, it would be as a consequence of differing interests as to how to deal with Taiwan.

Some observers believe that the People's Liberation Army (PLA) has deliberately aggravated cross-straits tensions in order to claim increased resources. Others believe China's current policy makers are manufacturing new waves of nationalism to substitute for their own declining legitimacy. A variant of this analysis is that Chinese rulers, lacking any authority or legitimacy themselves, cannot afford to stand down tensions or compromise any claims touching on questions of Chinese sovereignty, lest their political opponents use the nationalist cudgel to effect their undoing. But whatever the motive, it is clear that China and the United States face a dangerous and perhaps insoluble dilemma over the matter of Taiwan.

American credibility is critical to sustaining the ambiguous and inclusive status quo in the Taiwan Straits. Yet U.S. credibility is now commonly impeached by Chinese observers who note that the Vietnam era legacy of "force protection" dominates American thinking, superseding virtually all other considerations of policy effectiveness. The hasty stand-down in the Persion Gulf; the precipitous withdrawal from Somalia; the long, shameful gawking at the near annihilation of Sarajevo; and the war waged on Kosovo from a height of at least 15,000 feet—all seem a warrant to Chinese military planners to hold American warnings and commitments at a discount.

In January 1996, Chas Freeman, perhaps America's best professional diplomat, warned Chinese officials that a PLA move against Taiwan would be met by a vigorous American response. The Chinese were derisive. PLA Deputy Chief of Staff Xiong Guangkai replied: "In the 1950s you three times threatened China with nuclear strikes . . . and you could do that because we could not hit back. Now we can. So you are not going to threaten us again because in the end, you care a lot more about Los Angeles than Taipei."[65]

In March 2000, a widely read Chinese army paper, the *Haowangjiao Weekly*, in describing the scenario for taking Taiwan, argued "[t]he United States will not sacrifice 200 million Americans for 20 million Taiwanese and eventually they are going to back down." Once the way was cleared of American support, either by anti-ship missiles, nuclear threat, or a combination of electronic and political jujitsu, then China might use its arsenal of neutron bombs. "Even though we get a damaged Taiwan, it is better than not having Taiwan," the paper said.[66]

In a general sense, most of China's arsenal and plans are only of tangential concern to American military planners. John Culver, the CIA's military expert on China, told a National Defense University forum in 1998 that China's army is still largely the same force it was at the time the USSR collapsed—overwhelmingly a ground army with an inventory of weapons that, in most cases, has been deployed with the same units for up to 30 years.

Even with new Russian jet fighters, submarines, destroyers, and a whole array of new missiles, Culver argued, the Chinese army has created only a few "pockets of modernity."[67] The Chinese navy and air force are facing the obsolescence of their Soviet-era planes and warships; and about half of China's pre-1990 airforce is unflyable, according to current American estimates. On average, Chinese pilots fly far fewer training hours than those in any modern air force. Newer Russian SU-27 airplanes have had to be sent back to Russia for repairs before they could be flown. A number have already crashed. Russian SU-30s are said to be on order, but none appeared in the massive fiftieth anniversary October 1, 1999, fly-by over Beijing.

Chinese planners seem to be arguing from a different playbook. American strategy has largely been a product of a distinct tradition of efficient attrition. The Chinese, in contrast, have always stressed surprise, stealth, speed, and the ability to leverage small pockets of strength. China's military think tanks have loosed a torrent of optimistic plans for asymmetric war. A redacted CIA version of one Chinese military strategic document entitled "Unrestricted Warfare" was widely circulated among American defense intellectuals in 1999. "Unrestricted Warfare" called for the Chinese military to concentrate its efforts along a narrow range of technologies to "blind" the American military satellites so that U.S. ships and planes would not be able communicate with each other or acquire targets with confidence.[68] A concomitant terror campaign was suggested against financial exchanges, investment houses, banks, financiers, and other relatively soft targets. The upshot, according to "Unrestricted Warfare," would be sufficiently disruptive for the PLA to effect a fait accompli in Taiwan.

How the loss of George Soros, who was signaled out for assassination in "Unrestricted Warfare," would cripple the Seventh Fleet (or any real aspect of American military power) is unclear. In the first place, of course, most of American technology is hardened, redundant, and, in the end, American forces are in a kind of depth that makes Chinese plans seem a species of artful insouciance and self-delusion of the kind that led the Japanese to hope that Pearl Harbor would be determinative in knocking America out of the Pacific.[69]

But these kinds of planning discussions cannot fail to help mold expectations in the United States and in China, and in its PLA ranks. Such rhetorical inflation is liable (as in economic markets) to eventually produce a "bubble." And no matter how far-fetched they might seem, Chinese professions of impatience regarding Taiwan are backed by increasing Chinese political and economic capital. There is the chance, no matter what the cost, that they, like Germany with its Schlieffen plan, will eventually attack—no matter what the odds, lest (as the Germans finally calculated) time and opportunity irretrievably slip away.

NINETEENTH- AND TWENTY-FIRST-CENTURY PARALLELS

Like Germany, China's power is as much potential as actual. Whereas Germany had over 13.2 percent of world GDP, China's GDP in 1997 was 3.5 percent, an amount about half of what it was two centuries before.[70] As is the case with China, German reliance on international trade was substantial, amounting to some 38 percent of GNP before World War I. And as was the case with both America's and Germany's rise to power, most of China's growth appears to be spurred by imported capital.[71] Also as in the American case a century before, the major source of trade and investment is the potential adversary and its allies of the time.[72] Yet unlike America a century before, China is woefully lagging in measures of an educated work force, managerial expertise, and military sophistication. Indeed, scholars such as Paul Dibb and others have argued that in the newer technologies China is falling behind the United States, not catching up.[73]

Like the British in the Venezuelan instance, the Chinese do not understand how the United States can have a valid standing in the Taiwan Straits. China's current crop of diplomats is generally second rate and their quality seems to be declining as the best students in China's diplomatic academy are opting for careers in business or a life in America.[74] Nationalism, the great constant of rising powers at the end of the nineteenth century, is almost neurologically susceptible to either the Taiwan trigger or the accusation of arrogant American trampling of Chinese aspirations. Like Olney's blunderbuss—used to make Britain heed when otherwise the interest would have been dismissed altogether—China's anger is both operatically manufactured and real.[75]

Opera and Interests

But there is a danger to using well-staged diplomatic and military temper tantrums as an instrument of policy.[76] First, bluffs have proved hard to figure, and there are ample examples of great-power miscalculation in the face of small-power posturing. Second, the problem with bluffs, as in the problem of the diplomacy of coercive nuclear deterrence, is that each tantrum has to be larger lest it be subject to discount. At some point, the bluff might be called. Third, if the PLA's attempt to influence American elections in 1996 is any guide, this ability to actually gauge what the American political system will permit hardly seems well honed in China. Finally, bluffs can have immense unintended cost, even if they fail to trigger war.[77]

Not the least of these potential costs might be, as in the case of 1895, a financial panic. China's banks, especially, are dependent on a huge savings rate—over 43 percent of GDP is said to be held on deposit at very low interest rates.[78] Withdrawals, as well as a massive conversion of renminbi into dollars via Hong Kong despite currency controls, would be one likely result of war. Then too, there might well be a huge sell-off on the relatively thinly traded "red chip" indexes of the Heng Seng and in the "B" shares of the Shanghai market. The result of bluff—even if it "worked" and Taiwan capitulated—would be a disastrous blow to China's economy. The financial panic of 1895 was over before the year was out. The panic of 1997 and early 1998 skated substantially past China. New China has not really felt the discipline of a financial stampede and its vulnerability, indeed, fragility, is as high as any economy in the world.[79]

TROJAN HORSE OF PEACE? GLOBALIZATION IN APPEASEMENT'S STEAD?

Britain's decision to accommodate American claims at the end of the nineteenth century was abetted by a notion of ethnic, even familial intimacy. There may be an analogous phenomenon at work today in the emerging class of American-born Chinese and Chinese-born Americans who now comprise a huge portion of America's educated elite in university research and the high-tech industry. They, as well as the new multicultural tone of American politics, can help, perhaps, mitigate some great-power animus rife in the nineteenth century and early to mid-twentieth century.

Meanwhile, current trends indicate an American advantage in waiting matters out. Most of China's growth is in the export sectors; and most exports are to the United States, which now runs a trade deficit in excess of $70 billion a year with the PRC, the largest such "imbalance" in the world. The United States represents 42 percent or more of China's total foreign trade (with Japan a distant second, with about half the volume of trade as there is between the United States and the PRC) (nearly three times the dependency of Germany on Britain before World War I),[80] and total bilateral Sino-American trade adds up to about 10 percent of China's GDP.[81] But U.S. trade with China represents only 2.4 percent of total U.S. foreign trade and a tiny fraction of American national wealth.[82]

The relationship between China and Taiwan is also highly interdependent. There are, despite all kinds of restrictions, some 200,000 Taiwanese-based businesspeople resident in the PRC, manning some 40,000 firms. Taiwan is the PRC's second (or depending how it is measured, third) largest source of trade and investment capital after the United States. About half of Taiwan's computer-related production is outsourced in China.[83] For China, an attack on Taiwan would spell economic disaster of a scale unseen since the Cultural Revolution. It would also, of course, violate Deng Xiaoping's admonition, honored in the breach, that "Chinese do not kill Chinese."

There is, moreover, no compelling reason to believe that nuclear deterrence between China and the United States is any less stable than it has been when Mao was exhorting his cadres to "dig deep and store corn." Now most of the corn supplies have long been consumed and the shelters under Beijing converted to shopping malls and grocery stores. More Chinese have more to lose than ever before in war, and enough Chinese would find a war with America such an abomination that no Chinese government that waged it would likely survive. Even if America could somehow be militarily isolated, there would be the consequence of China's economic isolation. It is uncertain whether the present government, or even the current geographic definition of China, would survive.

The Future?

Partly in response to Chinese actions in the Straits as well as the remarkably abrasive and abusive rhetoric of Beijing, a loose coalition of American academics, members of Congress, think tank specialists, conservative journalists, and partisans of Taiwan have formed a self-styled "Blue Team" to sound a tocsin about a rising China. Alarmed by the PLA's increasing capability and domestic repression, overseas arms purchases, and arms transfers—and opposed to the so-called "Red Team" (those who favor the Clinton administration's policy of "constructive engagement" toward China), the Blue Team mobilized a significant public relations effort in 1999. The result was legislation to require the Pentagon to report annually to Congress on the Chinese–Taiwan military balance and new legislation to monitor Beijing's dismal human rights practices.[84] The center of the effort was the plan to defeat American acceptance of China into the World Trade Organization. That effort failed, but the attendant effort to portray China's small missile force as a threat gained some success; indeed, the national security team of President George W. Bush pledged a missile defense system that was directly tied to the PRC's tiny deterrent.

To be sure, China is a rising power. But "New China" is a work in progress. No country is changing faster; in no country is the future more cloudy. China could be a great power. It could come apart. Even for those immersed in China, the future is veiled in uncertainty. The China of tomorrow may proceed along the lines of the best hopes of today's globalists—that is, it would be more open, more democratic, more willing to deal with disliked elements of the status quo with offers of a Fabian menu of inducements.

It is only in the Taiwan Straits that there is a possibility of confrontation; and there is plenty of room for dithering. It would do good to remember the history of Anglo-German relations when, in the end, the worst was anticipated by both. A conflict in the Taiwan Straits, it should be underscored, would be a disaster for all, although China would, like Germany, certainly lose more.

Those who know American diplomatic history understand that it was only Mao's connection with Russia and the Korean War that made a relationship with China difficult for policy makers and public alike. Americans have invested much in the regeneration of China in the last 20 years. Recent study of American public opinion, even after the escalation of tensions generated from everything from Panama Canal scares to spy scandals, reveals no appetite for a "containment policy."[85]

For now, the American public seems indifferent, even generous to Chinese aspirations. Without a major test in the Taiwan Straits or some kind of apocalyptic (and public) human rights atrocity, as in June of 1989, American attitudes are likely to remain stable. In this sense, a general policy of propitiating China in as many ways as possible has substantial support, and, if history is any guide, makes sense.

NOTES

1. John M. Shalikashvili, Chairman of the Joint Chiefs of Staff, *The National Military Strategy of the United States* (Washington, D.C.: GPO, 1995).

2. A.J.P. Taylor, *The Struggle for the Mastery of Europe, 1848–1918* (Oxford: Oxford University Press, 1957), p. xxxiii.

3. Walter LeFeber, *The American Age: United States Foreign Policy at Home and Abroad since 1750* (New York: W. W. Norton, 1989), p. 12.

4. Paul Kennedy, *The Rise and Fall of the Great Powers* (New York: Vintage, 1987), p. 199.

5. Jon Tetsuro Sumida, *In Defense of Naval Supremacy: Finance, Technology, and British Naval Policy, 1889–1914* (Boston: Unwin Hyman, 1989); Robert K. Massie, *Dreadnought: Britain, Germany, and the Coming of the Great War* (New York: Ballantine Books, 1991).

6. Massie, *Dreadnought*, p. 426.

7. Kennedy, *The Rise and Fall of the Great Powers*, pp. 203, 226.

8. Clive Trebilock, "British Armaments and European Industrialization, 1890–1914," *Economic History* 26 (1973): 257.

9. Taylor, *The Struggle for the Mastery of Europe*, "Introduction"; Aron L. Friedberg, *The Weary Titan: Britain and the Experience of Relative Decline: 1895–1905* (Princeton, N.J.: Princeton University Press, 1988), p. 26.

10. Kennedy, *The Rise and Fall of the Great Powers*, p. 202.

11. Nathan Rosenberg and L. E. Birdzell, *How the West Grew Rich* (New York: Basic Books, 1986), pp. 190–212ff.

12. Walter Millis, *Arms and Men* (New York: G. P. Putnam's Sons, 1965), p. 133.

13. Robert L. Beisner, *From the Old Diplomacy to the New, 1865–1900* (New York: Thomas Crowell, 1975), p. 13.

14. Sumida, *In Defense of Naval Supremacy*, p. 8.

15. A. T. Mahan, *The Influence of Sea Power upon History* (Boston: Little, Brown, 1918), pp. 328–329.

16. Fareed Zakaria, *The Rise of a Great Power: National Strength, State Struc-*

ture, and American Foreign Policy, 1865–1908 (unpublished Ph.D. dissertation, Cambridge, Mass.: Harvard University, 1993), pp. 153, 204, 263 n.343.

17. William Appleman Williams, *The Roots of the Modern American Empire* (New York: Random House, 1969), pp. 358–359.

18. Foster Rhea Dulles, *The Imperial Years* (Binghamton, N.Y.: Thomas Y. Crowell, 1956), p. 46.

19. Alfred Thayer Mahan, *The Interest of America in International Conditions* (Boston: Little, Brown, 1910), p. 168.

20. H. W. Brands, *The Reckless Decade* (New York: St. Martin's Press, 1995), p. 292.

21. Charles W. Calhoun, *Golden Age Cato: The Life of Walter Q. Gresham* (Lexington: University of Kentucky Press, 1988), p. 212.

22. John A. S. Grenville and George Berkley, *Politics, Strategy, and American Diplomacy: Studies in Foreign Policy, 1873–1917* (New Haven, Conn.: Yale University Press, 1966), p. 133.

23. Walter LaFeber, *The New Empire: An Interpretation of American Expansion, 1860–1898* (Ithaca, N.Y.: Cornell University Press, 1963), p. 173ff.

24. William L. Scruggs, *British Aggression in Venezuela, or the Monroe Doctrine on Trial*, 2nd ed. (Atlanta, Ga.: The Franklin Publishing Co., 1895), pp. 23–24, 28–30.

25. Dexter Perkins, *The Monroe Doctrine, 1876–1907* (Baltimore, Md.: Johns Hopkins University Press, 1937), p. 136.

26. Henry James, *Richard Olney and His Public Service* (Boston: Houghton Mifflin, 1923), p. 101.

27. Ibid., p. 100.

28. Ibid., p. 110.

29. *Papers Relating to the Foreign Relations of the United States*, 2 parts (Washington, D.C.: GPO, 1896), Part 1, pp. 542–562.

30. Ibid., p. 562; Allan Nevins, *Grover Cleveland: Study in Courage* (New York: Dodd, Mead, 1938), pp. 642–643.

31. James, *Richard Olney*, citing Olney's daughter, p. 110.

32. Barbara Tuchman, *The Proud Tower: A Portrait of the World Before the War: 1890–1914* (New York: Ballantine, 1996), p. 35.

33. Charles Callan Tansill, *The Foreign Policy of Thomas F. Bayard, 1885–1897* (New York: Fordham University Press, 1940), p. 704.

34. Charles S. Campbell, *The Transformation of American Foreign Relations, 1865–1900* (New York: Harper and Row, 1974), p. 205.

35. Thomas Bailey, *A Diplomatic History of the American People*, 10th ed. (Englewood Cliffs, N.J.: Prentice Hall, 1980), p. 379; Beisner, *From the Old Diplomacy to the New*, p. 31.

36. Zakaria, *The Rise of a Great Power*, p. 231.

37. J.A.S. Grenville, *Lord Salisbury and Foreign Policy: The Close of the Nineteenth Century* ([London] University of London: Athlone Press, 1964), p. 59.

38. LaFeber, *The New Empire*, p. 266.

39. Wilson Beckles, *America's Ambassadors to England, 1785–1928: Narrative of Anglo-American Diplomatic Relations* (Freeport, N.Y.: Books for Libraries Press, 1969), p. 408.

40. Alfred L. P. Dennis, *Adventures in American Diplomacy: 1896–1906* (New York: E. P. Dutton, 1928), p. 28.

41. Brands, *The Reckless Decade*, p. 302.

42. *Selections from the Correspondence of Theodore Roosevelt and Henry Cabot Lodge, 1884–1918*, Vol. 1 (New York: Charles Scribner's Sons, 1925), pp. 200–205.

43. D. George Boyce, *The Crisis of British Power: The Imperial and Naval Papers of the Second Earl of Selborne, 1895–1910* (London: Historians Press, 1990), pp. 25–50ff.

44. LaFeber, *The New Empire*, pp. 274–275ff.

45. Ernest R. May, *Imperial Democracy: The Emergence of America as a Great Power* (New York: Harcourt, Brace, and World, 1961), p. 50.

46. Lamar Cecil, *Wilhelm II, Prince and Emperor—1859–1900* (Chapel Hill: University of North Carolina Press, 1989), p. 288.

47. Ex-Kaiser Wilhelm II, *My Memoirs: 1878–1918* (London: Cassell and Company, Ltd., 1922), p. 80.

48. Stephan R. Rock, *Why Peace Breaks Out: Great Power Rapprochement in Historical Perspective* (Chapel Hill: University of North Carolina Press, 1989), p. 223.

49. Cecil, *Wilhelm II*, p. 288.

50. Kenneth Bourne, *The Balance of Power in North America* (Berkeley: University of California Press, 1967), p. 240.

51. Blanche E. Dugdale, *Arthur James Balfour, First Earl of Balfour, KG, OM, FRS, Etc. O.M., F.R.S., etc., by his niece, Blanche E. C. Dugdale*, Vol. 1 (London: Hutchinson, 1936), p. 226.

52. Campbell, *The Transformation of American Foreign Relations*, p. 213.

53. Friedberg, *Weary Titan*, p. 163.

54. Stephen Gwynn (ed.), *The Letters and Friendships of Sir Cecil Spring-Rice: A Record*, Vol. 1 (London: Constable, 1929), p. 189.

55. William C. Windenor, *Henry Cabot Lodge and the Search for an American Foreign Policy* (Berkeley: University of California Press, 1979), p. 316ff.

56. Sensitive American observers note that the Deng Xiaoping phrase "tao guang, yang hui" (hide one's capacity and bide one's time) is again being heard in the corridors of think tanks and at academic conferences. But this time his words appear to have been removed from the essence of his position of seeking accommodation and eschewing assertiveness ("jue bu dang tou"). Willie Wo Lap Lam, "For Asia, Beijing Is All Smiles," *South China Morning Post*, June 30, 1990.

57. Yang Jiemian, "Summit Diplomacy and Strategic Partnership: Aspirations, Expectations, and Realization," in Peter H. Koehn and Joseph Y. S. Cheng (eds.), *The Outlook for U.S.–China Relations Following the 1997–1998 Summits: Chinese and American Perspectives on Security, Trade and Cultural Exchange* (Hong Kong: The Chinese University Press, 1999), pp. 54–55; Gaye Christoffersen, "China and the U.S.: Defining the Constructive Strategic Partnership," paper prepared for Senior Participants, Foreign Affairs College, Beijing, October 1999.

58. Bates Gil and Michael O'Hanlon, "Gil and O'Hanlon Hit Back," *The National Interest*, No. 58 (Winter 1999–2000): 118. In contrast, China's investment in education at all levels is at the lowest rate of all countries in the world. By Chinese estimates, total investment in education and the arts in the China is around

$1 billion out of a GDP of about $997 billion. See *BBC Monitoring*, London, May 29, 2000, "Text of report in English by official Chinese news agency Xinhua" (New China News Agency). The purchasing power parity–adjusted figures for Chinese military investment would put the figures at above $200 billion, making it the second largest military budget in the world.

59. Ding Shing, "The New Clinton Doctrine," Xiandi Guoji Guanxi, FBIS, August 20, 1999.

60. "Address to the Chinese National Defense University As Delivered by Secretary of Defense William S. Cohen," The National Defense University, Beijing, China, Thursday, July 13, 2000, DOD web site, viewed July 18, 2000.

61. For an analysis of the dynamics of nationalism as a politics of indignation, or resentment, see Liah Greenfield, *Nationalism: Five Roads to Modernity* (Cambridge, Mass.: Harvard University Press, 1992).

62. Kenneth N. Waltz, *Theory of International Politics* (New York: McGraw-Hill, 1979).

63. Thomas L. Friedman, *The Lexus and the Olive Tree* (New York: Farrar, Straus and Giroux, 2000).

64. Elizabeth Wishnick, "Russia in Asia and Asians in Russia," *SAIS Review* 20(1) (Winter–Spring 2000): 87–101.

65. Barton Gellman, "U.S. and China Nearly Came to Blows in 1996," *Washington Post*, June 21, 1998. Diplomats at the Foreign Ministry's Foreign Affairs College with long experience in the United States assured me during my tenure in the academic year 1999–2000 that Taiwan was an issue for which Americans would not fight, and that China, in circumstances that found Taiwan slipping even further away, would have no choice but to go to war.

66. *The Haowangjiao Weekly* detailed what seems to be the dominant scenario among Beijing military planners. First, the PRC would begin a campaign across China of demonstrations demanding action against Taiwan. The propaganda and agitation at home would be accompanied by increased armaments purchases of topline military goods from Russia. At the same time, American interests would be vitiated and complicated by huge trade deals—after all, China is pledged to spend some $750 billion on infrastructure development in the next decade and just a fraction of these contracts let to American suppliers would create a substantial pro-China constituency. If these actions did not yield the conjunction of American indifference and Taiwan accession to Beijing's demands, China would launch an armada of 200,000 fishing vessels carrying a force of two million men, protected by "an arsenal of secret weapons, the most advanced in the world—including laser weapons to disable the laser guidance systems of America's F-17s" and would take Taiwan. "If all else failed, the PLA would mobilize the country to take part in civil defense exercises to show the United States that China was preparing to survive a nuclear war." See "Newspaper Closed after Leaking Conflict Plan," March 20, 2000. *South China Morning Post*, Internet edition, viewed April 19, 2000.

67. John Culver, "Defense Policy and Posture II," in Hans Binnendijk and Ronald N. Montaperto (eds.), *Strategic Trends in China* (Washington, D.C.: National Defense University Press, 1998), p. 72.

68. Qiao Liang and Wang Xiangsui, *Unrestricted Warfare* (Beijing: PLA Literature and Arts Publishing House, February 1999) (FBIS translation), privately circulated, and see http://www.c4i.org/unrestricted.pdf.

69. These remarks were written before the September 11, 2001 attacks on Washington, D.C. and New York, but the attacks underscore the point. The site and locus of nearly 30 percent of America's treasury transactions and much of the human capital involved in American investment banking was wiped out in seconds. Within a week, however, Wall Street was back up and running at record volume; and the market damage—losses in capitalization of over a trillion dollars, nothing to be sneezed at, to be sure—was substantially recovered and repaired within weeks, though business activity ground to a halt for over a week, and there was substantial impetus toward a deepening global recession.

70. Gerald Segal, "Does China Matter?" *Foreign Affairs* 78(5) (September/October 1999): 24ff.

71. Paul A. Papaupanou and Scott L. Kastner, "Sleeping with the (potential) Enemy: Assessing the U.S. Policy of Engagement with China," *Security Studies* 9(1/2) (Autumn 1999–Winter 2000): 167–168ff.

72. Rosenberg and Birdzell, *How the West Grew Rich*, pp. 222–223.

73. Paul Dibb, "The Revolution in Military Affairs and Asian Security," *Survival* 39(4) (Winter 1997–1998): 98ff. For a good summary, see Solomon L. Karmel, *China and the People's Liberation Army: Great Power or Struggling Developing State?* (New York: St. Martin's Press, 2000).

74. The crop of young intelligence officers seems generally well-prepared, from my experience lecturing in Beijing to both groups of students.

75. On this point, see Andrew Scobell, "Show of Force: Chinese Soldiers, Statesmen, and the 1995–1996 Taiwan Straits Crisis," *Political Science Quarterly* 115(2) (Summer 1999): 233.

76. In China, the principle is called "resorting to force [in order to] press for peace." See Yo Ji, "Making Sense of the Taiwan Straits Crisis," *Journal of Contemporary China* 6 (Summer 1997): 300–301.

77. The Soviet missile bluff of the late 1950s and early 1960s cost the Soviets any hope for military strategic parity for 20 years.

78. The official figure is 37 percent. But most economists suspect it is higher. See "Banking Loopholes Earn Trouble as Personal-Savings Rate Escalates," *South China Morning Post*, September 4, 1998; and Wayne M. Morrison, "China's Economic Condition," *ISSIE Brief, IB98014*, Congressional Research Service, June 7, 2000, published by the National Council for Science and Environment, Washington D.C. http://cnie/nle/inter-10.html, viewed August 5, 2000.

79. Already, as one student notes, "magnitude of capital flight from China relative to both GDP and levels of domestic investment and savings appears to be noticeably higher than that for Russia." See Terry Sicular, "Capital Flight and Foreign Investment: Two Tales from China and Russia," *The World Economy* 21(5) (July 1998).

80. Papaupanou and Kastner, "Sleeping with the (Potential) Enemy," p. 168, especially n. 24.

81. China's Bureau of Statistics, *Statistical Yearbook of China*, various issues (Beijing: Publishing House of China's Bureau of Statistics, 1999–2000); "Wealth and Power: Those Illusive Goals," *The Economist*, April, 8, 2000. See, most authoritatively, Morrison, "China's Economic Condition"; and "China's Top-Ten Trading Partners Named," *Peoples Daily*, Internet edition, January 20, 2000. China's total trade volume in 1999 was said to be $319.5 billion in a nominal

economy of $997 billion. (The purchasing power parity economy is said to be larger by a factor of four or more.)

82. Morrison, "China's Economic Condition."

83. Greg Mastel, "WTO Means More Than Trade for China, Taiwan," *Journal of Commerce*, April 28, 2000; and Pierre G. Goad, "Asia's Gains and Losses," *Far Eastern Economic Review* 162(47) (November 25, 1999): 83.

84. http://www.icpsr.umich.edu. Viewed on July 10, 2000, Ryan Lizza, 2000. "On the Hill: The Red and the Blue." *The New Republic*. Web site viewed on March 27, 2000; and Nicholas Berry, "We Don't Need a Blue Team, or a Red Team: Taking Sides on China–Taiwan Relations," Center for Defense Information. Web site: http://www.cdi.org/asia/btn030100.html, viewed on February 23, 2000.

85. See Charles Tien and James Nathan, "American Ambivalence toward China," *Public Opinion Quarterly* 65 (April 2001): 124–138.

Chapter 7

On Coercive Diplomacy and the
American Foreign Affairs Experience

INTRODUCTION

In the heady aftermath of the Cuban Missile Crisis, an exultant Robert McNamara exclaimed that henceforth the only serious strategy could be "crisis management."[1] The analysis—that force could be supervised for discrete diplomatic ends—was exhilarating. National security defense intellectuals came to believe, in the aftermath of the Cuban Missile Crisis, that they had found some kind of resolution to the vexatious dilemmas attendant to force.[2] For nearly 200 years, force had seemed to expand beyond any sensible purpose. Yet, while the volume of potential destruction in war exceeded any meaningful object save deterrence of war itself, diplomacy had withered as a meaningful mechanism in moderating the conduct of states.

But in the early 1960s, a new nexus between force and order seemed to appear: Henceforth, it was hoped, force could be remarried to diplomacy. Justice's precursor—a stable, liberal, international regime—was the union's much-hoped-for issue. With properly refined techniques of statecraft, there would be no need for deterrence to come to any kind of unlimited test. If intelligent crisis management could find a way to discretely proportion force, if force could be made a calculable instrument of bargaining, then, it followed, the inner dynamic of Soviet expansionism could be tamed, and at long last the sibylline promise of an American century could be realized.

New doctrines of limited force held out the prospect that the sterile kabuki of diplomacy could be replaced by the management center, the telex, and a flexible and responsive military establishment. The hopes pinned to limited war conjured a memory of less lethal times. For the most part, from the mid-seventeenth century to the onset of the twentieth century, war and peace were ambiguous concepts, defined as much by legal artifacts as by the empirical reality of the battlefield. Wars usually began by declarations and ultimatums, and they ended with treaties and conferences. Short of war, there were frequent military maneuvers and demonstrations of intent undertaken in the absence of much public concern. European publics were largely unaware, ill-informed, and disengaged from war. The worst of most wars was fought at sea or in outposts distant to the capital. Battles might be intense, but the costs were limited to largely professional armies and navies. The stakes of these conflicts were relatively small. From the Treaty of Westphalia to the onset of the Napoleonic War, capitals and courts were rarely at risk. The consequences of defeat, in contradistinction to earlier practices, were neither slavery, slaughter, nor forcible conversion. Rather, a kind of custom of redistributive recompense evolved. Gains or losses were summed up and parsed out in the form of military alliances, dynastic marriages, or overseas colonies.

THE CLAUSEWITZIAN HERITAGE

To Clausewitz, both the warrior and the diplomat ought to have a kind of regulatory synergy, sharing an end not of victory but a better kind of peace.[3] War, to Clausewitz, was but a "stronger form of diplomacy,"[4] while the battlefield was merely an extension of the conference chamber. Clausewitz's specter was "pure war," which of "its own independent will . . . usurp[s] the place of policy the moment it [is] brought into being." Clausewitz's great fear was that war would become "pointless and devoid of sense"—a "thing unto itself."[5] Once war compelled animosities too intense, it lost its integration with the broader world of statecraft.[6] The ensuing carnage would only cease with annihilation, not just of the enemy's forces in the field, but of the enemy's state.

In the eighteenth century, as Clausewitz noted, an unlimited struggle was only a theorist's abstraction and not the reality of the battlefield:

[W]ar was still an affair for governments alone, and the people's role was simply that of an instrument . . . [T]he executive . . . represented the state in its foreign relations. . . . The people's part had been extinguished. . . . War thus became solely the concern of the government . . . [G]overnments parted company with their peoples and behaved as if they were themselves the state.[7]

With the American Civil War, war began to approach its terrible and absolute form. As a result, the best remaining rationale for war's employment was to defeat the causes of war itself. It was, Raymond Aron noted, "essential to inflate the purposes of victory," since "peace would be durable only if dictated unconditionally after crushing the enemy. The demand for total victory was not so much the expression of political philosophy as a reflex reaction to total war."[8]

By the mid-1950s, the Eisenhower administration had given atomic weapons a central place. Yet nuclear weapons were challenged as excessive even by those who depended on them. As Eisenhower himself, who was assailed by suggestions that he develop nuclear weapons that were more "useful," remarked:

No matter . . . how certain that within 24 hours we could destroy Kuibyshev and Moscow and Leningrad and Baku and all the other places . . . I want you to carry this question home with you. Gain such a victory, and what do you do with it? Here would be a great area from the Elbe to Vladivostok and down through South East Asia torn up and destroyed and without government. . . . I ask you what would the civilized world do about it? I repeat, there is no victory in any war except . . . through our dedication . . . to avoid it.[9]

Atomic "victory" could hardly be held to mean the bending of an enemy to one's will or even defeating his army, nor did it capture what Clausewitz had in mind when he wrote of war "in the extreme." Rather, victory implied the elimination of an enemy's society altogether. It was not "politics by other means," but what the Nuremberg lawyers spoke of when they wrote the laws of genocide.

THE DEPRECIATION OF DIPLOMACY AND THE RISE OF COERCIVE STATECRAFT

Not many elements of Soviet expansion seemed worthy of the risk or the moral liability of killing whole peoples. Yet, while nuclear weapons might paralyze one side, there was in the emerging American community of defense intellectuals a fear that these same weapons would embolden the Soviets. As Henry Kissinger explained:

It can be argued that fear of all-out war is bound to be mutual, . . . but . . . [i]f the Soviet bloc can present its challenges in less than all-out form, it may gain a crucial advantage. Every move on its part will then pose the appalling dilemma of whether we are willing to commit suicide to prevent encroachments, not one of which seems to threaten our existence directly, but which may be a step on the road to our ultimate destruction.[10]

The American concern was that the Soviets, without needing to concern themselves with their own public's apprehension of nuclear war, could present challenges that would find a large Western constituency for compromise. Once serious Western interests had been bartered, newer demands would ensue. Once encouraged, the process flirted with either a serious diminution of the Western position or war. It was a Hobson's choice, avoidable by ducking the conference chamber altogether. The Soviets seemed to view the work of diplomacy not as the adjustment of contending interests but, at a minimum, the search for brief respites and, at a maximum, a kind of policy jujitsu that would help leverage their opponents to the mat. Hence, for most of the "new strategists," the classic diplomatic enterprise, when it confronted Soviet power was, from the standpoint of American policy, worse than ill-conceived and fruitless—it was an invitation to disaster. As Kissinger argued:

To us, the willingness to enter conference is . . . a symptom of reduced tensions. . . . To the Soviets . . . , a settlement reflects a temporary, inherently unstable [relationship]. To us, a treaty has a legal and . . . a moral . . . force. In the Soviet view, a concession is merely a phase . . . Soviet doctrine prides itself on its ability to cut through spurious . . . good faith. "With the diploma," Stalin wrote, "words must diverge from acts. A sincere diplomat would equal dry water, wooden iron.[11]

The incandescent image of Neville Chamberlain's appeasement of Hitler burned with eidetic clarity in the collective memory of American policy makers. To William Bundy, longtime policy *doyen* and a senior architect of the American involvement in Vietnam, Munich was the "basic datum" of American foreign policy:

The rejection of armed action contribute[d] to the most ghastly human phenomena. To Kennedy, Johnson, Rusk, my brother [McGeorge Bundy] . . . McNamara, . . . [war] could prevent vast evil and open the way to progress. War was viewed . . . not as Catch-22 or MASH or even Patton . . . but as the only way to deal with world order.[12]

After the war, the great conferences during the war were an anathema. The Republican Party's platform of 1952, drafted by John Foster Dulles, denounced the Yalta conference's "secret understandings" which "aided communist enslavements."[13] The negotiators of Yalta had, it was charged, put the capstone on "twenty years of treason."[14]

Diplomacy was deemed a failure. After World War II, diplomats were accused at the least of having known the enemy too well—and at the most of deserting American interests for those of its adversaries. Secretaries Acheson and Marshall, and indeed the whole State Department, were pilloried. To Indiana Republican Senator William Jenner, for instance, General Marshall was a "front man for traitors . . . a living lie . . . an errand boy . . . a stooge, or a co-conspirator for this administration's crazy assortment of collectivists, cut-throats and Communist fellow traveling appeasers."[15]

FORCE AND DIPLOMACY IN THE COLD WAR

For most of history, force has been diplomacy's twin and its nemesis: the sum and symbol of diplomacy's failure. As Henry Kissinger wrote,

In any negotiation, it is understood that force is the ultimate recourse. It is the art of diplomacy to keep the threat potential, to keep its extent indeterminate. . . . For once power has been made actual, negotiations in the proper sense cease. A threat to use force which proves unavailing does not return the negotiation to the point before the threat was made. It destroys the bargaining position altogether[;] for it is a confession not of finite power, but of impotence.[16]

To the "new strategists," it was a great given that force could serve as a kind of functional diplomacy, wherein "adversaries" would bargain with each other through the mechanism of graduated increments of military force in order to achieve a "negotiated" accord. This odd and "vicious" "diplomacy of violence" gave a kind of perverse and pernicious twist to the ancient practices of official "gentlemen" who directed their energies toward the search for settlements. As Thomas Schelling explained, "The power to hurt is bargaining power," as its "only purpose, unless sport or revenue, must be to influence somebody's behavior to coerce his decisions or choice; to be coercive, violence has to be anticipated. And it has to be avoidable by accommodation. . . . To exploit it, is diplomacy—vicious diplomacy, but diplomacy."[17]

THE KENNEDY ADMINISTRATION: CLAUSEWITZ REDUX?

To the Kennedy team, foreign policy was hardly the array of minute and delicately crafted agreements that might take the hard edge off the more abrading aspects of international society, or that might make international relations more predictable and hence "orderly." Rather, diplomacy was an action tool of the Cold War. The lethal element of international relations was the Kennedy team's preoccupation. President Kennedy, and especially his Defense Secretary, Robert McNamara, grappled with the problem of central deterrence at a time when it was clear that the use of strategic weapons could be suicidal.

When Kennedy, urged on by Eisenhower, focused on the Laotian problem in 1961, the new president was startled to discover that the Joint Chiefs seemed obsessed with nuclear weapons. Robert Kennedy recalled the meetings on Laos in 1961 when the military unanimously recommended sending in at least 60,000 (and perhaps 160,000) U.S. troops, armed with tactical nuclear weapons.[18]

To the new defense planners, it was hoped that limited war could be restricted in its means and its purchase on the public. Any war might soon find arguments for a vast mobilization of effort. But a public thus pressed— and enthused with the effort—would soon demand everything for victory. Soon every instrument of force available would be tapped to defend troops, smash an enemy, and conclude the war with minimal American casualties. As Robert Osgood fretted, in his influential book *Limited War*, "if any democratic people . . . can be expected to sacrifice . . . without ever exerting [their] full military strength."[19]

The Kennedy-Johnson era planners proudly sought to tame a putative public dynamic that had caused commentators like George Kennan to doubt the public's capacity to respond in a measured fashion to challenge. A democracy, Kennan told a Chicago audience, shortly after he left the Truman administration,

is . . . similar to one of those prehistoric monsters with a body as long as this room and the brain the size of a pin: He lies there in his comfortable primeval mud—in fact you practically have to whack his tail off to make him aware that his interests are being disturbed; but, once he grasps this, he lays about him with such blind determination that he not only destroys his adversary but largely wrecks his native habitat.[20]

But the National Security managers of the 1960s believed they had stumbled on an unparalleled opportunity to educate Americans in the Clausewitzian imperative to measure force not by its emotional content but by its service to policy. Limited war in Asia might allow the American democracy to be disciplined to the requirements of its ascendant position. As a result, Americans could be tamed into refraining from chiliastic spasms with every military exertion. If the American war in Indochina were successful, the cost of each successive enterprise at arms need not risk a dangerous escalation to the cusp of nuclear war—and perhaps beyond.

PLAIN LESSONS ON THE NEW FRONTIER

The Kennedy administration was not prepared to be grabbed at the forelock by military machines, and was certainly unwilling to be a prisoner of military professionals whom it was starting to see as trigger-happy well before the Cuban Missile Crisis. The military's enthusiasm for preemptive attacks on the Soviet Union, and Air Force Chief of Staff General Curtis LeMay's wish to attack Cuba even the day after the Soviets announced the missiles were to be withdrawn, drew great walls of well-advertised scorn from the Kennedy national security *consiglieri*.

The clear conclusion of the new civilian defense planners was that the professional military either posed most of the risks, or exacerbated them in the Cuban Missile Crisis. As Robert Kennedy reflected in the aftermath:

"[T]his experience pointed out for all of us the importance of civilian direction and control."[21]

The initial "lesson" of the Cuban Missile Crisis—to all but a tiny select group of Kennedy intimates—was that Kennedy had determined events by dictating a virtual ultimatum. The chroniclers of the 1960s claimed the Soviets had merely capitulated. This was the expurgated sum of Bobby Kennedy's ultimatum to Dobrynin: "We had to have a commitment by tomorrow . . . [I]t was a statement of fact . . . [I]f they did not remove those bases, we would remove them."[22] Roger Hilsman, the senior State Department intelligence officer in the crisis, reached the only conclusion he could have from the "facts" as they were portrayed at the time: Khrushchev simply "backed down."[23] "Real negotiations," the Cuban Crisis seemed to confirm, did not have to occur until the United States acquired and employed an overwhelming position of strength and a maximum advantage in terms of coercive power. In the end, negotiations were, for America's opponents, a way to save face. With the right mix of force and toughness, the United States could prevail.

Three decades on, recent scholarship underscores a frightening truth: The "lessons" adduced from the Missile Crisis were not based on a true rendering of the facts. The military was as well orchestrated as portrayed; near misses abounded. There were overflights into Soviet territory that appeared to be precursors of atomic attack. U.S. unarmed missiles were readied and tested next to live missiles in a fashion that could have been interpreted as an augury of an American atomic attack on Russia—and invited an attempt to preempt. Soviet forces in Cuba may have been protected by tactical short-range atomic artillery. If the United States had invaded (as seemed likely until the last minute), the landing expedition would have been met by the kind of force that surely would have escalated.[24] Most important of all, Kennedy did make an explicit quid pro quo trade with Khrushchev. The United States would withdraw its missiles from Turkey soon after the Soviets withdrew their weapons from Cuba. But the trade—indeed, the conversations with Khrushchev and Soviet intermediaries—was restricted to all but four Kennedy advisors who, in turn, conspired to keep the president's willingness to negotiate at the precipice of war a secret for over two decades.

Most of these "lessons" were either wholly or partly wrong in their assessment of the facts of the Missile Crisis or in their assessment of the promise of the crisis' outcome. President Kennedy did, in fact, negotiate with the Russians vigorously in private, well before the *denouement* of the crisis—making it clear he was willing to remove the Jupiter missiles from Turkey in exchange for the Russian withdrawal of their missiles in Cuba. Kennedy was also willing to make the exchange public, if faced with the alternative of an invasion of Cuba or a public quid pro quo. Kennedy's advisors were largely excluded from the president's private determination to settle the crisis without arms. The ExComm, the ad hoc group of senior advisors who met more or less continuously during the crisis, did not, save for Dean Rusk and Robert Kennedy, know all the details of President Kennedy's exchanges with the Russians. The famous ExComm could not have managed events. Indeed, it was the president who was managing and negotiating with his advisors in order to coordinate the best public and bureaucratic perception of himself. Much of Kennedy's emphasis on firmness was more to impress the public, the allies, and his close advisors than to influence the Russians.[25]

In fact, during the Missile Crisis the use of force had not been orchestrated with anything like the precision that had been hoped at the time or advertised later. Indeed, many of the elements of U.S. deployments during the crisis could have easily been seen by Russian intelligence as precursors to atomic attack or actually part of an atomic onslaught.[26] If the military authorities had been heeded, atomic war was not just a distant probability but, given the presence of tactical nuclear weapons in Cuba, nearly certain.[27]

After Cuba, the long descent of classic diplomacy perceptibly accelerated. The legend arose that, in managing the Missile Crisis, the Kennedys only offered Khrushchev a face-saving method that would, in fact, "strengthen our stand."[28] For over two decades, surviving Kennedy faithful expunged and forswore any hint of compromise. The crisis was portrayed as a "test of will" that highlighted the Soviet transgression of the political-nuclear status quo. As Kennedy's Boswell put it, the president wanted to "concentrate on a single issue—the enormity of the introduction of the missiles and the absolute necessity of their removal."[29]

From the Cuban crisis on, policy alternatives to *dictats* predicated on strength had little currency if they were not at least framed in terms of coercion. A "moderate" in these terms was limited to suggesting limited violence. As Under Secretary of State George Ball explained his "devil's advocacy" about Vietnam (a "modest" troop ceiling of around 70,000 men and a series of bombing halts): "[I]f I had said let's pull out overnight or do something of this kind, I obviously wouldn't have been persuasive at all. They'd have said, 'That man's mad'."[30]

The very process of negotiations mutated into what was forthrightly called by Thomas Shelling "a diplomacy of violence."[31] The credit attending coercive strategies rose in inverse proportion to any esteem accorded the military. The new security managers believed they had discovered a modern alchemy of melding force to diplomacy. Subnuclear, and indeed subconventional violence, could in the right admixture be instrumental overseas and supportable at home. These confident assumptions were placed on a vast testing ground in Southeast Asia.

VIETNAM AND THE LIMITS OF COERCIVE DIPLOMACY

All the abstractions of the new doctrines of limited war—from the "pauses" and "squeezes," "signals," and "messages" that were adduced and validated by the Cuban Missile Crisis—manifestly failed in Vietnam. The theories and hopes of the liberal-intellectual force planners and social scientists of the 1960s came undone in the skies, jungles, villages, and rice paddies of South Asia. Gradual response, signaling, nation building, counterinsurgency—even containment and the great defense consensus of the Cold War—floundered.

Happily for "the health of the Republic," Colonel Harry Summers writes, in an influential essay, "a stab in the back syndrome never developed after Vietnam."[32] Yet any review of the last decade of national political discourse—and any cursory look at the military literature on the U.S. failure in Vietnam—yields an impression of a veritable blizzard of recrimination. Countless sober analysts who revisit the Vietnam War—especially those who were themselves involved directly—find that it would have been won but for a more supportive public, a better strategy, a more positive press, or a better kind of elective representative. Apace with these reflections is the sentiment—or the corollary—that the military was unduly restricted and, if only untethered from uncalled-for restrictions, the war would have been "won."[33]

Some assessments of the U.S. effort in Vietnam hold that the great flaw in American strategy was the failure to isolate the battlefield prior to Tet.[34] Some argue that if the Christmas bombings of 1972 had taken place in 1965, then the war could have been determined in America's favor.[35] To General T. R. Milton, the December 1972 bombing of North Vietnam was "an object lesson in how the war might have been won, and long ago," if only there had not been such political inhibitions.[36] "The shock was there; our enemy's will was broken."[37]

COULD THE "RIGHT KIND OF FORCE" DO THE TRICK?

Many of these analyses are a classic demonstration of a fallacy of argument, a *post hoc, ergo procter hoc* reasoning. To be sure, Hanoi was forced to agree to sign a peace accord in late December 1972, but it was the document it had already agreed to sign in October 1972—in other words, well before the bombing (that "would have won the war years ago") had even begun. Moreover, the agreement that Hanoi was "forced" to sign by dint of "Linebacker II" was overwhelmingly favorable to Hanoi's interests. The plain political fact was captured wryly by veteran diplomat John Negroponte, Kissinger's special advisor on Vietnamese politics: "We bombed the North Vietnamese into accepting our concessions."[38]

By the time of the Paris accords in January 1973, over 300,000 North Vietnamese troops occupied over 25 percent of the territory of South Vietnam.[39] If Nixon and Kissinger had seriously contemplated a viable South Vietnam, they would have accepted neither the North Vietnamese formula, wherein North Vietnamese troops would stay where they were in South Vietnam, nor the political formula placed in the Paris instrument at Hanoi's insistence that stipulated "two governments, one country"—a slogan that clearly dignified the North Vietnamese position that the war in Vietnam was not an international war between two states, but rather a civil war and hence the NVA troops were properly in the South with as much right as, say, Grant's army had a right to bivouac in Virginia.

If Kissinger thought South Vietnam had a long-term future, then the 17th parallel—the line that separated North and South Vietnam—would have been given at least some passing mention in the Paris formula. Similarly, if the Nixon administration had much hope for South Vietnam President Thieu's future, it seems unlikely that they would have accepted Hanoi's position that an NLF-dominated (National Liberation Front, or Vietcong) "National Council of Reconciliation" be folded into co-rule with the Thieu government. Finally, if the promise to aid the government of South Vietnam with bombing had been serious—that is, more than a sop tossed to the Thieu regime in the hopes that Thieu would sign an accord he knew spelled his own doom—then that commitment would not have been a private undertaking between the White House and the Thieu regime. As it was, lest the commitments be leaked and then be promptly rejected by Congress, neither the Congress nor the Joint Chiefs were informed of President Nixon's repeated promises to thwart any large-scale breach of the Paris accords with the massive use of U.S. air power. If a promise to use massive air power to support the post-Paris accords "peace" would have been rejected in 1973 by Congress, how could one expect that the commitment to use massive bombing would be honored when Nixon's last term had ended? In sum, and in truth, the Paris accords were hardly a vindication of American air power in delivering up to the conference table otherwise-unattainable concessions. The Paris accords were, instead, the Nixon-Kissinger diplomatic and public relations velum derived in contrivance with North Vietnam to dignify America's somewhat smarmy, but nonetheless inevitable, exit.

THE LIMITS OF AIR POWER

Contrary to the common current revision, U.S. Air Force commanders in Vietnam were not starved for air assets—or sufficient license—to bomb meaningful targets before 1968. General William W. Momyer, commander of the 7th Air Force, testified in 1967: "We are operating at about maximum effort . . . I do not believe . . . putting in additional forces would sig-

nificantly decrease . . . the movement of men and supplies to the South."
What was absent, General Momyer explained, was not air power, but manpower: "[S]ome kind of formalized ground campaign in which . . . the enemy [is] forced to . . . consume logistics faster than he can get down and
replenish them."[40]

Contrary to the critique that President Johnson did not understand the
need to isolate the battlefield, the president did approve a plan to isolate
Hanoi and Hanoi's supply train from the rest of the country.[41] As a result,
only a "single through-line was kept open at great expense in repair
crews."[42] But even that success was sterile, as many civilians in the Pentagon soon realized; as early as the summer of 1965, one authoritative
classified study conducted by 87 eminent scientists and scholars had concluded: "North Vietnam has basically a subsistence agricultural economy
that presents a difficult and unrewarding target system for air attack." The
finding shook McNamara, who never again proposed an increase in the
pace or intensity of bombing.[43]

Bombing to interdict North Vietnam's troops and supplies failed. Communist supply needs were small; seven two-ton trucks were estimated to be
able to supply all the Communist forces each day of combat, while North
Vietnam's allies supplied some 6,000 tons every 24 hours.[44] Notwithstanding two years of intense bombing along the infiltration routes to the South,
Hanoi managed to double the number of regulars each year. By 1967, an
estimated 100,800 out of some 225,000 Communist troops and active cadres had come from the North.[45] The only targets left relatively unscathed
were civilian population centers, a few small generators, and, for the most
part, trails in Cambodia and Laos. Many of the Communist forces in the
south depended on "taxes" and South Vietnam's own supply depots for
munitions and weapons. Even if all the risks attending to an expanded list
of targets and an expanded geography of operations had been discounted—
and heavier bombing were undertaken north, south, and even further
afield—the results hardly would have impacted at all the morale, victual-
ling, and arms of the Communists in the South.[46]

BOMBING, RISK, AND WIDER WAR

Harry Summers and other "revisionists" argue that an attack on Hanoi
in the mid-1960s could have broken Hanoi's political will. Mining Haiphong Harbor, invading Laos and Cambodia, and augmenting ground
forces were also advocated in the earlier stages of the war. But all these
suggestions carried risks, including the risk of failure. Bombing Hanoi, for
instance, might well have succeeded only in emptying the city, as indeed
happened in 1946 when Ho and his followers took to the jungles to war
against the French. And in any case, by the end of 1967 most civilians and
leadership with a reason to stay and work in Hanoi were dispersed, well-

bunkered, sandbagged, and screened by one of the densest anti-aircraft covers the world had ever seen.[47]

Simply eliminating North Vietnam ran heavy risks. Although the Soviets may have looked at the situation in Vietnam only as a function of their twin rivalry with the Chinese on the one hand, and the United States the other, they were willing to invest over a billion[48] dollars a year in the North's war. Moreover, from the mid-1960s to the early 1980s, the Soviets never receded from a challenge to one of their satellites. If Hanoi and Haiphong were bombed (and the amount that was coming through the port was not considered militarily significant, according to McNamara in his September 1967 testimony), perhaps the Russians would have acceded; or, perhaps they would have launched an unanswerable riposte elsewhere. As Walt Rostow reminded the president, bombing might well provoke the Soviets to "create a crisis in Berlin or elsewhere to offset the U.S. initiative."[49]

Further, an attack on North Vietnam's population centers risked placing the Chinese (who were considered, perhaps wrongly, far more radical than the Soviets) in the position of becoming the primary benefactors of North Vietnam. Hanoi, one American China expert reflected, was "one of China's closest allies."[50] If the Chinese proceeded to take casualties in any number (indeed, they did suffer losses by their own count of some 20,000), it might be sufficient to provoke them to enter the war with overwhelming numbers. The chance that China would enter the war was predicated on the considerable Chinese interests in the area. Over 170,000 Chinese "volunteers" served in Indochina. They manned anti-aircraft positions, repaired roads, and aided in supplying over a billion dollars a year in equipment.[51] Any invasion or large-scale bombing of Hanoi and further north toward the Sino-Vietnamese frontier would trigger many of the same calculations in Beijing that motivated Mao to enter the war in Korea in late 1950.

History is littered with inadvertent wars. Chinese interests at the time, as interpreted by North Vietnam, were to use the North Vietnamese as proxies, to weaken both North Vietnam and the United States, letting China pick up the spoils. But if the North were invaded, then there can be little doubt that some of the Chinese[52] involved in Vietnam's war would have engaged. Once China had become involved with large numbers of ground forces, the pressures on U.S. policy makers to use nuclear weapons would have been intense. Yet the cost of using nuclear weapons again in Asia would have exacted a heavy price in U.S. relations with Japan, and especially with Europe.

In sum, the *post hoc* prescriptions for a wider war look, in the light of cool reason, more like the common yearnings of all unsuccessful commanders for a second chance, and less like a prescription for real success. "Perhaps," concluded Earl Tilford in one of the Air Force's own reevaluations, "the bombing was not so much unsuccessful as it was irrelevant to the war in the South."[53] After Tet, the Vietcong were said to be on the ropes from a combination of the effects of Tet and the Phoenix program;[54] but in 1969 the U.S. embassy in Saigon estimated that some kind of Communist infrastructure still existed in 80 percent of rural Vietnam.[55] Kissinger, later, guessed that the United States faced some 225,000 guerrillas and an equal number of North Vietnamese regulars at the start of the Nixon administration.[56] By the end of the war, most U.S. government analysts had come to a conclusion, reached by the great British expert Sir Robert Thompson, that the battlefield was not amenable to meaningful isolation by air or on the ground. As Thompson put it:

A long jungle frontier cannot be sealed off. It is a waste of time and resources to build forts, frontier roads or forces, all of which will tie down a large body of troops for no effective purpose. Nothing can prevent small parties of men crossing such a frontier at any time.[57]

The case for a wider war made little sense. When, in 1970, Cambodia and Laos were subsumed in war, the consequence yielded not even a temporary military victory or surcease. The wider ambit of operations, forced on both the dwindling number of U.S. troops available for ground combat and the unwilling and unreliable Army of the Republic of (South) Vietnam (ARVN) forces, simply enervated the effort to shore up the South. A year later, ARVN forces came to predictable grief when they invaded Laos shorn of all but U.S. logistical help.[58] In retrospect, and as some U.S. Foreign Service officers noted at the time (the present author included), Cambodia's ambiguous neutrality had protected U.S. interests. As William Shawcross writes: "A Cambodia independent of Vietnam had been a principle of Chinese foreign policy at least since the Geneva Conference of 1954."[59] Before Nixon decided to widen the war, Cambodia's tentative political independence and neutrality had been significant bulwarks to North Vietnam's ambitions.

An earlier, wider war (except perhaps, as Kissinger later speculated, if it were fought in Laos in the early 1960s, where the local population was an adamant and able opponent of the Vietnamese) would have probably required more troops than the United States ever fielded or could have contemplated fielding, even if the reserves had been called up. The usual desired and necessary ratio for fighting small unit wars is a numerical combat superiority of 10 to 1. Given the classically extended U.S. "teeth to tail" ratio of fighting forces to logistic supply, a total force of five million would have been required by 1969 to subdue just the 500,000 forces fielded by North Vietnam and the Vietcong.[60] If the United States were involved in Laos and Cambodia on the ground, over time the numbers the United States would have had to put into combat (even if one counts on the aggregation of other friendly forces) would have been extraordinarily large. To subdue an insurgency, isolate the Indochinese battlefield effectively, and secure a working perimeter in which the South Vietnamese government might somehow legitimize itself might have easily required in excess of two million U.S. troops.

Moreover, guerrilla and small-scale wars are rarely short. The civil war in Greece after World War II, the British campaign in Malaya, and the war against the Huks in the Philippines all lasted a very long time. Given all these costs and risks of "winning," what president, if he had been given advanced knowledge of the tab, would have bellied to the bar of such a pricey venture?

WHAT MILITARY SOLUTIONS?

The war could have been taken early to Haiphong, to Laos and Cambodia, and even more men could have been sent. But it is doubtful that bombing could have ever secured the major object of the war: a viable government of South Vietnam that could be sustained after U.S. fighting forces left the field. The government of South Vietnam, a creature of American making if not American bidding, never managed to capture significant loyalty outside a narrow coterie of urban Catholics and some few elite army units. Even if the North Vietnamese and their associates had been isolated by air power and the forward deployment of large U.S. units, and even if there had been no entry of large numbers of Chinese troops in the South, and even if a full-blown war in Vietnam did not risk more valuable stakes in Europe (and the rest of the world), and even if the confidence of U.S. leadership had remained steadfast in the face of protests, there is no evidence that the government of South Vietnam could ever have gained sufficient legitimacy to insulate itself from its endemic insurgency.

Even when the Phoenix program started to wear away at the yeoman-level Vietcong/North Vietnamese presence in the South, the effort did not result in any gain by the government of South Vietnam.[61] In the absence of a viable government in Saigon, the only way to have won the war would have been to do away with any pretense at South Vietnamese independence and take over the functions of rule, as the French, Japanese, and the Chinese had all tried in Indochina. But, as Army Chief of Staff General Fred C. Weyand wrote, in 1976:

The . . . American military can . . . defeat enemy forces. . . . They can blockade enemy coasts. They can cut lines of supply and communication. . . . But . . . the Congress and the American people will not permit their military to take control of another nation's economic and social institutions.[62]

Earl Tilford, in a thorough review of the air campaign, concluded:

Short of the total obliteration of North Vietnam, something that was quite properly never considered by American leadership, it is quite unlikely any aerial firepower short of an all-out nuclear attack would have sufficed. In the final analysis . . . the war was not America's to win or lose. It was South Vietnam's war.[63]

U.S. strategy, after Tet, could only be achieved, wrote the Department of Defense Office of Security Affairs:

If the GVN [Government of (South) Vietnam] begins to take steps necessary to gain the confidence of the people . . . ARVN must also be turned into an effective fighting force. If we fail these objectives, a military victory over the NVN/VC main forces, followed by a U.S. withdrawal, would only pave the way for an NLF takeover.[64]

Many critics of the war in Vietnam complain that if more firepower and a greater geographic ambit for military operations had been allowed earlier, the war would have turned out differently.[65] But even if it were possible to find or develop a government in South Vietnam that did not inspire perpetual insurrection, and even if it were possible to insulate the battlefield from North Vietnamese reinforcements and resupply, a wider war seemed a poor alternative at the time and still does, in retrospect.

Since nearly every large unit engagement with NVA and VC forces was won decisively by U.S. forces, the effort in Vietnam could not rightly be called a battlefield failure; but there was a political failure to recognize that America had sacrificed a great deal for an ally who was poorly motivated and incapable of establishing its legitimacy in a society that demands security, if nothing else, as a precondition of loyalty.[66] Nothing the United States could accomplish on the battlefield would likely make its ally stronger or more legitimate. Indeed, the mere fact of the American presence went quite a way to establish North Vietnam's best point: The government of South Vietnam was a creature of the Americans and not the Vietnamese.

THE REAL STAKES

"The whole problem with the nuclear age," Kissinger once wrote, is that "until power is used, it is . . . what people think."[67] Appearances had been a critical objective in the Cuban Missile Crisis,[68] and for all the different explanations as to why Vietnam mattered, appearances were at the core of the interests in play in Vietnam. Kissinger, for instance, often said that one could argue a commitment to Vietnam on its own merits, but once large numbers of U.S. forces had been committed on the ground in combat, the matter of interests decided itself: "For what it involved now is the confidence in American promises. However fashionable it is to ridicule the terms "credibility," or "prestige," they are not empty phrases; other nations gear their actions to ours only if they can count on our steadiness."[69]

Presidents Kennedy and Johnson, first and foremost, hoped to give the appearance of expending significant effort and resources to support America's South Vietnamese ally. Few believed, after "Vietnamization" was announced, that the insurgency could be tamed and that the North Vietnamese forces could be held back indefinitely. The relative staying power of the United States and its allies versus that of North Vietnam seemed clear. In the absence of a plan to either outlast or overwhelm North Vietnam, U.S. strategy could only hope to give an *impression* of a valid effort. The U.S. design had two purposes. First, there was hope that the requisite but unpalatable decision to either withdraw or vastly expand the war could be deeded to another administration. Second, and perhaps more compelling if the internal memoranda of the decision making tell an accurate tale, the policy was configured to buttress the *appearance* of an earnest and effective effort.

Appearances were at the heart of U.S. credibility as an ally and hence at the whole structure of postwar U.S. foreign policy. As President Johnson wrote from his retirement "vantage point," if a valid effort were not perceived to have been rendered by the United States in Vietnam, (o)ur allies . . . throughout the world would conclude that word was worth little or nothing. [Moscow and Peking] could not resist the opportunity to expand their control into the vacuum."[70]

Appearances were at the heart of deterrence. As Kissinger wrote:

Deterrence is . . . greatest when military strength is coupled with the willingness to employ it. . . . Given the power of modern weapons, a nation that relies on all-out war as its chief deterrence imposes a fearful psychological handicap on itself. . . . The psychological equation, therefore, will almost inevitably operate against the side which can extricate itself from a situation only by the threat of all-out war.[71]

The disposition to wage conventional limited war, even if the war turned a cropper, was still valuable, therefore, in that it validated a willingness to shore up an ally and use power without nearing a nuclear abyss. As John McNaughton, Assistant Secretary of Defense and perhaps McNamara's closest advisor, wrote of U.S. aims:

70 pct.—To avoid a humiliating U.S. defeat (to our reputation as a guarantor).
20 pct.—To keep SVN (and then adjacent) territory from Chinese hands.
10 pct.—To permit the people of SVN to enjoy a better, freer way of life.

McNaughton further explained that, even if the Vietcong were not defeated, American involvement "would demonstrate the U.S. was a 'good doctor' willing to keep promises, be tough, take risks, get bloodied and hurt the enemy badly."[72]

Since the well-being of our nominee ally was accorded merely 10 percent, while "avoiding a humiliating defeat" derived 70 percent of the compulsion to fight in Vietnam, the ally's future was evidently less important than the reputation of its guarantor, at least in the sight of U.S. policy makers. The metaphor was one of a cool willingness to enter a bloody operating theater, wherein the patient might be disfigured, maimed, even done to death, as long as the *appearance* of a worthy effort was attempted.

To be sure, President Johnson himself was more than a "good doctor"; for there is little doubt that the president himself wanted to leave schools, dams, and a better life for the Vietnamese, just as he really yearned for a better life for the dispossessed of the United States.[73] Ultimately, however, Dulles, Kennedy, Johnson, and Nixon persisted in Vietnam not for the South Vietnamese, nor because there was a winning strategy at hand; but because it was feared that an erosion in the appearance of steadfastness and power would injure America's alliances and embolden American enemies. Indecision in Vietnam could, it was feared, precipitate the kind of test by aggressors that would necessitate larger wars for greater stakes, on the one hand, or risk either nuclear war or capitulation on the other. As Kissinger argued: "we had to remember that scores of countries and millions of people relied for their security on our willingness to stand by allies. . . . No serious policymaker could allow himself to succumb to the fashionable debunking of 'prestige' or 'honor' or credibility."[74]

The proximate goal of American firepower, of course, was to defeat the North Vietnamese and Vietcong; the ultimate goal, however, was to secure the American reputation, if, by nothing else, withdrawing after fighting a good fight and leaving the South Vietnamese with a plausible, though probably doomed, government. "A peace settlement," Kissinger wrote Nixon in the fall of 1971, in confirmation of this interpretation, "would end the war with an act of policy and leave the future of South Vietnam to historic processes. We could heal the wounds in this country as our men left peace behind on the battlefield and a *healthy interval* for South Vietnam's fate to unfold"[75] (emphasis added). John Ehrlichman, then counsel to President Nixon, recalled asking Kissinger how long he thought the South Vietnamese could hold out after the Paris accords had been signed in 1973. "About a year and a half" was the prophetic reply.[76]

DIPLOMACY: THE ROAD NOT TAKEN

In the end, the Vietnam War represented a failure to use diplomacy when it was relevant. As a result, a minor struggle was elevated into a major conflict. Between 1945 and 1955, there were ample opportunities to negotiate with Ho Chi Minh and his associates a settlement that would detach

Vietnam from China and insulate Vietnam from Russian dominance. In 1945–1946, France was playing a heroic bluff in attempting to win support for colonial position lest she collapse, on the one hand, or refuse to stand with Germany against communists on the other. In 1954, the Chinese and Soviets made it clear that they preferred a Vietnam that was relatively weak, and probably neutral, in the Titoist sense. In 1957, Russia even proposed admitting both Vietnams to the United Nations; but the United States dragged its feet because it would have legitimized a Communist regime in a divided state with perhaps some strained implications for United States policy in a divided Germany or Korea.

To be sure, Ho had been nothing less than a dedicated Leninist since the 1920s. And to be sure, by 1961, there was a growing constituency in the United States for Ngo Dinh Diem's regime. But what would an American Bismarck or Tallyrand have done if he had pondered the Indochina question instead of Dean Acheson, John Foster Dulles, Dean Rusk, and Robert McNamara? Would a great statesman have worked with Ho Chi Minh and his associates, as American administrations worked with Tito in Yugoslavia from 1948 and Gomulka in Poland from the late 1950s, and even Ceaucescu in Romania in the 1960s and 1970s? Or would he have embraced the alternative of creating a fictive South Vietnam, in petulant defiance of the 1954 Geneva agreements? Could a Hamilton or Jay, or any serious statesmen of the American past, have held fast to Bao Dai and Diem? Would the great statesmen of yesterday have invented a jack-leg imitation of NATO in Asia in order to contain Communism in Asia as in Europe? Or, would they have made a distinction between the interests at risk in Southeast Asia and Central Europe? The questions answer themselves.

DIPLOMACY AND FORCE: CAN LIMITED INTERESTS BE FUNDED BY LIMITED FORCE?

The revisionist view of Vietnam weighs heavily on contemporary military doctrine. General Colin Powell, while chairman of the Joint Chiefs, recalled the consequences of limited force: "This isn't some syndrome I'm suffering. . . . As a major and a captain, I saw what doing otherwise produced in Vietnam."[77] The U.S. military is alive to the truth that the United States' goal of appearing as a steadfast ally in Vietnam was achieved at a cost disproportionate to any real American interests. America's war in Southeast Asia was waged without any accounting of how the conflict was viewed by major allies and adversaries, whom the war was ostensibly to impress in the first place. Indeed, the whole usual matrix of interests to costs was fatally askew in Indochina. The great military rodomontade of recent years has been that civilian policy makers are being schooled to ask if diplomatic ends are congruent with the military demands for "clear and unambiguous objectives" configured to achieve "decisive means and results" after "all other nonviolent policy means [have] failed."[78] As General Powell put it in his last press conference in uniform: "My philosophy is . . . simple: Match political expectations to military means."[79]

But the contemporary conventional military wisdom that required policymakers to assure military planners that "force is a last resort . . . used in an overwhelming fashion" to achieve "clear and measurable objectives" contradicts Clausewitz's careful observation that:

Sometimes the political and military objective is the same—for example the conquest of a province. In other cases, then, the political object will not provide a suitable military objective. In that event another military objective must be adopted that will serve the political purposes and symbolize it in the peace negotiations.[80]

Clausewitz could not conceive of letting political considerations override "purely" military considerations. As Clausewitz wrote: "Subordinating the political point of view to the military [is] absurd, for it is policy that has created war. Policy is the guiding intelligence and war only the instrument, not vice versa. No other possibility exists, then, than to subordinate the military point of view to the political."[81]

For Clausewitz "[w]hen people talk as they often do, about harmful political influence on the management of war, they are not really saying what they mean. Their quarrel should be with the policy itself, not its influence."[82] Hence, Clausewitz advanced his famous dictum that war is "never . . . autonomous but always an instrument of policy."[83]

CONCLUSION: THE BURDEN OF THE RECENT PAST AND THE TASK AHEAD

Since the mid-1980s, Clausewitz has been both embraced in discourse and abandoned in fact by U.S. policy makers. Ever since Secretary of Defense Caspar Weinberger, in 1984, announced a new "doctrine,"[84] U.S. armed forces have labored under an expanding list of restrictions, foremost among which is the conviction that force should meet a three-part test. First, force "should not" be committed "unless the particular engagement or occasion seemed vital to our national interests." Second, the recourse to arms has to receive the "full sanction of the American people." Third, then, as General Powell put it, force can be mustered, but only when it is brought to bear in an "overwhelming" fashion.

President Bush, in a speech to West Point cadets, attempted to aerate the edifice of strictures Mr. Weinberger and General Powell had erected against the use of all but nearly apocalyptic levels of firepower. Bush tried to admit flexibility by taking issue with the military's new fixation—"vital" interests. As Mr. Bush put it: "The relative importance of an interest is not a guide. Military force . . . might be the best way to protect an interest that qualifies as important, but less than vital." Mr. Bush also rejected the notion that force should be "overwhelming"; rather, the criterion he offered was that force be "effective, where its application can be limited in scope and time and where the potential benefits justify the potential costs and sacrifice."[85]

In the Clinton administration, Secretary of Defense Les Aspin explicitly tried to escape from the Weinberger and Powell kinds of cautions, stating: "Real leadership requires a willingness to use military force, and force can be a useful backdrop to diplomacy, a complement to it, or, if need be, a temporary alternative."

In fact, in Aspin's initial pronouncements on force there was an unashamed echo of Clausewitz: "Suppose," Clausewitz once wrote:

one merely wants a small concession from the enemy. One will only fight until some modest quid pro quo had been acquired, and a moderate effort should suffice for that. The enemy's reasoning will be much the same. . . . [W]e must be willing to wage such minimal wars which consist in merely threatening the enemy with negotiations held in reserve.[86]

Yet the summary dismissal of Secretary Aspin and his closest political advisors, and Aspin's manifest failure to deal with the ascendant chiefs, gave rise to the conclusion that Colin Powell's patrimony was the enduring demand that military forces be used, as Powell put it, "only when there is a clear-cut military objective" and "only when we can measure when the military objective has been achieved."

In the 1990s, American policy practice reversed the Clausewitzian insistence on the supremacy of policy over any autonomous logic attendant to arms. As senior civilians working in the Pentagon told one defense correspondent, the Joint Chiefs "exercise an incredible veto. . . . There is no interest on the civilian side of this building in challenging the Joint Staff."[87] Indeed, the new wisdom stands the Clausewitzian relationship between policy and strategy on its head. "[I]f there's one story that is going to be written out of Desert Storm and Just Cause and everything else we've done," Colin Powell explained, "it's how political objectives must be carefully matched to military objectives and the military means and what is achievable."[88]

Notions that are not "concrete" but nonetheless hardly empty of meaning—such as validating the power of the United Nations to keep peace, or ensuring that there is a price to pay for aggressor states, or punishing war crimes and genocide—would apparently be abandoned if the Powell/Weinberger strictures invariably apply. It can be no surprise that in the salad days of the Powell/Weinberger inhibitions, those profound goals of post–World War II U.S. foreign policy—demonstrating a price of genocide, or buttressing the unity of NATO, sustaining the validity of NATO and UN commitments, or combating terrorism—were at a discount, since they have no immediate military referent. With the regnant Powell/Weinberger strictures serving as predicates of national security policy, even central deterrence was at risk of consignment to the back shelves of our collective store of interests, inventoried under the rubric: "too hard."

NOTES

1. Cited by Coral Bell, *The Conventions of Crisis: A Study in Diplomatic Management* (London: Oxford University Press, 1971), p. 2.

2. At least this was the lesson of the crisis derived by many of the "New Strategists." The term is not mine; rather its paternity belongs to James E. King, a pivotal member of a community of scholars, among whom are included Bernard Brodie, Arnold Wolfers, Denis Healey, P.M.S. Blackett, Henry Kissinger, B. H. Liddell Hart, Herman Kahn, Edward Meade Earle, Michael Howard, Alexander George, Robert Osgood, Pierre Gallois, John Blackett, Thomas Schelling, Raymond Aron, William Kaufman, and Leo Szilard. King's enormous, two-volume, still unpublished manuscript, as well as his private correspondence, holds a germinal place in the intellectual history of strategic thought. Most of the first generation of "New Strategists" read at least part of his manuscript. The present author holds all of King's papers, including an unpublished book-length manuscript on Clausewitz. The present book is both in Jim King's debt and in his honor.

3. Carl von Clausewitz, *On War* (Michael Howard and Peter Paret, eds. and trans.), with introductory essays by Peter Paret, Michael Howard, and Bernard Brodie, and a commentary by Bernard Brodie (Princeton, N.J.: Princeton University Press, 1984), Book Two, chapter 2, p. 146.

4. Ibid., pp. 488, 501.

5. Ibid., Book One, chapter 1, p. 88; Book Eight, chapter 6B, p. 605.

6. Ibid., Book Eight, chapter 6, p. 706.

7. Ibid., Book 8, chapter 8, pp. 583, 589–591; and see Book One, chapter 2, p. 647.

8. Raymond Aron, *The Century of Total War* (Boston: Beacon Press, 1954), p. 28.

9. In a 1954 conversation with military officers, cited in Robert H. Ferrell (ed.), *The Dairy of James C. Hagerty* (Bloomington: Indiana University Press, 1983), p. 69.

10. Henry Kissinger, *Nuclear Weapons and Foreign Policy*, abridged ed. (New York: W. W. Norton, 1969), p. 11.

11. Ibid., pp. 59–60.

12. Transcript of Remarks by William P. Bundy, University of Delaware, October 16, 1973. Also see Jeffrey Record, "Perils of Reasoning by Historical Analogy: Munich, Vietnam, and the American Use of Force Since 1945," *Occasional paper Number 4* (Maxwell Air Force Base: Center for Strategy and Technology, Air War College, Montgomery, Ala.), March 1998.

13. Theodore Draper, "Neoconservative History," *New York Review of Books* 32 (January 16, 1986): 5; Stephen Ambrose, *Eisenhower*, Vol. 1 (New York: Simon and Schuster, 1983), p. 543.

14. One can pick his authority. Mine are Charles Webster, *The Art of Diplo-*

matic Practice (New York: Barnes & Noble, 1962), p. 42; and Ernest Satow, *A Guide to Diplomatic Practice*, Vol. 1 (London: Longman's, Green, 1922), pp. 1–4.

15. Congressional Record, 81st Congress, 2d Sess., 96, 1414–1417.

16. Henry A. Kissinger, "The Congress of Vienna," *World Politics* 8 (July 1956): 277.

17. Thomas C. Schelling, *Arms and Influence* (New Haven, Conn.: Yale University Press, 1966), p. 2. Schelling, an economist, was senior officer in the Department of State in the 1960s.

18. Arthur M. Schlesinger Jr., *A Thousand Days: John F. Kennedy in the White House* (New York: Fawcett Crest Books, 1967), p. 315. There was the impression that the preferred goal was 160,000 troops to be equipped with tactical nuclear weapons. See Schlesinger, *A Thousand Days*, p. 316.

19. "Perhaps," Osgood cogitated, "the people must be artfully cajoled into undertaking new courses of action by indirection . . . by disguising new imperatives." Robert Endicott Osgood, *Limited War: The Challenge to American Strategy* (Chicago: University of Chicago Press, 1957), pp. 279–281.

20. George Kennan, *American Diplomacy, 1900–1950* (New York: New American World Library, 1959), p. 59.

21. Robert Kennedy, *Thirteen Days* (New York: New American Library, 1969), p. 119.

22. Ibid., p. 108.

23. Roger Hilsman, *To Move a Nation* (Garden City, N.Y.: Doubleday, 1967), pp. 226, 215.

24. The Soviet ground commander was, he now says, prepared to respond with tactical nuclear weapons. See, on this point, James Nathan's essay in James A. Nathan (ed.), *The Cuban Missile Crisis Revisited* (New York: St. Martin's Press, 1992), p. 36 n.116; and John Newhouse, "A Reporter at Large Socialism or Death," *The New Yorker*, April 27, 1992, p. 70ff.

25. On this point, see Elizabeth Cohn, "President Kennedy's Decision to Impose a Blockade in the Cuban Missile Crisis: Building Consensus in the Excom after the Decision," in Nathan (ed.), *The Cuban Missile Crisis Revisited*, pp. 219–236.

26. See Scott D. Sagan, *Limits of Safety* (Princeton, N.J.: Princeton University Press, 1993), pp. 117ff; Richard Ned Lebow and Janice Gross Stein, *We All Lost the Cold War* (Princeton, N.J.: Princeton University Press, 1994), indicates that Soviet generals took a U2 overflight of Siberia as a potential precursor for an American attack (pp. 139–140).

27. Nathan (ed.), *The Cuban Missile Crisis Revisited*.

28. Theodore Sorensen, *Kennedy* (New York: Bantam Books, 1969), p. 699.

29. Schlesinger, *A Thousand Days*, p. 810. Before the Senate Foreign Relations Committee, Secretary of State Dean Rusk was asked by Senator Bourke Hickenlooper to affirm that a "deal" or "trade" had in "no way, shape or form, directly or indirectly, been connected with the settlement . . . or had been agreed to." Rusk replied, "That is correct, sir." "Briefing on Cuban Developments," January 25, 1963, Executive Sessions of the Senate Foreign Relations Committee (Historical Series) Vol. 15, pp. 105–106, 111. In 1963, McNamara told the House Appropriations Committee: "without any qualifications whatsoever there was absolutely no deal . . . between the Soviet Union and the United States regarding the removal of

the Jupiter weapons from either Italy or Turkey." U.S. House Appropriations Committee, Department of Defense Appropriations for 1964, 88 Cong., 1st Sess., 1963, pt. I, p. 57. This was also McNamara's position in 1968 when he wrote, in an introduction to Robert Kennedy's memoir: "Perhaps his [JFK's] most difficult decision was the refusal, against the advice of his weaker brethren . . . to bargain the security of the Western world by yielding to the specious Russian offers of a face saving accommodation at the expense of America's allies." Kennedy, *Thirteen Days*, p. 18. McGeorge Bundy writes of this outright swap: "As far as I know, none of the nine of us told anyone else what had happened. We denied in every forum that there was any deal." McGeorge Bundy, *Danger and Survival: Choices about the Bomb in the First Fifty Years* (New York: Vintage, 1988), p. 434. Roger Hilsman, the Senior State Department intelligence officer in the crisis, reached the only conclusion he could have from the "facts" as they were portrayed at the time: Khrushchev simply "backed down." Hilsman, *To Move a Nation*, p. 226; and Dean Rusk's phrase, recalling a childhood game, "we were eyeball to eyeball, and the other fellow blinked," was said to have told it all.

30. Leslie Gelb and Morton Halperin, "The Ten Commandments of the Foreign Affairs Bureaucracy," *Harper's* 244 (June 1972): 36.

31. Schelling, *Arms and Influence*, p. 2.

32. Harry G. Summers Jr., *On Strategy: The Vietnam War in Context* (Novato, Calif.: Presidio Press, 1982), p. 11.

33. Many in the military accepted this view. See "Review" by Lloyd J. Mathews in *Parameters* 5(2) (1976): 88–90. See also William C. Westmoreland, "Vietnam in Perspective," *Military Review* 59 (January 1979): 34–43, a speech to the U.S. Army Command and Staff College, April 11, 1978.

34. Summers, *On Strategy*, p. 77.

35. Admiral U. S. Grant Sharp, U.S. Navy (Ret.), "We Could Have Won in Vietnam Long Ago," *Reader's Digest* (May 1969): 118.

36. T. R. Milton (U.S. Air Force Retired), "USAF and the Vietnam Experience," *Air Force Magazine* 58(6) (June 1975): 65; Mark Clodfelter, *The Limits of Air Power: The American Bombing of North Vietnam* (New York: The Free Press, 1989), p. 201.

37. Jim and Sibyl Stockdale, *In Love and War: The Story of a Family's Ordeal and Sacrifice during the Vietnam Years* (New York: Harper and Row, 1984), p. 432.

38. Nguyen Tien Hung and Jerrold L. Schecter, *The Palace File* (New York: Harper & Row, 1986), p. 46. John Negroponte was interviewed on this point in 1985.

39. Since the NLF was known to be dominated by North Vietnam. See Tien Hung and Schecter, *The Palace File*, p. 111.

40. Senate Committee on the Armed Services, *Hearings before the Preparedness Investigating Subcommittee on the Armed Services*, 90th Cong., 1st Sess., August 9, 15, 16–25 (Stennis Hearings), *Testimony* of Lt. Gen. William W. Momyer, August 16, 1967, Vol. 2, p. 132–168ff.

41. Earl Tilford, *Setup: What the Airforce Did in Vietnam and Why* (Montgomery, Ala.: Maxwell Air Force Base, Air University Press, 1991), p. 148.

42. General William W. Momyer, *Airpower in Three Wars* (Washington, D.C.: Government Printing Office, 1978), p. 311.

43. The Jasons Report, dated August 29, 1966 is found in the *Pentagon Papers*, Gravel Edition (Boston: Beacon Press, 1971–1972), pp. 116–119. James King supervised the study. Also see Deborah Shapley, *Promise and Power: The Life and Times of Robert McNamara* (Boston: Little, Brown, 1993), p. 559ff.

44. The numbers are Karnow's, in Stanley Karnow, *Vietnam: A History* (New York: Penguin, 1983), p. 455. Some put the daily requirement of NLF and NVA forces much lower.

45. Tilford, *Setup*, p. 138; Clodfelter *The Limits of Air Power*, p. 134. On the order of battle controversy, see James J. Wirtz, "Intelligence to Please? The Order of Battle Controversy during the Vietnam War," *Political Science Quarterly* 106(2): 244ff.

46. See the Rand study conducted by Konrad Kellen, cited in *A Profile of the PAVN Soldier in South Vietnam* (RM 5014 ISA/ARPA) (June 1966), and *Conversations with Enemy Soldiers in Late 1968/Early 1969: A Study in Motivation and Morale* (RM 6131/1 ARPA) (September 1970).

47. Karnow, *Vietnam*, p. 459.

48. Michael Tatu, "Moscow, Peking, and the Conflict in Vietnam," in Anthony Lake (ed.), *The Vietnam Legacy* (New York: Pegasus, 1976), p. 21.

49. Nonetheless, U.S. intelligence estimates held that a Soviet intervention was "extremely unlikely." Yuen Foong Khong, *Analogies of War* (Princeton, N.J.: Princeton University Press, 1992), p. 168.

50. John W. Carver, "The Chinese Threat in the Vietnam War," *Parameters* 22(1) (Spring 1992): 75.

51. Ibid., p. 76.

52. In December of 1965, the intelligence community estimated a near 50–50 probability that U.S. escalation might trigger the introduction of Chinese forces. *Pentagon Papers*, Vol. 4 (1964), Gravel Edition (Boston: Beacon Press, 1971), p. 668, and Vol. 4 (1968) pp. 254–256, and pp. 46–48.

53. Tilford, *Setup*, p. 138.

54. Phoenix was a plan that managed to kill an estimated 20,000, including a very high proportion of local V. C. leadership. Some 28,000 were captured, and another 17,000 defected. See Neil Sheehan, *A Bright Shining Lie: John Paul Van and America in Vietnam* (New York: Vintage (Random House, 1988), p. 733.

55. See Robert W. Komer, "Impact of Pacification on Insurgency in South Vietnam," *Journal of International Affairs* 25(1) (1971): 48–69; Karnow, *Vietnam*, pp. 602–605; Sharp, *Strategy for Defeat*, p. 396. The Vietcong lost some 40,000 of their numbers, almost 80 percent. Moreover, their brutality, upon their defeat at Hue, exposed many of their pretensions as reformers and nationalists. George Herring, *America's Longest War* (New York: Wiley, 1979), p. 187.

56. *Pentagon Papers*, Vol. 3 (1964), Gravel Edition (Boston: Beacon Press, 1971), p. 668, and Vol. 4 (1968), pp. 254–256 and pp. 46–48. See the Staff study for Clark Clifford indicating, "we know that despite a massive influx of 500,000 U.S. troops, 1.2 million tons of bombs a year, 400,000 attack sorties per year, 200,000 KIA in three years, 20,000 U.S. KIA . . . our control of the countryside is now essentially at pre-1965 levels." *Pentagon Papers*, Vol. 4, p. 555. See Kissinger, *Diplomacy*, p. 679.

57. Sir Robert Thompson, *Defeating Communist Insurgency* (New York: Frederick A. Praeger, 1966), p. 154.

58. The timing of the Laotian invasion was highly politicized but had been hurried, instead of delayed (as Kissinger successfully insisted) so that less U.S. logistical aid and air cover than might be optimal was available. As H. R. Haldeman, Nixon's Chief of Staff, wrote: "This new action in Laos would set us up so we wouldn't have to worry about problems in '72, and that of course . . . is most important." Cited in Walter Pincus, "Haldeman: Reelection Drove Nixon Policy," *Washington Post*, May 18, 1994, p. A6.

59. William Shawcross, *Sideshow: Kissinger, Nixon and the Destruction of Cambodia* (New York: Simon and Schuster, 1979), p. 387. Shawcross concludes on this point: "Back in March and April [of 1970] the administration had the freedom of choice in reacting to events in Cambodia. . . . [I]t could have compelled the return of Sihanouk or, at least, an attempt by Lon Nol, to preserve the country's flawed neutrality. This would have . . . probably meant a government dominated by Hanoi . . . and the [use of] sanctuaries. But as the suppressed National Intelligence Estimate had pointed out, [anything] short of permanent occupation of the sanctuaries would always pose a military problem for a South Vietnamese government; that was a fact of both geography and revolutionary warfare" (p. 165).

60. The NVA, VC order of battle number is Kissinger's. Ibid.

61. See Gunter Lewy's "Review of William Colby's *Lost Victory*," *Parameters* 20(3) (1990): 111.

62. Cited by Summers in *On Strategy*, p. 79.

63. Earl H. Tilford Jr., "Why and How the U.S. Air Force Lost in Vietnam," *Armed Forces and Society* 17(3) (1991): 339.

64. Cited in Lewy, "Review," p. 130.

65. Sharp, *Strategy for Defeat*; Momyer, *Air Power in Three Wars*, p. 339.

66. This is perhaps the most solid point of Francis Fitzgerald's otherwise flawed but quite brilliant *Fire in the Lake* (New York: Vintage Books, 1972).

67. Cited by Jonathan Schell, *The Time of Illusion* (New York: Alfred A. Knopf, 1967), p. 354.

68. Since deterrence rests as much on a psychological relationship as it does on the balance of forces, a shift from the well-advertised "missile gap in reverse" of the year before to a position where, as Kennedy fretted, "they look like they're coequal with us" was bound to be unsettling. If, as Kennedy summed up the experience in public a few months later, the Soviets had succeeded in keeping their missiles in Cuba, "it would have politically changed the balance of power." Off the Record Meeting on Cuba, October 16, 1962, 6:30–7:45 P.M., JFK Library, pp. 57–58. "It would have appeared to, and appearances contribute to reality." McGeorge Bundy, in *Danger and Survival*, p. 452.

69. Henry Kissinger, "The Vietnam Negotiations," in *American Foreign Policy* (New York: W. W. Norton, 1969), p. 112.

70. Lyndon Johnson, *Vantage Point* (New York: Holt, Rinehart and Winston, 1971), pp. 151–152.

71. Henry Kissinger, *Nuclear Weapons* (New York: Harper and Row, 1957), cited by Schell, *The Time of Illusion*, pp. 351–352.

72. *The Pentagon Papers The Defense Department History of United States Decisionmaking on Vietnam* (New York: Bantam Books for the *New York Times*, 1971), p. 255; and the Gravel Edition of *The Pentagon Papers* (Boston: Beacon Press, 1971), Vol. 4, p. 393.

73. Lyndon B. Johnson, "Patterns for Peace in Southeast Asia," *Department of State Bulletin* 41(1348) (April 26, 1965): 607.

74. Henry Kissinger, *The White House Years* (Boston: Little, Brown, 1979), pp. 226–235.

75. "Decent interval" instead of "healthy interval" (as used in the text herein) had been used by Kissinger in various private academic settings in 1967 and 1968, before he came to Washington. The text is a memo from Kissinger to Nixon, September 18, 1971, cited in Walter Isaacson, *Kissinger* (New York: Simon and Schuster, 1992), p. 485.

76. Tien Hung and Schecter, *The Palace File*, p. 209. The bombing was to reassure and to pressure the Thieu administration. Thieu himself feared assassination if he did not capitulate to the Nixon administration's forceful insistence that they go along with the accords. Tien Hung and Schecter, *The Palace File*, pp. 80–81; John Ehrlichman, *Witness to Power* (New York: Simon and Schuster, 1982), p. 316.

77. Transcript, National Press Club Luncheon Speaker, National Press Club, September 28, 1993; Richard H. Kohn, "Out of Control: The Crisis in Civil-Military Relations," *The National Interest* 35 (Spring 1994): 12.

78. Colin Powell, "U.S. Forces: Challenges Ahead," *Foreign Affairs* 71(5) (Winter 1992/3): 38–40.

79. Transcript, National Press Club Luncheon Speaker, National Press Club, September 28, 1993.

80. Clausewitz, *On War*, Book One, chapter 1, p. 81.

81. Ibid., Book Six, chapter 8, p. 607.

82. Ibid., Book Six, chapter 8, p. 608.

83. Ibid., p. 87; and Summers, *On Strategy*, p. 95.

84. Speech by the Honorable Caspar Weinberger, "The Uses of Military Power," November 28, 1984, *Defense Issues* (January 1985) p. 35.

85. George Bush, "The Uses of Military Force, the President's Difficult Choice," *Defense Issues* 8 (November, 1992), p. 3.

86. Clausewitz, *On War*, Book Six, chapter 8, pp. 604–605.

87. Paul Quinn-Judge, "Doubts of Top Brass on the Use of Power Carry Great Weight," *Boston Globe*, April 20, 1994, p. 12.

88. David Roth, *Sacred Honor: A Biography of Colin Powell* (Grand Rapids, Mich.: Zondervan Publishing House, 1993), pp. 195–196; and Kohn, "Out of Control," p. 12.

Chapter 8

Conclusion

The calculus of the 1990s sought not to balance effort to interest; rather, it postulated that, absent a central focus, the American people will not abide a fight for principles—especially abstract principles of international order. As former Secretary of State Lawrence Eagleburger reflected on his tenure—at the height of the siege of Sarajevo in the mid-1990s:

If the Soviet Union still existed . . . I would have told you we should have been in there with both feet. . . . In a world where we are no longer at sword points with the Soviet Union, the decisions the U.S. has to make with regard to when it will intervene . . . are much more difficult and always—I don't know how else to say this—always will depend on our judgment on what the American people are prepared to tolerate. In that sense, Vietnam never goes away.[1]

The demands of military writers in the 1990s that policy makers deliver crisp objectives and absolute deadlines stem from an urge that, as long ago as Clausewitz, could be recognized as a canard. The military held that matters regarding force were becoming too technical for the hoary Clausewitzian symbiosis between war and policy making to still appertain.[2] Thus, contemporary Pentagon planners insisted that "military power should be used only when there are clear-cut military objectives," "end points," and "exit strategies."

Even when *political* objectives might be clear enough, when *military* objectives seemed too fuzzy, force was precluded unless and until, as General Powell insisted, "we can measure [how] the military objective has been achieved."[3]

The constitutional implications of the near veto the American military seemed to exercise by means of its doctrinal manipulation over American policy makers in the 1990s was worrisome enough. And the empirical assumptions of the reticence of the 1990s for the most part slipped examination. To be sure, when plenteous force was employed in Panama and Grenada, the immediate results appeared an unvarnished success. Conversely, in those areas where limited means were attempted—Central America and Lebanon—the results were clouded and indeterminate. But these observations need great qualification.

At first look, it is easy to term the early 1980s mission in Lebanon as ill-conceived; and the suicide bomber's murder of some 200 U.S. peacekeepers at the Beirut airport only seems to underscore the mission's apparent failure. Yet the United States *did* have serious interests in Lebanon in the early 1980s, for it *was* important to give the Israelis an incentive to withdraw from their misbegotten policy of controlling a vast security zone from their northern frontier to the suburbs of Beirut. Moreover, the United States' interest in a stable peace in the area required that the Palestinian Liberation Organization's family members—women, children, and old people—not be exterminated by rampaging Christian Phalangists. A sovereign Lebanon, free of Syrian domination, was also a valid goal of U.S. policy. American and allied peacekeeping forces—albeit, perhaps much larger forces than the one deployed—were relevant to the stakes. The trouble with the U.S. deployment in the Levant was not that the mission was unclear; it was that it was not achievable in the short run with the force at hand. But absent the stomach and force levels to confront Syria and its protégés, the folly of a modest deployment tasked beyond its means was clear enough—after the bombing of the marine barracks—to provoke a withdrawal.

In Central America, neither the U.S.-backed Contras in the 1980s, nor U.S. trainers, nor even U.S.-trained forces, were sufficient for an early realization of the goal of achieving non-Communist, stable, democratic governments. But the United States did achieve eventual success in that the Sandinistas agreed, in 1990, to an election which resulted in their defeat. In large part, of course, U.S. goals were achieved because the great Sandinista benefactors, the Soviets and Cubans, were facing ruin and collapse. But even more, U.S. goals were realized because the United States stuck with a small, surrogate force for a very long time. It was not overwhelming arms but a slow grinding persistence that carried the day. As one U.S. military advisor wrote: "The hallmark of U.S. policy was durability . . . [W]e threw enough money into [it] hoping the problem would go away. Luckily, it did."[4]

In Nicaragua, a small investment paid handsomely, whereas in other instances in Central America where overwhelming force was used—Panama and Grenada[5]—conditions were arguably worse and more unstable than they were before the intervention.[6] In the case of the 1991 Gulf War, after one of the greatest and most lopsided military victories since Agincourt, the balance of power in the region was left little improved from the standpoint of American interests. To be sure, Iraq was weakened, but not sufficiently to stop Saddam Hussein's depredations against his own people. Common Iraqis fell victim to even more repression as they were pauperized by the harsh UN-sponsored embargo. Meanwhile, Iran was emboldened ideologically and fortified politically by Saddam's defeat. The classic goal of war—"a better kind of peace"—was never really considered by the Bush policy *apparat* prior to, or even during, hostilities.[7] After the Kurd and Shia opposition to Saddam had been effectively eviscerated, the Bush administration threatened Saddam with displacement; but the option, like so much in the last year of the George H. W. Bush administration, was little cultivated and, in the end, withered from neglect.

In the case of Somalia, some 28,000 U.S. forces did, in late 1992 and early 1993, prevent starvation from spreading, and U.S. forces were successful in stabilizing Mogadishu and most of the rest of the stricken countryside. In March 1994, when the United States departed, leaving some 3,000 troops in a logistics role, a successful verdict on the Somalia mission was possible. But the effort in Somalia, like the effort in Lebanon, had two stages. And, like Lebanon, the second stage proved disastrous. From the June 1993 slaughter of a Pakistani contingent of UN soldiers to a fatal October 1993 urban firefight that cost 18 U.S. Rangers their lives, Mohammad Farah Adid's gunmen bloodied and embarrassed U.S. forces working with the UN. American efforts to support the UN in Somalia were virtually abandoned when a date set in cooperation with Congress resulted in an almost total U.S. withdrawal at the end of March 1994.

Even before the disastrous October 1993 ambush of rangers by Adid's gunmen, U.S. military observers were trying to determine the "lessons" of "Operation Restore Hope," as the Somalia undertaking was deemed. As Colonel F. M. Lorenz, the U.S. Army's Legal Advisor to Operation Restore Hope, said:

End state conditions for a future U.S.-led humanitarian operations must be set before the U.S. commits forces to such operations. End state conditions include not only the circumstances that will permit the United States to withdraw from the commitments, with its mission complete, but also the terms for contemplating the transition to whatever force will follow.[8]

There were in some quarters suspicions that President George H. W. Bush had mounted the Somali intervention in December 1992 not because it was in U.S. interests, but because of the two sets of claimants on U.S. attention—Yugoslavia and Somalia. Somalia looked easier, even though few argued that it was more important. And although Operation "Restore Hope" was not the kind of effort initially advertised (i.e., an exercise from which the United States could disengage within 60 days), it might none-theless serve the purpose of staying the hand of U.S. intervention in Yu-goslavia.

In Somalia, there were few real national security interests in feeding the hungry if they had to be balanced against significant U.S. casualties. Yet mission "creep" took it to the point where the United States attempted to undo one contender and his clan seeking power in favor of others. Like Lebanon, the U.S. peacekeeping had mutated, perhaps inevitably, into peacemaking. Neither effort could withstand the resulting images of Amer-ican dead and wounded. Western aid and attention dribbled away. As U.S. troops departed, the worst cholera in 20 years swept the countryside. Sixty thousand people in the capital had no way to feed themselves and 150,000 Somali refugees remained in neighboring Kenya. The lesson learned by the executive officer of the 10th Mountain Division, Lt. Col. Raoul Archem-bault, was, "You can't solve social problems with military force." One prominent Somalia businessman commented: "They gave it a good try. But the Americans set deadlines. In our society we have no deadlines."[9]

The urge of military planners to seek "end states" and "end dates" in a few punchy sentences delivered in the opening paragraph of a mission state-ment[10] was only fortified by the Somali experience.[11] In the light of So-malia, Panama, Nicaragua, and Lebanon, one can only sympathize with those military who do not want to be in the business of pursuing jobs they perceive more rightly to be the business of social engineers. But the fact is that social problems *are* relieved by force. Nazism and slavery are two instances that come to mind.

As Jeffrey Record, a longtime analyst of and participant in the Vietnam War, concludes,

To the extent that the [Weinberger-Powell] doctrine purports to be a warning against another Vietnam, it is almost certainly unnecessary. The very experience of the Vietnam War remains the greatest obstacle to its repetition, and even if it weren't, there are probably no more Vietnams lying in wait. . . . [T]here is probably no non-industrial state or faction in the foreseeable future that could replicate the remarkable performance of the Vietnamese communist forces . . . Iranian, Pas-daran, Nicaraguans . . . , Lebanese, Iraqi . . . Somali and . . . Serbs . . . may be vex-ing . . . [but] they could not hold a candle to the North Vietnamese . . . and main force Viet Cong.[12]

Madeleine Albright, as U.S. delegate to the United Nations, complained of the first Clinton administration response to Yugoslavia's aggression:

There was this doctrine that you'd be dealing with a crazy dictator [and then U.S. forces had to take] six months to prepare and [then there was the requirement that] the earth was flat and [then] you'd use overwhelming force and[then] somebody else would pay. But those circumstances don't come along very often.[13]

General John Shalikashvili, Powell's successor, claimed, more cautiously, "A president must have in his tool bag, in addition to the diplomatic tools, the economic tools, also the tool of military power to protect American interests."[14]

But the Clinton administration's guidelines on peacekeeping made it plain that "next time," U.S. troops would be sent into areas only when it was deemed that U.S. interests are "fully engaged." In sum, the test of "vital interests" had been modified as the "trigger" for U.S. troops, but not by much. Moreover, U.S. troops would only be committed to areas wracked by civil war *after* the outlines of a settlement appear acceptable to all sides.[15]

"Nation building," said Clinton's first National Security Adviser, Anthony Lake, had been scratched off the list of U.S. interests, not because it was not valuable, but because it was too burdensome and problematic for the kinds of force the United States might be willing to commit.

In addition, the U.S. troops would not operate under United Nations command; rather, they would be autonomous, responsible only to the president who, it was said, would have to seek "congressional support for [the] operation."[16] The quickly amended Clinton administration take on force, PDD 25—which in its early incarnation was a prescription to realize the hopes of President Clinton and advisors such as Peter Tarnoff that the United States could unburden itself through a more active UN—became less an enabling document to fund U.S. interests through multilateral endeavors, and more a kind of public stockade wherein U.S. interests would be cuffed by every considerable stricture the military had hammered on since the early 1980s.

CLAUSEWITZ ON HIS HEAD: THE FUTURE OF AMERICAN FOREIGN POLICY UNDER THE NEW RULES

With the new military writ as part of contemporary military culture of the 1990s, U.S. diplomacy could not help but be enfeebled; for a precise "end state" could hardly be relevant, for instance, to otherwise perfectly valid constabulary missions, whether they be drug interdiction, eradication of terrorist bases, or peacekeeping in the Sinai.

Some good uses of force go on for a very long time, including most limited wars. The British war in Malaya lingered for 12 years. U.S. efforts to help against an endemic Maoist insurgency in the Philippines have been going on since World War II. Moreover, if the mission is seen as relatively short, or if there is a specification of a time or a condition which *perforce* leads to withdrawal, an inevitable and perhaps fatal advantage is given to U.S. adversaries. Hostile elements could feign meeting precise, but necessarily cursory, specifications—they could sign an agreement, they could agree to withdraw to relocation points, and so on—only to resume safely after U.S. forces had been withdrawn. Initial mission statements could be met or complied with; but after withdrawal had been effected, the military situation could radically change. President Clinton claimed he was "wrong" to have given two such deadlines in Bosnia, but the urge for clarity remains a preeminent goal of political planning.

One of the unarticulated but apparent conditions of the military writ of the 1980s and 1990s was that only a small number of casualties were permissible. One can reflect with distress how this inhibition encouraged those who wish us little well, such as the likes of Saddam Hussein, who told April Glaspie on July 25, 1990,[17] without refutation, that the U.S. cannot tolerate "tens of thousands" of deaths. Within a week, Saddam was in Kuwait. Saddam Hussein may have been disabused, at least for a time; but other thugs from Haiti to Serbia to the mountains of Kabul did not seem to have gotten the message. As one senior Serbian official told a Belgrade television audience: "Clinton ha[d] his own problems. . . . He can't afford to have even a few soldiers killed in Bosnia."[18]

As long as the United States seemed to indicate an intolerance of casualties, as seems to be the latent agenda of the War Powers Act and the Weinberger-Powell military wisdom, decision makers would be confronted with the fickle effects of events as they played out on television, and their effects on Congress and public opinion.

If a withdrawal would be triggered by dint of some number of specified losses in excess of the permissible (or by some condition putatively met by malefactors), renewed U.S. intervention is all but precluded. If an "end state" were indicated whenever the United States takes "too many" casualties, the incentive only increases to bloody the United States, on the one hand, and for the United States to restrain its use of force, on the other.

Deterrence is fundamentally psychological, a calculus of will and interests. The evidence of will is an ability to take a good deal of discomfort. If it is discovered, as a matter of doctrine, that the United States cannot stomach casualties, future Saddams, and Osama bin Ladens would be emboldened. Some will get away with it, and some will not. But the mere proliferation of temptation and the resultant episodic and successful forays of some aggressors would inevitably embolden others, leaving the possibility that one day an aggressor armed to the teeth, perhaps with a nuclear or biological capability, will challenge the United States, leaving Americans the same unhappy choice confronted during the heyday of the Cold War— the use of apocalyptic force or capitulation.[19]

CONCLUSION: THE SHADOW OF POWER

The burden of policy is less to find clear military objectives than it is to find pertinent policy objectives. Force, if managed subtly, casts its own penumbra—what Acheson once described as the "shadow of power."[20]

What one military commentator, Edward Luttwak, once termed "active" and a "latent" "suasion"[21] need not require that policy makers be prepared to escalate from small deployments (or small, punishing expeditions) to all-out war. Indeed, if policy is credibly attached to interests, force in modest sum signals intent and reinforces one's own position while giving pause to others. Power has to be credible, to be sure; but it need not—unless the whole history of "gunboat diplomacy" speaks a lie—always be followed by huge and overwhelming undertakings.[22]

Deployments can symbolize, at the same time, both intent and threat. Before the events of September 11, 2001, however, there was a vast depreciation of "presence missions." When, for instance, senior U.S. State Department officers requested a Sixth Fleet "sail-by" in the Adriatic when Dubrovnik was shelled from the sea in the opening days of Serb aggression against Croatia in September 1991, they were dismissed by Larry Eagleburger, Acting Secretary of State, because he could not imagine "what the next steps were."[23] If it had been similarly required that "clear . . . measurable military objectives" had needed to be adduced in advance throughout the American experience, then the deployment of B-29s to England during the Berlin Airlift in 1948 (as well as the more recent dispatch of U.S. soldiers to Macedonia) would never have been possible.

Because the preclusive call for "overwhelming force" and well-known, definable "end states" had become "doctrine" and because the most spectacular victory in arms was Desert Storm, more subtle uses of force were little discussed. Yet, "active suasion" and "latent suasion" need to be considered significant ingredients of the reservoir of military-diplomatic influence. To be sure, presence missions risk, on the one side, becoming stale with overuse and on the other being discounted because the instruments of the mission are unfamiliar and misunderstood. Nor can the most modest coercive display be tested, as was the case when the USS Harlan County was chased from a Haitian pier in October 1993 by the sight of an unruly mob waving sticks. Nor did the long years of the Serbian defiance (despite the profligate rain of NATO fly-bys in Bosnia and then Kosovo) augur well for "expressive diplomacy" backed by military power.[24]

Exploitable military power ought to exist short of massive firepower. The agent of exploitable power, whether it be ships or planes or armed peacekeepers, has to be recognizable as capable of calling forth large and probable punishment if it is to be effective. But it need not signal a commitment of resources beyond the interests in question.

The relationship between force, order, and justice is worth keeping in mind, lest one fail to acknowledge the essentially destructive damage a depreciation of force can do to a nation's reputation—and, in the American case, the real harm that could befall the world community if American power reverts to simple all-or-nothing policy dyads of policy alternatives.[25] In early 1984, when Chairman of the Joint Chiefs General John Shalikashvili argued (in language first rejected by the State Department but then adopted by the White House)[26] that one cannot use air power in the siege of Gorazde on the grounds that it would favor one side over another, he missed, it would seem, the whole point of what use force would be when one side, Serbia, was clearly intent on continuing its aggression even while claiming it was doing no such thing. Indeed, according to Western intelligence sources, Serbs eagerly took Shalikashvili's statements as a "green light."[27]

In June 1995, President Clinton pressed French President Jacques Chirac to lobby Congress to refrain from arming the Muslim-led Bosnian government. When President Chirac returned to Paris, he pronounced the leadership position of the free world to be "vacant." For a while, apparently the message had sunk in: An unwillingness to use ambiguous instruments of coercion and to validate threats with the use of force, when called for, undermined alliances, weakened prior commitments, and emboldened rogue states and terrorists. Even Mr. Clinton, in a July 1995 breakfast meeting with his national security team, confessed that the administration's performance in Bosnia "is killing the U.S. position of strength in the world." But in subsequent sallies forth in Kosovo, or Afghanistan, the response was tentative and constrained by the first mission, as it was put, of "force protection."[28]

In the late winter of 1999, Yugoslav forces began killing and rounding up hundreds of civilians and forcing thousands more to flee their homes. President Clinton said a NATO air campaign would "save the lives of innocent civilians in Kosovo from a brutal military offensive." When the Yugoslav forces refused to desist, and the expulsion proceeded, an altitude floor of 15,000 feet was placed on NATO aircraft. Many targets were hard to discern from three miles up and some ordinance, especially cluster bombs, could only function effectively at 3,000 feet. But U.S. planes and service personnel suffered no losses save embarrassment of the Yugoslav army marching out of Kosovo, virtually intact, after a bombing campaign that lasted more than 70 days.[29]

When then-candidate Clinton campaigned in 1992, one of the few foreign policy positions he articulated clearly was that there was a "high cost" to "remaining silent and paralyzed in the face of genocide."[30] The delay in engaging in Bosnia had cost, by former U.S. Ambassador Warren Zimmerman's woeful estimate, some 100,000 dead and 2.5 million people driven from their homes. Finally, after three years of increased horror, a much embarrassed Secretary of State Warren Christopher and the president he served seemed to have realized that America's failure to use arms threatened American leadership and credibility. Still, no force materialized to meet the ever braver words of American policy makers until, finally, Richard Holbrooke moved the unusually preoccupied president to action in the spring and summer of 1995.

But it was neither shame nor strategic insight that motivated policy.

Rather, it was the realization that a nearly inadvertent promise to send American forces to extract UN forces in Bosnia would probably end in significant casualties. And, if such an extraction could be sustained at all, it would leave all of Bosnia abandoned (as other UN-guaranteed "Safe Areas" such as Srebenica were left to the sanguinary reality of Serb "ethnic cleansing," i.e., massacre.) In the end, even more significant than the sheer dicey prospects for rescue of the U.S. "peacekeepers" was the probable breakup of NATO if the United States stood aside any longer, which finally allowed the Clinton administration to recover its collective backbone.

Even then, the military insisted on a huge force, with the initial suggestion of 500,000 men (whittled down to some 20,000 troops) and a 12-month "exit" schedule. The peace finally negotiated at Dayton at the end of 1995 gave power to the U.S. Commander, Admiral Leighton Smith, analogous to that given the occupier of Japan, Douglas MacArthur, who of course brought constitutional government to that country. But so concerned did Admiral Leighton Smith, the Commander of 60,000-strong international forces in Bosnia, seem to be with "force protection" that, in the withering reflections of the Dayton accord's architect, Richard Holbrooke, he tended to find "civilian aspects of the task beneath him."[31] President Clinton told his military Chief, General John Shalikashvili, "I know there has been ambivalence among some of your people . . . about Bosnia, but that is all in the past. I want everyone here to get behind the agreement."[32] Even then Admiral Smith, Holbrooke emphasizes, was unwilling "to use his *authority* to do more than he was *obligated* to do" by direct order or the need to keep casualties to a minimum.[33] So successful was the latter effort that years passed without a single mortality in action. But the requirements of the Dayton accord lingered as the Serb government set its sights on Kosovo.

In December 1992, President George H. W. Bush said, in a letter to Serb President Slobodan Milosevic, that the United States was prepared to use force against the Serbs if they tried to drive ethnic Albanians from Kosovo, a province in which Serbs are a small minority. In 1998, the Serbs attacked whole villages and forced thousands from their homes. Secretary of State Madeleine K. Albright, National Security Adviser Samuel R. "Sandy" Berger, and America's toughest negotiator, special envoy Richard Holbrooke, all seemed stymied once again. Without approval of the UN Security Council, NATO would not act. And the United States did not have the clout with Russia to push a resolution through the UN Security Council, Clinton policy makers claimed—notwithstanding a simultaneous Russian petition to U.S.-dominated multilateral financial institutions for tens of billions of dollars. Finally, when the exasperated Secretary of State mustered a NATO consensus, it was predicated on a twofold proposition: first, that it would be a short-term exercise; and second, that NATO ground troops would not be called upon to enter into combat. The first condition proved illusory;

the campaign lasted 78 days, and though it did little damage to Serb forces, it did immense damage to the Serbian economy. The second condition, that ground forces not be employed, prolonged the campaign and probably made the plight of the suffering Kosovars worse.

In the case of earlier threats to use "targeted" force against Saddam's weapons of mass destruction in that late winter of 1998, there was the added curious fact that the crisis was precipitated by the unanswered question as to where Saddam's most destructive forces were in the first place.[34] After months of stalling, and presumably moving his chemical, biological, nuclear, and who knows what other kinds of weapons, Saddam invited international inspectors in to begin the charade again. U.S. forces quietly dissipated and American policy makers, perhaps sensibly enough, considered another try at rapprochement with Iran. But "containment" without power would take more than diplomatic reconnoitering. And the missing ingredient, credible force, withered from disuse.

For nearly a decade, from Serbia and the Gulf to Haiti, Korea, and Taiwan, a parade of hollow threats has hobbled American statecraft. Indeed the whole process of escalating threat, followed by embarrassing tergiversation, seems to have served only to further separate force from the service of diplomacy. At long last, General Shalikashvili admitted to a *New York Times* reporter later that usable force and alliance leadership were inextricably wed: "We thought we could somehow let them be on the ground and we would be in the air and that would be enough. . . . There is a very important lesson that you cannot be in an alliance with nations and somehow step back from a leadership position."[35]

But in the second Clinton administration, ever-more-exuberant technological enthusiasts dominated military discourse, claiming that United States military power has undergone a "revolution" that avoids commitments on the ground of immense numbers of troops—practically all troops, for that matter. This brave new epoch is said to be characterized by new sophistication in reconnaissance, surveillance, command, control, military organization, communications, computing power, stealth, and accuracy.[36]

Technological optimism is nothing new regarding waging warfare from a distance, if at all, and with minimum costs.[37] In 1921, an Italian General, Giulio Douhet, suggested that the new technology of his time—machine guns, poison gas, and especially, aircraft—had come to nullify prior military experience.[38] Warfare between large land armies had become simply obsolete. The new technology of arms left no place, in Douhet's view, for the classic miseries of war—such as "natural forces like wind and weather and psychological disruptions of purpose like boredom, terror, and self-destructiveness"—except in the dimming recesses of memory.[39]

The new technological optimists admitted that those groups that are most likely to be resistant to American power may possess the most diabolical weapons. But the new RMA (Revolution in Military Affairs) "school" of American power remained convinced that a gamut of male-factors would be manageable from space—or, at least from great distance—and at low cost. Of course, the current wave of technological optimism, especially in the Air Force, may be whistling up ever more missions for air power, and at the same time, preempting the argument for funding ground forces as mere "political" and "police" issues not worthy of military consideration. Yet, a military doctrine—or even a military cast of mind—that dismisses constabulary and political nuisances as terrorism, and internecine war and the like as being either technical problems or beneath their dignity as professionals, avoids confronting the most likely sorts of instability American planners face in attempting to sustain and nurture world order.

The technological optimism of adherents to the RMA school subsumed every military mission, from central deterrence[40] to urban warfare, wiping the battlefield of gore, and especially, American misfortune. As a 1995 group of air power strategists at the Air Force's Air University at Maxwell Air Force Base enthused:

> By 2020, real-time responsiveness of sensor-to-shooter systems must become a reality. For the first time in history, this responsiveness will allow the striking force to maneuver fires rather than forces over long ranges, and allow direct and simultaneous attack on many of the enemy's centers of gravity.[41]

By centers of gravity, the new doctrines did not mean, necessarily, military forces, but rather a variant of the kind of bombing on industrial targets and leadership that was attempted in World War II. As Colonel John Warden, the architect of the Gulf War campaign prior to the ground assault, put it, variants of strategic bombing will make possible "the return of Clausewitzian decisive victories in place of attrition warfare."[42] Warden stated that "Contrary to Clausewitz, destruction of the enemy military is not the essence of war; the essence of war is convincing the enemy to accept your position, and fighting his military forces is, at best, a means to an end; and, at worst, a total waste of time."

But Warden misunderstands what Clausewitz calls "*war in the abstract*," and "*actual war*" which "*is often removed from the pure concept postulated by theory*"[43] (emphasis in the original). "Disarming" and even defeating the enemy, writes Clausewitz, "need not be fully achieved as a condition of peace. . . . Many treaties have concluded . . . even before the balance of power has been seriously altered."[44]

And, of course, all of Clausewitz's (and Warden's) "centers of gravity" are not equal. It is one thing to target advanced industrialized countries, but quite another to extirpate religious figures, warlords, criminal gangs, nationalists, ethnic secessionists, terrorists, and conspirators. One wonders how many "real-life" situations would, in fact, lend themselves to the following description of American capability offered by Colonel Warden, who asks:

Can we not put a combination of AC-130s and helicopters in the air equipped with searchlights, loudspeakers, rubber bullets, entangling chemical nets, and other paraphernalia? When groups are spotted, they first receive a warning to disburse. If they don't, they find themselves under attack by non-lethal, but unpleasant, weapons. If these don't work, lethal force is at hand. It may be very difficult to prevent an individual from skulking around. . . . Single individuals, however, constitute a relatively small tactical problem.[45]

Similarly, the Maxwell Air Force planning group anticipated: "[A]ir and space power . . . forged into means that can effectively deny people the use of the street for looting property or mobbing human victims, (so) the dark shadow of one of the most vexing problems of the future will have been drawn back.[46]

Dr. Carl Builder, one of America's leading air power theorists of the 1980s and 1990s, imagines an American military future populated by exclusively American high-tech air- and space-borne Excaliburs dominating world politics. As the British were able to use the Royal Air Force (RAF) to conduct police operations in Iraq in the 1920s, Builder suggested modern space and air technologies would offer "tools to exploit . . . the use of the ground."[47]

But the inconvenient historical reality is that the RAF in 1920 sought only to coerce Arab tribesmen into some rather minor matters, that is, to ensure that tribesmen paid their taxes and were suitably awed by British arms so that they might reduce their attacks against caravans. It was hardly the same as a resounding crusade, like the one Osama bin Laden declared in 1998: "to kill the Americans and their allies—civilians and military—is an individual duty for every Muslim who can do it in any country in which it is possible to do it."[48]

To be sure, there were some who were critical of the air force doctrine of the 1990s. As James S. Corum concluded (in a rather accidental restatement of Clausewitz): "People are more susceptible to coercion by force [from the air . . . and presumably, anywhere else] when they have little motivation to resist the will and strength of an outside party."[49]

To Clausewitz, the psychological (which he classified as the "moral" element of war) and the physical aspects of conflict are "composed in equal parts." Indeed, the "moral" is probably the stronger, for as Clausewitz observed, "One might say the physical seems little more than the wooden hilt, while the moral facts are the precious metal, the real weapon, the finely-honed blade."[50]

In sum, will (as Clausewitz knew) is the greatest "force multiplier" of them all. Commitment was the critical component of conflict in Vietnam. It was central to the Palestinian struggle in the 1980s when, for instance, the Israeli air force massively employed modern American F-15s and precision-guided munitions against terrorist encampments in southern Lebanon—engendering virtually no abatement of terrorist activity against Israel.

The use of Israeli fighters, helicopter gun ships, and tanks did little to stem the conflict over the West Bank and the violence of late 2000–2001. It remains to be seen what American air power might be able to do against Al Qaida, the shadowy terrorist network at the heart of the conspiracy to destroy the World Trade Center, the Pentagon, and other targets in September of 2001.

Air power, to be sure, was effective in Bosnia. But it is less certain that new missions in this early part of the new millennium will only rarely feature adversaries like the underarmed and often inebriated thugs like the Bosnian Serbs surrounding Sarajevo. Nor can there be real confidence that others will be forever restrained from acquiring the kinds of weapons which the United States now all but monopolizes. The American "unipolar moment"—a time of unrivaled American dominance—at the end of the Cold War cannot last without allies and concomitant respect for the credible use of American power (not that the only element of respect, of course, is useful force).

In the post–Cold War era, in conflicts in Central Africa, the Balkans, and the Middle East, technology hardly touched the classic factors of willpower and territorial control. Hence, Colonel Warden's dictum that "the new physical reality of accurate weapons means that few [American] men need be or should be exposed" to mortal risk, though proved right in practice, appears more a function of current military caution and doctrine and less a correlate of the imperatives of national interests.[51]

Eventually, Americans will have to come to grips with the cost of the vexatious legacy of ambitions for a particular kind of world order and the means necessary to sustain that order.[52] It has been the hair on the hot dog of the otherwise beautiful American ambition: World power requires sustained commitments, resources, money, and occasional investments payable in the lives of America's fighting forces. But without a credible capability to use moderate force, fate rather than statecraft determines the future. Overreliance on multilateral force—or unilateral force, for that matter—to enforce peace can, of course, detract from conventional diplomacy; but an inability to call upon force helped to neuter the diplomacy of the late 1990s and the early third millennium.

Among the most effective symbolic uses of force are ground troops in great numbers.[53] But after Somalia, and the hasty post-hostilities withdrawal after 100 hours of ground war in Kuwait, even ground forces have been vitiated.

The lesson that Osama bin Laden, the apparent mastermind of the terrorist cartel Al Qaida, drew from the American aversion to casualties is revealing. As bin Laden told ABC newsman John Miller on May 28, 1998:

We have seen in the last decade the decline of the American government and the weakness of the American soldier, who is ready to wage cold wars and unprepared to fight long wars. This was proven in Beirut when the Marines fled after two explosions. It also proves that they can run in less than twenty-four hours, and this was also repeated in Somalia. . . . The youth were surprised at the low morale of the American soldiers. . . . After a few blows, they ran in defeat. . . . They forgot about being the world leader and the leader of the new world order. [They] left, dragging their corpses and their shameful defeat.[54]

If we denude ourselves of some of the minimalist options pertaining to force, we leave ourselves too open to chance—and the initiatives of others. Especially in the post–Cold War era, facing adversaries who do not bear easy summation, the burden of strategy is to find suitable and commensurate levels of coercive force. The reverse, to reject objectives that cannot be achieved with diplomacy alone, is fraught with danger. If force is rendered irrelevant (except to overwhelming threats that become manifest only after all diplomatic palliatives are exhausted) or, as a last resort,[55] then disorder and anarchy will be given a license unseen since America's rise to world power.

Clausewitz's insistence on a better kind of peace will always be illusory without a measure of force that is less than apocalyptic. America's experiment with abandoning force, except in cases when all the markers were blindingly clear, was at least as risky as striking with too little force when the political/military objectives were of compelling urgency. The last two-thirds of the twentieth century saw a vast depreciation of diplomacy, and at the end of the twentieth century, the decline of diplomacy was attended by a generalized inability to muster the will and the means to make any resurrection of diplomacy a credible servant of order.

George W. Bush rightly declared the attack of September 11, 2001 a "new kind of war." Earlier strictures regarding force protection, exit strategies, and end points were abandoned. This war, said Secretary of Defense Donald Rumsfeld, is not going to see defining moments: "Needless to say, there is not going to be a D-Day, as such, and I'm sure there will not be a signing ceremony on the *Missouri*, as such. . . . It is something that will involve a sustained effort over a good period of time."[56]

Victory, said Rumsfeld, will be found only when Americans can be "satisfied" that they "are going to be able to live their lives in relative freedom." But the process of "routing out evildoers,"[57] as Mr. Bush defined America's task, has an elasticity as worrisome as it is impractical. Deputy Defense Secretary Paul Wolfowitz, former Dean of Johns Hopkins University, went as far as to suggest that the United States would "end states" that supported terrorists. The remarks were widely debated, amended and even, in the case of Secretary of State Colin Powell, rebuked.[58] Yet, in the end, it was clear that the Bush administration had embraced an enormous agenda.

At long last, the Powell–Weinberger straightjacket regarding exit strategies and end points was jettisoned. But there loomed a danger of embracing missions too broad to be believable without an effort as heroic as the rhetoric. As Clausewitz warned nearly two centuries earlier, setting out to over-throw an enemy—to annihilate him—is to "presuppose a great physical and moral superiority, or a great spirit of enterprise, an innate propensity to extreme hazards."[59] The hazards, a list of horribles as broad as the imagination, were abundantly clear after September 11, 2001. And also clear were the imperatives of focus, determination, and proportion between ends and means.

NOTES

1. Transcript, "While America Watched," March 16, 1994, ABC News Special, p. 7.

2. John E. Shephard Jr., "On War: Is Clausewitz Still Relevant?" *Parameters* 20(3) (September 1990): 90.

3. Edwin Arnold Jr., "The Uses of Military Power in Pursuit of National Interests," *Parameters* (Spring 1994): 7, 10ff.

4. Victor M. Rosello, "Lesson from El Salvador," *Parameters* (Winter 1993–1994): 106. Perhaps the contest was worthwhile, although the paucity of subsequent efforts to seal apparent victory in Salvador and Nicaragua with economic and political resources seems to indicate that U.S. interests were largely symbolic of larger Cold War interests, rather than any hemispheric well-being.

5. Conditions were not much improved economically or politically in Grenada. See Mark Kurlansky, "Post-Invasion Prosperity Stalled by Financing Shortage," *Chicago Tribune, National Edition*, October, 1, 1986, p. 8C; and Peter Copeland, "Grenada Still Living on Hopes: Post Invasion Dreams Fail to Turn into Reality," *Chicago Tribune*, February 19, 1986, p. 9C. The failure of promised aid left Grenadians with "a low-keyed, bitter resentment," said Dessima Williams, a Brandeis sociology professor who was Grenada's UN ambassador. "Goodbye Grenada," *Boston Globe* (editorial), May 13, 1994, p. 20.

6. After reducing Panama's GDP by over 30 percent with an embargo and an invasion, and after killing hundreds of Panamanians—and 27 American soldiers—all that was certain was that Panama was not less free from drugs and drug money. Indeed, Panama, as the *New York Times* put it in mid-1991, became a drug exporters' "free for all." Joseph B. Trester, "Cocaine Is Again Surging Out of Panama," *New York Times*, August 13, 1991, p. A1. The best and most balanced discussion of the invasion can be found in Alan Ned Sabrosky, "Panama: 1989: Deposing a Dictator," *Small Wars and Insurgencies* 1(3) (December 1990); and Peter Clavert, "The U.S. Intervention in Panama," *Small Wars and Insurgencies* 1(3) (December 1990): 303–315.

7. Conversations with senior State Deparment Persian Gulf Task Force personnel, December 1990–May 1991.

8. F. M. Lorenz, "Law and Anarchy in Somalia," *Parameters* 23(4) (Winter 1993–1994): 39.

9. Ibid., p. 1.

10. Elliot A. Cohen, review of Mark Clodfelter's *The Limits of Air Power: The American Bombing of North Vietnam* (New York: The Free Press, 1989), in *Parameters* 20(2) (June 1990): 115.

11. Patrick J. Sloyan, "A Look At . . . The Somalia Endgame: How the Warlords Outwitted Clinton's Spooks," *Washington Post*, April 3, 1994, p. C3.

12. See Jeffrey Record, "Perils of Reasoning by Historical Analogy: Munich, Vietnam, and the American Use of Force Since 1945," *Occasional Paper Number 4* (Maxwell Air Force Base: Center for Strategy and Technology, Air War College, Montgomery, Alabama, March 1998), pp. 24–25.

13. Steven Erlanger and David E. Sanger, "On Global Stage, Clinton Finds Balance as Leader," *New York Times*, July 29, 1996 (web site).

14. Ibid.

15. Elaine Sciolino, "New U.S. Peacekeeping Policy De-emphasizes the Role of the UN," *New York Times*, May 6, 1994, p. 1.

16. These were Clinton National Security Adviser Anthony Lake's words. See Daniel Williams, "Joining the Pantheon of American Missteps," *Washington Post*, March 26, 1994, p. 18; and Paul Lewis, "U.S. Plans Policy on Peacekeeping," *New York Times*, November 18, 1993, p. 7.

17. The transcript can be found in the *New York Times*, September 23, 1990.

18. The remark was made by Mihajilo Markovic, leader of the former Communist (now Socialist) Party. Markovic is a close aide of Serbian President Slobodan Milosevic. Markovic's remarks cited by Roger Thurow, "Serbs Bet That West Won't Risk the Thing They Fear: Ground Troops," *Wall Street Journal*, April 21, 1994, p. A10.

19. The above was written well before this book was scheduled to go to press. Now, as the press deadline nears, force of nearly unimaginable destructiveness was loosed on New York, and subsidiary attacks leveled part of the Pentagon. Words of foreboding have become the saddest kind of prophecy.

20. See Dean Acheson, *Present at the Creation* (New York: W. W. Norton, 1969), p. 405; and, also on these points, Commodore James F. McNulty, "Naval Presence—The Misunderstood Mission," *Naval War College Review* (September–October 1974): 21–31; James A. Nathan and James K. Oliver, *The Future of United States Naval Power* (Bloomington: Indiana University Press, 1979), pp. 65–82.

21. Edward Luttwak, *The Political Uses of Sea Power* (Baltimore, Md.: Johns Hopkins University Press, 1974).

22. James Cable, *Gunboat Diplomacy: A Political Application of Limited Naval Force* (London: IISS, 1971).

23. Interview with Peter Jennings, ABC Special, "While America Watched." Transcript, Journal Graphics, March 16, 1994.

24. From January to May of 1990, NATO ruled out intervention in Kosovo. The aim was to isolate the province from other Albanian populations (i.e., Albania itself and Macedonia). But on June 9, 1998, British Prime Minister Tony Blair attacked "Serbian barbarity," citing Serbian actions against Albanians in Kosovo. It was a clear attempt to rally support for Mr. Clinton, as Margaret Thatcher had done for President Bush in August 1990 during the confrontation with Iraq. Blair proposed a UN resolution authorizing the use of force. But Russian Foreign Minister Yevgeny Primakov reminded NATO that any action should be approved by the UN in advance. French Foreign Minister Hubert Védrine and some of the European states welcomed the Russian caution, which was seconded by Secretary General Kofi Annan. The United States was, however, able to get NATO to conduct aerial maneuvers over Macedonia and Albania on June 15. But a day later, Russian

President Boris Yeltsin received Slobodan Milosevic in Moscow and informed him that Moscow would steadfastly resist a NATO intervention by the UN. NATO resolve collapsed. Then American interests waned as Serb–Kosovar violence increased. With Kosovar armed resistance increasing, the U.S. search for alternatives to the Kosovar leader Ibrahim Rugova, who had adopted a strategy of nonviolence, became increasingly dubious. Rugova joined the long list of forlorn and abandoned American associates in the Cold War and after. Alain Joxe, "On the Brink of War in Kosovo: NATO at a Loss," *Le Monde Diplomatique* (Barry Smerin, trans.), July 1998 (LeMonde-diplomatique web site).

25. Robert E. Osgood and Robert W. Tucker, *Force, Order, and Justice* (Baltimore, Md.: Johns Hopkins University Press, 1976), esp. chapter 1, pp. 3–41.

26. Michael R. Gordon, "U.S. Officials Debate Policy to Halt Serbs," *New York Times*, April 6, 1994, p. 1. To be fair, Shalikashvili's comment was echoed by none other than the president, who told reporters a little over a week later: "I have to clarify, if there is any real doubt, that the United States has no interests in this war and [in] trying to gain advantage for one side or another." The United States was "firm, but provocative and not [going to] try to change the military balance." Cited by Elaine Sciolino, "U.S. Policies under Siege," *New York Times*, April 16, 1994, p. 5. Two days later, Serb tanks rolled into the "safe havens" in the center of Gorazde and fired directly at people with their main cannons.

27. See "Washington Whispers: Bosnia: Did Pentagon Statements Give Green Light to Serbs?" *U.S. News & World Report*, April 25, 1994, p. 27.

28. Dana Priest, "NATO Rules Out Relief Flights as Too Risky," *Washington Post*, April 15, 1999, p. A27.

29. Shape News Summary & Analysis, November 22, http://www.fas.org/man/dod-101/ops/docs99/sa221199.htm.

30. Elaine Sciolino, "Bosnia Policy: Shaped by U.S. Military Role," *New York Times*, July 29, 1996 (web site).

31. Richard Holbrooke, *To End a War: From Sarajevo to Dayton—and Beyond* (New York: Random House, 1998), p. 328ff.

32. Ibid., p. 316.

33. Ibid., p. 328.

34. Adam Garfinkle, "Anatomy of a Farce," *The National Interest* 52 (Summer 1998): 123–126, for an unsubtle, but not wholly unwarranted criticism.

35. Sciolino, "Bosnia Policy."

36. See, as representative, Michael Mazarr, Jeffrey Shaffer, and Benjamin Ederington, *The Military Technical Revolution: A Structural Framework* (Washington, D.C.: Center for Strategic and International Studies, March 1993), p. 58; Joseph Nye Jr. and William Owens, "America's Information Edge," *Foreign Affairs* 75(2) (March/April 1992): 23ff.; Elliot A. Cohen, "A Revolution in Warfare," *Foreign Affairs* (75)2 (March/April 1996): 44ff.; Robert Pfaltzgraph and Richard H. Schultz (eds.), *War in the Information Age* (McLean, Va.: Brassey's, 1997).

37. See Lt. Col. Richard H. Estes, then Air Force Chief, Strategy and Policy Division, "Giulio Douhet: More on Target Than He Knew," *Airpower Journal* 4(4) (Winter 1990): 68–78.

38. Giulio Douhet, *The Command of the Air* (Dino Ferrari, trans.) (1942) (reprint, Washington, D.C.: Office of the Air Force History, 1983), pp. 30, 394.

39. Paul Fussell, *Wartime: Understanding and Behavior in the Second World War* (New York: Oxford University Press, 1989), p. 15.

40. Col. John A. Warden III, USAF, "Air Theory for the Twenty-First Century," in Barry R. Schneider and Lawrence E. Grinter (eds.), *Battlefield of the Future: 21st Century Warfare Issues* (Montgomery, Ala.: "Maxwell AFB, Air University Press, 1995).

41. Jeffrey McKitrick et al., "The Revolution in Military Affairs," in Schneider and Grintner (eds.), *Battlefield of the Future*.

42. Cited by John Orne, "The Utility of Force in a World of Scarcity," *International Security* 22(3) (Winter 1997/1998): 153.

43. Carl Von Clausewitz, *On War* (Michael Howard and Peter Paret, eds. and trans.), with introductory essays by Peter Paret, Michael Howard, and Bernard Brodie, and a commentary by Bernard Brodie (Princeton, N.J.: Princeton University Press, 1984), Book Three, chapter 3, p. 91.

44. Ibid.

45. Warden, "Air Theory for the Twenty-First Century." See also Col. John A. Warden III, "Air Power for the Twenty-First Century," in Karl P. Magyar (ed.), *Challenge and Response: Anticipating U.S. Military Security Concerns* (Montgomery, Ala.: Maxwell AFB, Air University Press, 1994), pp. 328–329.

46. McKitrick et al., "The Revolution in Military Affairs."

47. Carl H. Builder, "Doctrinal Frontiers," *Airpower Journal* 9(4) (Winter 1995): 12.

48. http://www.mideastweb.org/osamabinladen2.htm.

49. James S. Corum, "Airpower and Peace Enforcement," *Airpower Journal* 10(11) (Winter 1996): 18–19.

50. Clausewitz, *On War*, Book Three, chapter 3, pp. 184–185.

51. Warden, "Air Power for the Twenty-First Century," p. 330ff.

52. On the American tendency to overreach and underfund an ambitious policy, see Robert W. Turker, "The Future of a Contradiction," *The National Interest* 43 (Spring 1996): 18ff.

53. Barry M. Blechman and Stephan S. Kaplan, "Armed Forces as a Political Instrument," *Survival* 19 (July/August 1977): 168–174.

54. Cited by Bernard Lewis, "The Revolt of Islam," *The New Yorker*, November 19, 2001, pp. 62–63.

55. Caspar Weinberger, *Fighting for Peace* (New York: Warner Books, 1990), pp. 448–449.

56. CNN News Conference. Transcript, Pentagon News Briefing. Aired September 25, 2001, 12:17 P.M. ET.

57. Jane Perlez, David E. Sanger, and Thom Shanker, "From Many Voices, One Battle Strategy," *New York Times*, September 23, 2001 (web site).

58. "One has to say it's not just simply a matter of capturing people and holding them accountable, but removing the sanctuaries, removing the support systems, ending states who sponsor terrorism." "U.S. to Respond with Sustained Military Action," *Houston Chronicle*, September 14, 2001.

59. Clausewitz, *On War*, Book Eight, chapter 5, p. 601; Rick Atkinson, "How Wars Are Won," *Washington Post*, September 16, 2001.

Bibliographical Essay

CHAPTER 1

There has been a recent spate of compelling works on Westphalia settlement and the nature of international politics. Among the most important is the skeptical argument of Stephen B. Krasner, "Rethinking the Sovereign State Model," *Review of International Studies* 27 (December 2001, Special Issue): 17–42 and Derek Croxton, "The Peace of Westphalia and the Origins of Sovereignty," *International History Review* 21 (1999), as well as Croxton and Anuschka Tischer's exhaustive guide, *The Peace of Westphalia: A Historical Dictionary* (Westport, Conn.: Greenwood Press, 2001). Croxton and Tischer's coverage is a great help to anyone who wishes to begin to work through the vast historiographical swamp of the Thirty Years War.

Readers might also wish to consult the classic article on the legal meaning of Westphalia written by Leo Gross, "The Peace of Westphalia, 1648–1948." The article can be found in Gross, *Essays on International Law and Organization* (Dobbs Ferry, N.Y.: Transnational Publishers, 1984), pp. 3–21. A wonderfully written introductory article is Geoffrey Parker's "The Thirty Years' War," *History Today* 32 (August 1982): 50–51. A little more detailed but extremely readable is A. W. Ward's "The Peace of Westphalia," in *The Cambridge Modern History*, Vol. 4 (Cambridge: Cambridge University Press, 1996), pp. 395–433.

A very neat classic synthesis for the uninitiated is Charles W. Kegley Jr. and Gregory A. Raymond, *Exorcising the Ghost of Westphalia: Building International Peace in the New Millennium* (Upper Saddle River, N.J.: Prentice-Hall, 2002).

The best scholarly, though immensely readable, study in English remains that of C. V. Wedgwood, *The Thirty Years War* (New Haven, Conn.: Yale University Press, 1939). Geoffrey Parker is one of the best contemporary historians of the era. See Parker (with contributions by Simon Adams et al.), *The Thirty Years' War*, 2nd ed. (London: Routledge, 1997). Also useful is Ronald Asch, *The Thirty Years War: The Holy Roman Empire and Europe, 1618–48* (New York: St. Martin's Press, 1997) and Herbert Langer, The *Thirty Years' War* (Poole: Blandford Press, 1978).

The reader who would like to know a bit more about the immediate Hapsburg missteps that led to one of the great catastrophes of European history should consult the finely crafted book by Charles Howard Carter, *The Secret Diplomacy of the Hapsburgs, 1598–1625* (New York: Columbia University Press, 1964).

For a fine authoritative synopsis of the relationship between military innovation and state building, see Geoffrey Parker, *The Military Revolution: Military Innovation and the Rise of the West, 1500–1800* (New York: Cambridge University Press, 1996).

CHAPTER 2

The scholarly work on Louis XIV and his times is immense. Many of the classic works in English are by John Baptist Wolf. See Wolf (ed.), *Louis XIV: A Profile* (New York: Hill and Wang, 1972); and Wolf, *Louis XIV* (New York: W. W. Norton & Co., 1969), *The Emergence of the Great Powers 1685–1715* (New York: Harper & Brothers, 1951), and *Toward a European Balance of Power: 1620–1715* (Chicago: Rand McNally & Co., 1970).

Other useful books are John C. Rule (ed.), *Louis XIV and the Craft of Kingship* (Columbus: Ohio State University Press, 1969) and Philippe Erlanger, *Louis XIV* (Stephen Cox, trans.) (New York: Praeger, 1970). Nancy Mitford spent much of her adult life in France and has a fine sense of language. Mitford's *The Sun King* (London: Penguin, 1995) shines with detail and mordant wit.

A wonderful if not necessarily authoritative read is Winston S. Churchill, *The Age of Revolution* (New York: Dodd, Mead & Co, 1957). Also still interesting is Voltaire's *The Age of Louis XIV* (Martyn Pollack, trans.; preface by F. C. Green) (New York: Dutton, 1978). Useful on the diplomatic context of Louis' time is Sir Herbert Butterfield, "Diplomacy," in Ragnhild Hatton and M. S. Anderson (eds.), *Studies in Diplomatic History* (London: Longman, 1970), pp. 363ff. A good, readable introduction to early European and American diplomacy is Henry Kissinger's *Diplomacy* (New York: Simon & Schuster, 1994).

Pierre Goubert's *Louis XIV* (Anne Carter, trans.) (New York: Pantheon, 1970) is a trenchant and expert attempt, as Goubert puts it, to "set Louis

XIV in relation to his kingdom and his time, and ultimately to consider yet again the problem of the great man in history." As for Louis' policies, they were, says Goubert, "a long series of mistakes."

Web sources include Saint-Simon's portrait of Louis XIV from "Parallele des trois premiers rois Bourbons" (written in 1746), in J. H. Robinson, *Readings in European History*, 2 vols. (Boston: Ginn, 1906), 2:285–286. Scanned by Brian Cheek, Hanover College, November 12, 1995, http://history.hanover.edu/early/louisxiv.htm. There is also an interesting site in French, http://www.urich.edu/~jpaulsen/louisxiv.html.

CHAPTER 3

A powerful statement that European politics before the French Revolution were mere extensions of the dictums of raison d'état is Albert Sorel, *Europe and the French Revolution: The Political Traditions of the Old Regime* (Alfred Cobban and J. W. Hunt, eds. and trans.) (Garden City, N.Y.: Anchor Books, 1971).

The common understanding of the eighteenth-century international system as a "golden age" is reflected in the following volumes: Walter L. Dorn, *Competition for Empire: 1740–1763* (New York: Harper & Brothers, 1940); Edward Vose Gulick, *Europe's Classical Balance of Power* (New York: Norton, 1955); and Ludwig Dahio, *The Precarious Balance of Power* (New York: Vintage Books, 1962).

The work on Frederick is huge. There are two standard works in English. One is Gerhard Ritter, *Frederick the Great: A Historical Profile* (Peter Paret, trans. and intro.) (Berkeley: University of California Press, 1975). The other, of great use, is Thomas Carlyle, *History of Frederick II of Prussia, Called Frederick the Great*. Carlyle's 21 volumes are now a book online project put on the World Wide Web by volunteers at Project Gutenberg. See: http://www-2.cs.cmu.edu/~spok/metabook/fgreat.html.

Nancy Mitford's *Frederick the Great* (New York: Harper & Row, 1970) is easily one of the most readable and engaging looks at Frederick. Another jaundiced portrait of Frederick is Nathan Ausubel's *Superman: The Life of Frederick the Great* (New York: Ives Washburn, 1931). A more generous take is Albert Sorel, *Europe under the Old Regime* (New York: Harper & Row, 1964). Another remarkable Internet site is Frederick the Great "Military Instructions," translated by Lieutenant Colonel T. Foster, http://www.sonshi.com/frederickthegreat.html.

Journalist and historian Giles MacDonogh's *Frederick the Great: A Life in Deed and Letters* (London: Phoenix Press, 2000) is a sympathetic look at Frederick's battle gifts as well as his place in the cultural history of middle Europe.

On the classic European system as one of consensus see, among others, Hans J. Morgenthau, *Politics among Nations* (New York: Alfred A. Knopf,

1948) and Edward Vose Gullick, *Europe's Classical Balance of Power* (Ithaca, N.Y.: Cornell University Press, 1955). The seminal work of Herbert Butterfield and Martin Wright also should be consulted. See Butterfield and Wright's *Diplomatic Investigations: Essays in the Theory of International Politics* (Cambridge, Mass.: Harvard University Press, 1968). Especially useful are the essays by Butterfield and Wright on the balance of power.

CHAPTER 4

For Clausewitz on war and the French Revolution, nothing in English equals in clarity and depth the studies of Peter Paret. See Paret's *Carl von Clausewitz: Historical and Political Writings* (Peter Paret and Daniel Moran, eds. and trans.) (Princeton, N.J.: Princeton University Press, 1992). Another indispensable study of Paret and Daniel Moran is their *Understanding War: Essays on Clausewitz and the History of Military Power* (Princeton, N.J.: Princeton University Press, 1992). See also Paret's *Clausewitz and the State: The Man, His Theories, and His Times* (Princeton, N.J.: Princeton University Press, 1976) and his seminal essay on Clausewitz in Peter Paret (ed.), *Makers of Modern Strategy: From Machiavelli to the Nuclear Age* (Princeton, N.J.: Princeton University Press, 1986), pp. 186–213.

Paret also has an important set of essays and commentaries in his translation of Clausewitz's *On War*. Paret's equals in breadth, if not depth, in the study of war and Clausewitz are Michael Elliot Howard and Bernard Brodie. See the essays in Carl von Clausewitz, *On War* (Michael Howard and Peter Paret, eds. and trans.), with introductory essays by Peter Paret, Michael Howard, and Bernard Brodie, and a commentary by Bernard Brodie (Princeton, N.J: Princeton University Press, 1984).

Michael Howard has several other important studies of Clausewitz. See his *Clausewitz* (New York: Oxford University Press, 1983) and *Clausewitz On War* (Washington, D.C.: Library of Congress, 1998).

Howard's other essays have inspired much in this book, including his *The Invention of Peace: Reflections on War and International Order* (New Haven, Conn.: Yale University Press, 2000), *The Lessons of History* (New Haven, Conn.: Yale University Press, 1991), *Studies in War and Peace* (London: Temple Smith, 1970), and *War in European History* (New York: Oxford University Press, 2001).

Bernard Brodie's work, along with the work of Crane Brinton, Gordon A. Craig, Felix Gilbert, and Edward Mead Earle, is extremely useful. See their *Makers of Modern Strategy: Military Thought from Machiavelli to Hitler* (Princeton, N.J.: Princeton University Press, 1944). Brodie's review essay, "Clausewitz: A Passion for War," *World Politics* 25(2) (January 1973): 288–308, is compelling. Also not to be ignored is Brodie's "In Quest of the Unknown Clausewitz" (a review of Paret's *Clausewitz and the State*), *International Security* 1(3) (Winter 1977).

One of the most useful web pages for the reader of this book (alas, discovered well after this book was in production) is the Clausewitz home page, http://www.clausewitz.com/CWZHOME/CWZBASE.htm, replete with professional bibliographic essays, the searchable, original English language translation of Clausewitz's *On War* by J. J. Graham (1873), *Principles of War* by Hans W. Gatzke (1942), and more. It is a terrific scholarly resource.

For the place of the French Revolution in the growth of international society, I am especially indebted to Paul W. Schroeder and T.C.W. Blanning. See Schroeder, *The Transformation of European Politics, 1763–1848* (New York: Oxford University Press, 1994) and Blanning, *The French Revolutionary Wars, 1787–1802* (London: Arnold, 1996) and *The Origins of the French Revolutionary Wars* (London: Longman, 1986).

For the significance of the jeremiad of Edmund Burke, one should look at the readable and important study by Jennifer M. Welsh, *Edmund Burke and International Relations* (New York: St. Martin's Press, 1995). Even more compelling on Burke is Conor Cruise O'Brien's *The Great Melody: A Thematic Biography and Commented Anthology of Edmund Burke* (Chicago: University of Chicago Press, 1992).

Also useful are the books of Jeremy Black, *British Foreign Policy in an Age of Revolution: 1783–1793* (Cambridge: Cambridge University Press, 1994) and David Armstrong, *Revolution and World Order: The Revolutionary State in International Society* (Chicago: University of Chicago Press, 1993).

CHAPTER 5

Important for this chapter is Carl von Clausewitz, *The Campaign of 1812 in Russia* ([Francis Egerton, Lord Ellesmere], trans.) (London: J. Murray, 1843), reprinted with an introduction by Sir Michael Howard (New York: Da Capo Press, 1995). On the other side there are the important observations of General De Caulaincourt, *With Napoleon in Russia* (edited and abridged by Jean Hanoteau) (New York: Grosset and Dunlap Universal Library, 1935). Also useful is the unusually clear military study by David H. Chandler, *The Campaigns of Napoleon* (New York: Macmillan, 1966).

For the diplomacy of the end of the Napoleonic Wars, Henry A. Kissinger's *A World Restored* (New York: Grosset and Dunlap, 1964) is a good place to start. Also worth consulting, especially for the British position, is Harold Nicholson, *The Congress of Vienna* (London: University Paperbacks; Methuen, 1946) and Sir Charles K. Webster, *The Congress of Vienna: 1814–1815* (New York: Barnes & Noble, 1963). Felix Markham, *Napoleon* (New York: Mentor Books, 1963) is a fine short book on an inexhaustible subject. Not to be ignored is Peter Paret's "Napoleon as Enemy," in Clarence B. Davis (ed.), *Proceedings of the Thirteenth Consortium on Revolutionary Europe* (Athens, Ga.: Consortium on Revolutionary Europe, 1985).

Paul W. Schroeder's collected works are indispensable in making one's way to a meaningful understanding of the French Revolution, the Congress system, and the origins of the modern notion of collective security. See Schroeder's *The Transformation of European Politics, 1765–1848* (Oxford: Clarendon Press, 1994). See also "Did the Vienna Settlement Rest on a Balance of Power?" *American Historical Review* 97(3) (June 1992): 683–735; "The 'Balance of Power' System in Europe, 1815–1871," *Naval War College Review* (March–April 1975): 18–31; "The Transformation of Political Thinking, 1787–1848," in Jack Snyder and Robert Jervis (eds.), *Coping with Complexity in the International System* (Boulder, Colo.: Westview Press, 1993), pp. 47–70; "Old Wine in Old Bottles: Recent Contributions to British Foreign Policy and European International Politics, 1789–1848," *Journal of British Studies* 26(1) (January 1987): 1–25; "The Nineteenth Century Balance of Power: Balance of Power or Political Equilibrium?" *Review of International Studies* (Oxford) 15 (April 1989): 135–153; and, importantly, "Napoleon's Foreign Policy: A Criminal Enterprise," *Journal of Military History* 54(2) (April 1990): 147–161.

The literature on the Concert of Europe is substantial, but the work of Evan Luard is particularly good. See his *Types of International Society* (New York: Free Press, 1976); *War in International Society: A Study in International Sociology* (New Haven, Conn.: Yale University Press, 1987); and *The Balance of Power: The System of International Relations, 1648–1815* (New York: St. Martin's Press, 1992). Also important for the concert system is F. H. Hinsley's *Power and the Pursuit of Peace: Theory and Practice in the History of Relations between States* (London: Cambridge University Press, 1967). Worth reading too is Richard Elrod's "The Concert of Europe: A Fresh Look at an International System," *World Politics* 28(1) (January 1976).

CHAPTER 6

No one who studies the competition between the United States and Great Britain at the end of the nineteenth century in South America can start anywhere other than with Walter LaFeber's *The New Empire: An Interpretation of American Expansion, 1860–1898* (Ithaca, N.Y.: Cornell University Press, 1963). Also important is the early work of Ernest R. May. See May's *Imperial Democracy: The Emergence of America as a Great Power* (New York: Harcourt, Brace, and World, 1961).

Dexter Perkins' *The Monroe Doctrine, 1876–1907* (Baltimore, Md.:

Johns Hopkins Press, 1937) is useful, as is John A. S. Grenville and George Berkley's *Politics, Strategy, and American Diplomacy: Studies in Foreign Policy, 1873–1917* (New Haven, Conn.: Yale University Press, 1966).

I am grateful to Fareed Zakaria for allowing me to look at his finely crafted Ph.D. dissertation, *The Rise of a Great Power: National Strength, State Structure, and American Foreign Policy, 1865–1908* (Cambridge, Mass.: Department of Government, Harvard University, 1993). Zakaria's book, derived from his dissertation, is also useful and, of course, more accessible. See Zakaria, *From Wealth to Power: The Unusual Origins of America's World Role* (Princeton, N.J.: Princeton University Press, 1998). Also useful is Aron L. Friedberg, *The Weary Titan: Britain and the Experience of Relative Decline, 1895–1905* (Princeton, N.J.: Princeton University Press, 1988) and Paul Kennedy, *The Rise and Fall of the Great Powers* (New York: Vintage, 1987).

On Germany, Lamar Cecil's *Wilhelm II, Prince and Emperor 1859–1900* (Chapel Hill: University of North Carolina Press, 1989) is indispensable, as is John C. G. Röhl's *The Kaiser and His Court: Wilhelm II and the Government of Germany* (Cambridge: Cambridge University Press, 1995).

Some of the best work on China's view of great power politics is that of Gaye Christoffersen. See her "China and the Asia-Pacific," *Asian Survey* 36(11) (1996): 1067–1085. I also profited from her "China and the U.S.: Defining the Constructive Strategic Partnership" (paper prepared for Senior Participants, Foreign Affairs College, Beijing, October 1999).

CHAPTER 7

The materials on Cuba and the Cuban Missile Crisis are so immense that they defy description and categorization. I have some prejudice in offering my own work as a good summary on Cuba. See James A. Nathan, *Anatomy of the Cuban Missile Crisis* (Westport, Conn.: Greenwood Press, 2001) and Nathan (ed.), *The Cuban Missile Crisis Revisited* (New York: St. Martin's Press, 1992).

On strategy and limited war, one would do well to consult the work of Douglas A. Blaufarb, a station chief in Laos in the early 1960s. See Blaufarb, *The Counter-Insurgency Era: U.S. Doctrine and Performance, 1950 to the Present* (New York: Free Press, 1977). Also useful are the Ph.D. dissertations of James J. Brask, *Counterinsurgency as an Instrument of American Foreign Policy: A Framework for the Analysis of Vietnam Counterinsurgency Evaluation* (Department of Political Science, Northern Illinois University, 1990) and Richard T. Shultz, *The Intellectual Origins and Development of Counterinsurgency Theory in American Foreign Policy Doctrine: The Vietnam Case Study* (Miami University, 1976). I am especially indebted to the work of Stephen P. Rosen. See his "Vietnam and the American Theory of Limited War," *International Security* 7 (Fall 1982): 83–

113. See also Robert A. Pape, *Bombing to Win: Air Power and Coercion in War* (Ithaca, N.Y.: Cornell University Press, 1996) and Mark Clodfelter, *The Limits of Air Power: The American Bombing of North Vietnam* (New York: Free Press, 1989).

On contemporary military policy and civil-military relations I am indebted to the work of Andrew J. Bacevich, Charles Dunlap Jr., and Richard H. Kohn. See Bacevich, "Civilian Control: A Useful Fiction?" *JFQ: Joint Force Quarterly* 6 (Autumn/Winter 1994–1095): 80–83 and "Tradition Abandoned: America's Military in a New Era," *The National Interest* 48 (Summer 1997): 16–25; Dunlap, "Origins of the American Military Coup of 2012," *Parameters* (Winter 1992–1993): 2–20; and Kohn, "Out of Control: The Crisis in Civil-Military Relations," *The National Interest* (Spring 1994). See also Colin Powell, John Lehman, William Odom, Samuel Huntington, and Richard H. Kohn, "An Exchange on Civil-Military Relations—Comment/Reply," *The National Interest* (35) (Spring 1994): 3–17; and Powell, Lehman, Odom, Huntington, and Kohn, "Exchange on Civil-Military Relations," *The National Interest* (36) (Summer 1994): 23–31. See also the important article by Kenneth J. Campbell, "Clausewitz and Genocide: Bosnia, Rwanda and Strategic Failure," *Civil Wars* 1 (Summer 1998): 26–37 as well as Campbell's "Once Burned, Twice Cautious: Explaining the Weinberger-Powell Doctrine," *Armed Forces & Society* 24 (Spring 1998): 357–374.

CHAPTER 8

On the sad inability to respond to the Balkan challenge in a timely fashion—or, for that matter, to confront the question of what the purposes of American power might be—see Richard Holbrooke, *To End a War: From Sarajevo to Dayton—and Beyond* (New York: Random House, 1998). After this book went to press, David Halberstam's *War in a Time of Peace: Bush, Clinton, and the Generals* (New York: Scribner, 2001) appeared. Halberstam writes well and offers a good deal of detail, but is disappointing in that both his narrative skills and analytic power are not what one has come to expect after his seminal *The Best and the Brightest* (New York: Fawcett, 1992, 20th anniversary ed.).

In the lead of those who question the utility of Clausewitz are Air Force planners. Foremost is retired Col. John Warden III, the leading intellectual of the Gulf War. See Warden, "Air Power for the Twenty-First Century," in Karl P. Magyar (editor-in-chief), *Challenge and Response: Anticipating US Military Security Concerns* (Maxwell AFB, Ala.: Air University Press, August 1994); "Air Theory for the Twenty-First Century," in Barry R. Schneider and Lawrence E. Grinter (eds.), *Battlefield of the Future: 21st Century Warfare Issues* (Maxwell AFB, Ala.: Air University Press, 1995), available online at http://www.airpower.au.af.mil/airchronicles/battle/

bftoc.html; and "The Enemy as a System," *Airpower Journal* (Spring 1995): 40–55. See also Maj. David S. Fadok, John Boyd, and John Warden, *Air Power's Quest for Strategic Paralysis* (Maxwell AFB, Ala.: Air University Press, February 1995). For a first-rate criticism of the regnant military doctrines of force protection, see Jeffrey Record, "Force-Protection Fetishism: Sources, Consequences, and (?) Solutions," *Airpower Journal* (Summer 2000), http://www.airpower.maxwell.af.mil/airchronicles/apj/apj00/sum00/record.htm. A first-rate web resource is "Defense and the National Interest." This web site's "aim is to foster debate on the roles of the U.S. armed forces in the post–Cold War era and on the resources devoted to them." It is an excellent resource of sites otherwise passed over. See http://www.d-n-i.net.

Index

About the Author

JAMES A. NATHAN is Khaled bin Sultan Eminent Scholar and Professor of International Relations at Auburn University, Montgomery. A former foreign service officer, he has taught at the Army War College and the Navy War College and lectured widely to professional, military, and diplomatic audiences worldwide. He is the author of seven books on U.S. foreign and security policy, and has published articles in the *New York Times*, the *Washington Post*, the *Los Angeles Times*, *Foreign Policy*, *World Politics*, *The Nation*, and other popular and scholarly publications. He is director of the Alabama World Affairs Council and a long-time member of the Council on Foreign Relations. His most recent book is *Anatomy of the Cuban Missile Crisis* (Greenwood, 2000).